The Voice

The Voice

A Memoir

Thomas Quasthoff

RECORDED BY MICHAEL QUASTHOFF

Translated from the German by
Kirsten Stoldt Wittenborn

PANTHEON BOOKS, NEW YORK

Library of Congress Cataloging-in-Publication Data

Quasthoff, Thomas.
[Stimme. English]
The voice / Thomas Quasthoff.
p.   cm.
Includes discography (p. 225) and index.
ISBN 978-0-375-42406-9
1. Quasthoff, Thomas. 2. Bass-baritones—
Germany—Biography. I. Title.
ML420.Q37A32 2008
782.42168092—dc22   [B]   2007039089

www. pantheonbooks.com

CONTENTS

Downtown   3

If You Can Make It There   7

I Got the Blues   36

All the World's a Stage   70

All I Need Is Music, Music, Music   99

Sympathy Is Free, Envy You Gotta Earn   129

On the Road Again   161

Life Is a Total Work of Art   195

Coda   219

Discography   225

Index   229

The Voice

Downtown

February, downtown Hanover. The Tavern Inn, a beer hall-cum-restaurant, is packed. At the bar, the proprietors, Armin and Gerrit, are chatting with regulars beneath the holiday decorations (Christmas, not Valentine's Day, and in this place they'll stay up until Easter). In the rear to the right squat the brothers Quasthoff, hefty sausage sandwiches and glasses of beer before them. Michael, the tall one, chews. Thomas, the little one, speaks:

TQ: "So I say to myself, why should I write my autobiography? I'm doing fine. I'm not a famous alcoholic, I haven't cheated anyone to get my money, I don't sleep with prominent women, and as of yet I have no plans to die."

MQ *[Takes a gulp of beer]:* "You don't?"

TQ: "Definitely not."

MQ: "Then we'll have another round." *[He waves in the direction of the bar.]* "Armin, Gerrit, two more Pils, please."

TQ: "Anyway, this literary agent wouldn't take no for an answer. She insisted that a celebrity's life is always interesting, and that I am, after all, a very famous singer—"

MQ: "Sure, but most celebs write their autobiographies because they aren't famous anymore."

TQ: "That's what I said, but she said my story is something special."

MQ: "That's a valid argument. Thalidomide victim who was denied admission to the Music Academy sings his way from body

cast to Grammy. What a story! It has everything: intense child
hood, battle against the monster bureaucracy, drama, love, insanity. Finally, triumph in America, the land of limitless possibility!
The republic can always use success stories."

*Gerrit, a giant Dutchman in exile, arrives with two fresh
beers.*

GERRIT: "There you go, gentlemen."

MQ: "Thanks a lot, Gerrit. Listen, Tommy is supposed to write
his biography. Would you like to read it?"

GERRIT: "Of coursh, soundsh rrreeally intereshting, the sto-
rrries of the shinging, the trrraveling, the famoush conductorsh,
and the beautiful tenorsh." *[Walking away]* "Jusht fantashtic."

MQ: "There you have it."

TQ: "And what comes of it? Half-truths and highbrow kitsch."

MQ: "Whatever pleases is allowed."

TQ: "Leave Goethe out of this."

MQ: "Alright, then, consider Mr. Frisch: Truth cannot be
shown, only invented."

TQ: "You write the book, then. You're a pro when it comes to
making things up."

MQ: "I'd rather order another Pils." *[He holds up his glass.]*
"Do you want one?"

TQ: "Please."

MQ: "Armin, Gerrit, two—"

DIETRICH ZUR NEDDEN: "Make it three, please."

*Zur Nedden, publisher about town and the brothers' pal, raps
on their table and drops onto the bench.*

DZN: "What's new?"

TQ *[Grinning]*: "Micha is writing up my life. A publishing
house wants to make a book of it."

MQ: "What a load of bull."

DZN: "Why? It's not the worst idea. Tommy has lots to talk

about and usually it's damn funny. I'm sure quite a few people would love to read it. Besides, you wouldn't be doing it for free."

MQ: "The publishers' guild is glad to hear that."

DZN: "Anyway, it's better when you write your life yourself. You've already rejected offers from two publishing houses. After the third Grammy, they won't bother to ask. They'll just have someone write it, and then you have no idea who'll go digging through your life."

TQ: "That's a good point. I don't even want to think about some of the nonsense that's been written about me in the papers."

MQ *[Empties his glass and takes a deep breath]:* "Assuming we write the book, we've got to do it right. Realistic. We owe that to Mom and Dad."

TQ: "Exactly. No prisoners. Everybody gets what he deserves, for better or for worse."

DZN: "Well, it sounds like you'll have fun."

MQ: "We'll have a lot of fun. But I can think of some people who'll have nothing to laugh about."

DZN: "As long as they aren't celebrities—then you just have to change their names."

TQ: "What about your name?"

DZN: "Not necessary. I am a person of integrity, through and through. The world might as well know that."

MQ: "When he's right, he's right. That's why Didi is buying the next round."

DZN: "Persuaded." *[Lifts his arm]*

ARMIN *[Shows him three fingers]:* "Got it. Be back right away."

MQ: "So what should we start with?"

TQ: "How about my first performance in New York? 1998. You came with me. Remember how much fun we had? We drove to Cape Cod and met Felicitas, who was giving a lecture in the Goethe-Institut Boston—"

MQ: "—crazy Tony was there—"

DZN: "—and your Renatchen, don't forget about her."

MQ: "True. It was great. Especially when the strange guy from your concert agency in the bar—"

TQ: "That's how we could do it."

MQ: "Then we go back in time: the trial of the cast, the years in the Saint Ann's Home, school—"

TQ: "—the first singing lessons—"

MQ: "—we can't forget Father's singing number with Peter Frankenfeld—"

TQ: "ARD Competition, Grammy, opera, a few truths about the music industry, beautiful travel adventures. Done."

DZN: "There you go. The book writes itself."

ARMIN [puts the tray down]: "Here you are, gentlemen, three fresh five-minute beers. Enjoy."

MQ [Grumbles]: "Illusion is short, regret is long."

TQ: "Schiller."

DZN: "Die Glocke" (The Bell). [Raising his glass]: "See you at the book fair."

If You Can Make It There

"Brrroeek," drones the jackhammer. "Brrroeek, brrroeek." When it rests you can hear the radiator grumbling and the baseline murmur of traffic rising up from Columbus Circle to the fifth floor of the Mayflower Hotel. Somewhere police sirens are shrieking. New York is a loud city, even at one o'clock in the morning. Again, "BRRROEEK." Next door a clonk, and now someone's curses. Or did that come from the construction workers below, the ones who've been racking my nerves for the past three hours? I hope they get paid a nighttime bonus for this nastiness.

I slide off the much-too-soft mattress and turn on the television. Through the news floats John Glenn, eighty years old and still dreaming of space—zap—"the mysterious prostitute murderer of Newark. Seventeen victims since 1994"—zap—a fat man in a green apron pours "rich molasses-based sauce" over a gigantic rack of pork ribs. "Spicy but not spicy enough," according to the fat guy, who then holds up "the best garlic paste in the world"—zap—on the History Channel General Patton chases Rommel's Africa Corps through the Libyan desert. Once again, serves those old Nazis right. In Libya grenades explode, soundlessly now because the jackhammer is at it again, right below my window. "Brrroeek, brrrrrroeek, brrroeek." Shattered, I switch off the box and pace the room.

This is just super. Tomorrow, November 13, 1998, Gustav Mahler's *Des Knaben Wunderhorn (The Youth's Magic Horn)* is on the program at Avery Fisher Hall. It is my long-desired debut with the New York Philharmonic. The baritone parts are high and not entirely simple. I need a clear head and a lot of sleep, but so much for that. All I can do now is seek out a soothing tonic. I call my brother, Michael, who is three rooms down with girl-friend, Renate, and who most definitely cannot sleep either. Thank God, those two are always up for a late beer, and for any other nonsense I propose.

In the hallway outside their door I can already hear Renate. "Sleepless, helpless, sleepless," she sings as her red mane peeks around the door.

I counter with *Don Giovanni:* " . . . night and day it's toil and sweat for a master hard to please."

"To Wolfgang Amadeus Mozart and the German Union Fed-eration, which guarantees the working class its rest," Micha grumbles, cracking open three bottles of beer. The New York con-struction workers, unimpressed, continue to flatten the earthly realm with their diabolical tools. At the window, we silently drink our beer and gaze out over Central Park, which yawns like a gigantic black hole against the illuminated concrete blocks of midtown Manhattan.

I, too, have to yawn. "What time is it?"

"Just past three," Renate says sympathetically. Micha fetches more beer. He holds the bottle up to the pallid moon and pro-claims: "Du bist die Ruh, / der Friede mild, / die Sehnsucht du, / und was sie stillt." ("You are rest / and gentle peace; / you are longing / and what stills it.")

"Rückert," I say.

"Hit," nods Renate.

"Prost," Micha says, stone faced. One beat later we have to laugh. There is nothing like a solid humanist education. We are a good team.

"Eeeeeeeeeeeeeeaaaaaaaay." The next morning the jackhammer is still ranting when "Mr. Quasthoff takes his voice for a spin," as the chambermaid calls it, with a charming smile, when she drops off the footstool that allows me to conduct my ablutions. "Eeeeeeeeeeeeaaaaaaaaaay." It might not be lovely to hear, but it does loosen the vocal cords. Despite the trying night I passed, I am content: the voice is in place.

After a leisurely shower I put the footstool in front of the sink, climb up, and grimace at what I see in the mirror.

"Crippled arms and legs, no laughing matter." That's how a tabloid paper once put it, but I see the situation differently. Here is a four-foot three-inch concert singer without knee joints, arms, or upper thighs, with only four fingers on the right hand and three on the left. He has a receding hairline, a blond pig head, and a few too many pounds around his hips, and he is in a superb mood. All he needs now is a shave.

Half an hour later we sit down for breakfast at the Carnegie Deli, corner of Seventh Avenue and Fifty-fifth Street. It's part of New York legend—because it appears in at least two Woody Allen movies, because it serves the best kosher pastrami sandwich in the city, and because of the linen napkins the manager hands out to his regulars, like Kinky Friedman and his buddy Ratso, while the other customers make do with paper (according to Kinky, who includes this detail at least once in each of his crime novels).

Needless to say, our napkins are paper. "It's all BS. Everybody gets paper napkins here," my brother mumbles through a mouthful of pastrami.

Renate checks her watch. "Guess it's still a little early for the boldfaced names."

"I bet you not," Micha says, pointing towards the bar with his fork. The genteel older lady who has just sashayed in may not be Kinky Friedman, but she is sporting a hat whose size and shape would make any Texan green with envy. It is purple, to match her dress. As she makes her way towards us, we see that her right hand clutches a pen and her left, a notebook. Her voice sounds like a rusty bell:

"Oh, you are the fabulous singer! What a pleasure to see you. Please, give me an autograph." I turn violently pink, as if my face is struggling to match her outfit, and then do her the favor. How did she recognize me? She says she has seen my face on CBS, and *The New York Times* published a praiseful piece by the feared critic Anthony Tommasini. She has tickets for tonight.

"Naturally! We know you in this town, honey," her voice shrills through the place as she leaves our table and teeters back to hers.

Nice, I think, a little kooky, but a nice lady. I don't expect other people to recognize me, but on our way back to the Mayflower, as we cut through Central Park, I have to give another half dozen autographs. They haven't mistaken me for Danny DeVito—they really do want *my* signature on the shopping lists, newspapers, and ticket stubs they hastily fish out of pockets and purses. Everyone says New Yorkers are rude and tough, but it's amazing how open and friendly these people are. Not to mention crazy about music! Everyone wishes me "good luck" for the concert. I can use it.

I don't usually suffer from stage fright, and appearances in the United States are nothing new for me. I have sung in Washington and Seattle, in Chicago, Portland, and Boston; in Eugene, Oregon, I am a regular guest at the Bach Festival organized by my mentor and friend Helmuth Rilling. But this is my first appearance in New York. The fact that I am staying on the Upper West Side and in a few hours will be standing in one of the most beautiful concert halls of the world—with the New York Philharmonic—makes my heart race after all. Or is it just the hotel elevator? My conventionally shaped readers should know: elevators are, for people of my format, indispensable, but when they are crowded (and they usually are crowded) they are also a terrible trial (a blow below the belt, so to speak). To make matters worse, the Mayflower's tourists seem determined to buy up half of the city. I don't believe they care what they carry out of the boutiques of Madison Avenue or Bloomingdale's, Saks, or Macy's; after all, most of that stuff is available in Osaka, Lyon, and Düsseldorf. What's important is the shopping bags themselves with their fine and, one hopes, recognizable writing, which, back home, will induce envy and indicate restless hip-hunting and international creditworthiness.

About three dozen of these hunters and gatherers are now packing themselves and their purchases into the elevator. A stampede is nothing compared to this; only by resolutely exercising my stentorian voice can I secure a spot. While the cabin slowly rises my spirits sink. The air is thick and warm. Wedged in between purses, boxes, and plastic bags, beset by protruding behinds, trouser legs, and nylon-covered ladies' thighs, before we reach even the second floor I begin to feel like a piece of cheese melting on a grilled sandwich. The five floors I have to travel feel more like fifty.

Once in my room I fall onto my bed and count "seven . . . eight . . . nine . . . out." Technical KO. I take two aspirin and try to chase away misery with the Ross Thomas dime novel Renate brought me from the Village. It starts with the sentence "It began like the end of the world will begin: with the phone ringing at three a.m." "At least it's only noon," I think, some consolation. Then the aspirin takes effect and I drift off into the realm of dreams, a calm and pleasant place with no telephone. Thus apocalypse is kept at bay and—voilà—after two hours of deep sleep, the worst is over. I feel better. The last bit of nervousness is filed away under "creative tension," and professional routine takes its place.

Performing music is not unlike rock climbing. Before you begin you check your gear super-carefully: Does the tailcoat have to be ironed again? Is the hanky beautifully folded? Would the white turtleneck be better today, or the black one? Are the patent leather shoes shining? Where are the black socks, and where is the bloody comb? Then you review the score mentally, concentrating on the difficult ridges, gorges, and overhanging rocks. Finally, you need a strengthening refreshment. Not exactly "six eggs, sunny side up, with hot cocoa," the kind of thing Anderl Heckmair would put away before fastening his bundle and climbing across the wall of Eigernord. No, something easily digestible that won't turn your stomach into a stone pit encroaching on your diaphragm. For me, a few cookies usually suffice, rinsed down with juice or water.

After the snack comes the most important preparation of all: warming up the voice. I once again jump into a hot shower, for nothing massages the voice better than sultry air full of warm droplets. The vocal stretching lasts a half hour or forty-five minutes, depending on the repertoire. For higher parts, like Mahler's *Wunderhorn Lieder*, it takes a little bit longer.

At four o'clock sharp Micha comes to help me don my professional attire. Though not absolutely necessary—I can usually manage by myself—it simplifies the procedure. Unlike me, he is able to crouch with ease to peer beneath the tables, cabinets, and dressers that combs, shoehorns, and socks have a way of retreating to just before a concert. You know the axiom—"Things disappear when you need them most." What treacherous law of life is behind this I have never made out, and unfortunately, neither has science. Probably all efforts to solve this problem are quashed by lobbyists of the textile and accessories industries.

"Got one!" My brother is triumphantly waving a sock when Linda Marder calls. Blond, capable, roughly my age, Linda is my New York agent and a truly cool person. Together with her colleague Charles Cumella, she sits in a small office on Ninety-sixth Street and handles all my business between Boston and San Francisco. They take care of good—that is, artistically interesting—engagements and, more important, reject the bad ones. They coordinate PR, negotiate contracts, and make sure I am decently compensated. They even find the least taxing flight connections and book convenient hotels for my tours. In short, Linda and Charles make sure that I am okay and that no one takes advantage of me. As one says here, they do a very good job.

Linda reminds me of the New York Philharmonic's request that I make myself available after the concert for the so-called ten-minute smile, a euphemism disguising a uniquely American triathlon. Exercise number one: thirty minutes of hand shaking; exercise number two: forty minutes of small talk; and finally, the dinner obstacle course, complete with asparagus hurdles, a maze of cutlery, and a squadron of boiled lobster. In the United States cultural institutions don't get a single cent from public funds but get by entirely on sponsors, donations, and entrance fees. That means that without the goodwill of private donors, the concert tonight could not take place. So I will show up, cultivate some goodwill, and, I hope, meet some interesting people.

"You will," Linda assures me. "By the way, Avery Fisher Hall has been sold out for weeks."

"Wow." I imagine the hall filled with three thousand people. I have never sung in front of such a mighty assemblage.

"Are you nervous?"

"Not anymore. I am just happy to be able to perform here."

"Very good, Tommy, that's the right attitude!"

Meantime, Micha has dug up the second sock. When the shoe-horn reveals itself, I glide into my patent leather slippers and am on my way, even though it's a bit early. Avery Fisher Hall is only fifteen minutes away, and I like walking a bit before a concert. I stroll up Central Park West until the twin towers of the San Remo and El Dorado appear in the distance. Stars like Marilyn Monroe and Groucho Marx used to live at the San Remo, later to be replaced by Diane Keaton and Dustin Hoffman. Shortly after spotting them, I make a left onto Sixty-fourth Street, and the building canyon frames one of the most magnificent temples of secular modernity in the world: Lincoln Center for the Performing Arts.

Every year five million aesthetic pilgrims visit these fifteen acres, home to four theatres and two concert halls that offer up the best of dance, drama, classical music, and jazz. The center-piece is the Met, the Metropolitan Opera House, which resembles a Bauhaus version of the Athenian Parthenon, its face covered with high arched windows. Next door the New York State Theatre hosts the City Ballet, while the Philharmonic makes its home in Avery Fisher Hall. Who can believe that gangs like Leonard Bernstein's Jets and Sharks ever dominated the neighborhood, and in the middle of the last century? Not two decades later, in May 1959, the gangs were history. Bernstein lifted the conductor's baton, the Juilliard Chorus belted "Hallelu-jah," and President Eisenhower plunged his shovel into the flat-tened slum floor. Lincoln Center was born.

At Avery Fisher Hall's stage door, the doorman looks surprised as he nods hello. It's only five, and I am early—as usual. "You are always and everywhere too early," my brother would tease me if he were here. "Too early for trains, too early at the airport, too early for dinner reservations. If you go on like the devil, friend Hein will send you to the grave way before your time as punishment." For me, "being there at the right time" is the only effective strategy for coping with the inscrutability of life. Lateness and dawdling are suspect to me. Besides, I hate rushing about unnecessarily. My brother, on the other hand, is your typical last-minute man, a jolly solipsist who believes that all the world has nothing better to do than wait for him. As you might imagine, when the two of us travel together, sparks fly. I sit and seethe, insisting that the time to depart has passed and angrily kicking whatever I can, as Micha calmly lights another cigarette, peruses the *Süddeutsche*, and calls me a hectic neurotic. It's quite a drama.

For the past two days I have been working on a different two-man sketch, this one with a stagehand called Jim. It goes like this:

JIM: "Hi, little big man."
QUASTHOFF: "Hi, big belly."
JIM: "Everything's okay with Gustav Mahler?"
QUASTHOFF: "Yes! He rests in peace. I hope the concert doesn't raise him."

Jim's roly-poly belly jiggles like pudding as he laughs at our routine, sending sunny chuckles burbling up to the ceiling. It's fair to say that the acoustics here are brilliant.

On the stage, I inspect my workplace one last time before the concert. Our contract includes a memo that my agency sends to every organizer. "Thomas Quasthoff needs for the concert: a podium, about three by three feet, sixteen to twenty inches high (roughly corresponds to a conductor's podium without rail), with two steps and a chair (if possible with adjustable height), a wooden score console."

These requirements are neither extravagances nor affectations; they are related to my disability. It is exceedingly difficult to stand throughout a longer concert (even my "normal" colleagues can manage passages that last hours only by taking breaks to sit down). And when ecclesiastical or orchestral works are performed, there are always several soloists arrayed alongside the conductor, not unlike a soccer team. Without a podium bringing me up to eye level, the maestro would need the visual field of an owl to get his commands across to the tot surrounded by a forest of high tenors and baroque altos. Similarly, I would be forced constantly to locate the prompter behind the backs of my colleagues. I would sway like a reed, which would not exactly amplify my aesthetic appeal and might even give some viewers the idea that I had had a nip before the concert. This is the math: 20-inch podium + 36-inch chair + 27-inch seated baritone = seeing and being seen. The podium holds the heavy score books for me and makes turning the page much easier; it should be made of wood, a material that, when it comes to podiums, pits itself more reliably against the gravitational forces than metal.

What other condition must obtain if we are to have a successful performance?

The fortitude of all those involved is necessary. Whoever has spent his youth interpreting songs for audiences in school auditoriums and small town halls knows exactly what I mean. Well do I recall the many nights I had to focus on maintaining my balance atop a stack of fruit crates while trying not to wake the cultural official snoring blissfully in the first row. After all, he had been coaxed into attending because we hoped he would throw some subsidies our way. I managed to sing in spite of it all, but don't ask how.

At the Zombie Club in Wennigsen we never even got that far. I was singing with a soul band at the time. Beside me the keyboard player sat atop a precarious plywood platform. Right after the instrumental intro the entire construction collapsed with a bang. We survived, but the electric piano and the amplifier unfortunately did not. The rest of the band tried to save what could be saved, but two numbers later the subwoofer gave up, and the concert was over. And what was our reward? Expenses, jeers, and a bump on the head as big as a potato dumpling. That's the music business.

This is something different, though; that's all in my past. And it's high time Tony Shalit appeared. Sure enough, here is the knock at my dressing room door. In comes a man in his late fifties, elegant yet impish, his face tan, his features sharply chiseled, his icy grey hair sparse above a high forehead. With a nonchalant movement his sunglasses disappear into the breast pocket of his sport coat. Then he beams and throws his arms around my neck and plants a moist kiss on my cheek.

"Hallo, Sweetheart, wee gates?"

"Everything is great."

"Alright, then, you will be good tonight. You will be formidahbel."

"Hmm."

"You will dazzle New York."

"Hmm."

"Don't say 'hmm,' say 'yes!' " Tony is stilting euphorically from wall to wall, looking like a mating marabou. "The best orchestra in the world with the best singer in the world. That will make history."

"Tony, come on."

"I talked about it with Colin Davis. I said to him—"

"Tony, sit down!!!" I would rather not know what he said to Davis. Sir Colin is not only the head of the London Symphony; not only one of the great interpreters of Mozart, Sibelius, and Berlioz; and not only a knight of Her Majesty Elizabeth II. Tonight he is the conductor of the New York Philharmonic. I would be mortified if he decided that Mr. Quasthoff and his herald were suffering from a Napoleon complex. Tony, on the other hand, does not give a damn. From Bayreuth to Sydney he enjoys a solid reputation in the music community as a seasonal eccentric, bon vivant, and free radical. Now he wheezes as he drops into an armchair, ready as always to have the last word.

"I *know* it will be woonderbah."

"We'll see."

"What do you mean, 'see'? You have to stroke my ears, not my eyes."

That's how it has been with us for years. A decade ago we were both chugging through the Mediterranean on a luxury cruise ship, Tony as a passenger, I in the capacity of "Cultural Diversion" (and in good company, too: also aboard were the violinist Vladimir Spivakov, the god of cello Mstislav Rostropovich, and his wife, the celebrated opera diva Galina Vishnevskaya). It was my first cruise and my first excursion into the world of hundred-dollar tips. I found many things bewildering: who knew that one could change one's outfit seven times a day, and what exactly was this nouvelle cuisine, which took pains to stretch into five courses what at our house fits comfortably on one plate? Having to prove myself alongside some of my musical heroes didn't make things any easier, and I paced the deck feeling like an impostor until Tony rescued me. He heard my first concert, declared it "magnificent," and took me under his wing. Tony was the captain's buddy, the stars' buddy, the waiters' buddy—in short, a friend to one and all. He ordered the right wines, made the right conversation, and conducted himself with intelligence and wit all day and all night. How he did it? At first I thought he managed thanks to his curious diet: for breakfast he would have a joint with tea; at lunchtime, a joint with fish; and at night he would supplement his salad with some grass. But this wasn't it. Plenty of our powerful and successful shipmates would have a martini with their coffee, but Tony was something special: a free spirit who cultivated the unconventional—at times veering into the highly comical and even kinky—not for its own sake but because he believed obstinacy, independence, and tolerance to be fundamental human rights. Of course, this position can only be taken by those who can afford it, as Tony can. As an international lawyer he made a fortune by finessing a way for Australian companies to access the American market. At fifty he put work aside and decided to devote himself to family and a few hobbies, above all the obsession of his life: music. So when he is not sailing across the Indian Ocean, buying valuable books and art, or hopping into a helicopter in search of fresh caviar, he is following singers and conductors around the globe like a well-off Deadhead.

Since that cruise we have been fast friends, and whenever he can Tony escorts me on my tours—a guarantee of lots of fun. Something crazy always happens, often occasioned by the seemingly unlikely stimulus of Tony's tendency to embark on exhausting excursions through music history. He'll start with Monteverdi and end by saying, "I just don't know what this Schönberg wanted." In a museum café, fine, but at the butcher's counter of a German supermarket such behavior can raise blood pressure to unimagined heights, especially in the line behind him. Tony is a polished man of the world and archromantic who can be moved to tears by the first notes of the *Tannhäuser* overture. But he is also from New York, where boys learn in kindergarten never to leave a verbal injury unanswered. And so Tony turns around, makes a face like Robert De Niro in *Cape Fear*, and barks that "Krauts," having begun and lost two world wars, should know better than to meddle in other people's business. Once that has been clarified he can order, ever so calmly, half a pound of "bloody roast beef" and march to the register, not deigning to dignify his audience with so much as a glance. In a world whose inhabitants increasingly resemble the products of Playmobil, Tony should be protected as an endangered species.

But he has got to get on his way now. A gong resounds from the speaker above the door of my dressing room, indicating that the concert will begin in twenty minutes. I accompany Tony for part of the way so I can watch the entry of the New York audience from the foyer, an instructive spectacle for a native of Old Europe. What strikes me first is the complete absence of that solemn, respectful murmur that has been flowing around German stages since the days of Goethe and Schiller. Instead one enjoys the relaxed atmosphere, the matter-of-fact attitude with which the Americans have—yes, I will put it this way—made use of their cultural temples. One sees humans of all skin colors, all age and income groups, though here it is harder than it is at home to tell the well-to-do from the just-scraping-by. Of course, even here one finds the class-conscious parade of custom-made suits, impressive jewelry, and designer wardrobes, but most visitors wade in jeans and sneakers through the ankle-deep merchandise. Some carry shopping bags, others are gobbling up a last-minute tuna burger, while others still read in comfortable corners perfect for lounging. Do these masters of the universe study the evening's program bulletin? No, their attention is held by the sports section of the *Post*, which proclaims today that the Rangers once again lost to Boston. I suppose that "The Sentry's Nightsong" ("I cannot and may not be merry") will most certainly hit a nerve in the auditorium later tonight.

This fundamentally democratic casualness, though it is very likable, has its drawbacks. For example, towards the end of a not-so-compelling performance, half of the audience jumps up and scurries towards the exit, drowning the final bars in a cacophony of rustling clothes, clattering chairs, and querulous maneuvering, even as the conductor urges the orchestra to a stubborn yet helpless forte. No problem, a pizza baker from Seattle once told me, pointing out that he donated five thousand tax-deductible dollars to the opera each year, earning himself not only a spot on the brass plaque in the foyer but also the right to get his car out of the garage before the inevitable traffic jam. I suppose it depends on how you look at it. Personally, I view *Homo Americanus*'s habit of valuing the classical arts no higher than other forms of intelligent entertainment—whether film or basketball—as a true achievement of civilization. It does not harm the quality and professional appreciation of artists; rather, the opposite is true.

Returning to the backstage area, I notice that even the aces of the New York Philharmonic are tense like racehorses before the start. A cloud of scales, shreds of melody, and tangles of chords mingle with the aromas of hair gel, perfume, sweat, and rosin. Musicians are warming up their instruments, loosening their lips and fingers, wandering around or standing together in little groups. The gong sounds for the second time. The countdown is on—only ten minutes left. Last puffs on cigarettes, here a dress adjusted, there a bow tie, kisses exchanged, and, following old theatre custom, colleagues spitting over each other's shoulders.

"See you," a clarinet is calling out to me. Then the orchestra has got to go on stage.

Colin Davis opens the evening with the *King Lear* overture by Hector Berlioz and Frank Martin's *Petite Symphonie Concertante.* The Mahler lieder are scheduled for after the break, so I can still sit for a while in my dressing room, do a few voice exercises, and follow the concert via loudspeaker and TV monitor. When the first notes float through the hall I stare at the screen. The sound quality of the transmission is, well, not the best, but one imagines it must sound wonderful in the hall. After a while I want to know for sure and stalk over to the right side entrance of the stage. Through the narrow opening I see the percussionists, compact men who smash their sticks mightily and precisely onto the skins. I see hairdos and violin bows fly, and I see Sir Colin, calmly bringing the romantically bubbling *King Lear* prelude to a climax. He is directing a near perfect sound body: fully trained, with highly sensitive nerve paths and resilient muscles, driven by a center force pulsating somewhere between the oboes, violins, and violas. It is from there that the ear presumes a mighty stream of energy to spring forth and electrify the musicians up to their fingertips at all times. Frank Martin once said good music worked like "an organism." The New York Philharmonic sounds like that of a blessed dancer, so light-footedly does the orchestra trip across the sound carpet rolled out by Berlioz, a pre-Mahlerian wealth of color; with a sleepwalker's security the orchestral sections follow even the most subtle shifts of the *Petite Symphonie.*

I have been rehearsing with the Philharmonic for two days, so I already know their magnificence. But I simply could not have imagined that, when it comes down to it, they can play two classes above what I have heard. Inger Dam-Jensen, my Danish colleague, is similarly impressed when, after the break, we are preparing to march into the hall. Normally one allows ladies to go first. Not me. At least not on stage. The old elevator problem! Inger is a tall, slim blonde. I am four feet and three inches. My trotting along behind her would look slightly curious. I am reminded of little Oskar, Günter Grass's growth-defying tin drummer. Through five hundred pages the little guy strides ahead at all times. A military image, from the world of parades, the well-versed reader will say. I don't believe it. It is an ironclad aesthetic law, similar to the golden ratio: the shortest must come first. Whoever can remember the cartoon cowboy Lucky Luke and his eternal adversaries, the four Dalton brothers, will know what I mean: the nefarious quartet always confronts Lucky in tiers, standing on the prairie like one of Nebuchadnezzar's ziggurat towers (one might also say like a staggering joke). The same principle holds in the ranks of profiled figures in ancient Egyptian images, in which the small one, whether he, she, or it, always belongs *in front of* the big one. Then again, in our particular case the idiom "age before beauty" makes the point just as well.

Inger and I are now crossing the orchestra front. The moment of passage from the twilight wings onto the stage is something magical for me, again and again. It is hot and blindingly bright out there. The spotlights create sparkling reflections on the tin and polished wood of the string instruments, while the glittering stage light draws a dark curtain before the rows of seats. One senses rather than sees the murmuring crowd. After one or two steps applause suddenly swells up out of the darkness, much like the first breaker of a rising tide thrown against the shore. The sound gains even more force as Sir Colin climbs the podium and lowers his curly grey head with a smile. But as soon as he turns his back to the audience, this friendly gentleman takes on the aura of an emperor. "He mounts the rostrum, clears his throat and raises his baton; silence falls," Elias Canetti writes of the conductor, and he knows why it must be so and no other way: ". . . since, during the performance, nothing is supposed to exist except this work, for so long is the conductor the ruler of the world."

Sir Colin has lowered the baton, and the orchestra has begun building the score, layer by layer, working towards a mighty march and battle noise. The sentry—in this case, your humble narrator—launches the first stanza into the parquet with corresponding verve: "Ich kann und mag nicht Froehlich sein! / Wenn alle Leute schlafen, / So muss ich wachen, / muss traurig sein." ("I cannot and may not be merry, / when all the world's asleep. / So I must guard / and must be sad.") Inger tries to whisper into my ear that there is no reason for depression since "im Rosengarten, / im gruenen Klee" ("in the rose garden, among the green clover") the maiden awaits her soldier. Besides that, there is God's blessing, which can also be relied upon "on the field," at least for him who believes in it. With this her lovely, enticing soprano glides across a floating cadence of major triads, which Mahler, at the end, tips over into the twilight (an E-minor chord, to be exact). That is when the poor sentry realizes that this tenderly eroticized image of nature is nothing but dream, and the man realizes that trust in God was misplaced, for "He is King / He is the emperor / He leads the war." ("Er ist Koenig! / Er ist Kaiser! / Er fuehrt den Krieg.")

The Philharmonic is establishing this tragedy in such an inspired manner, and our voices bringing it alive in such perfect harmony, that applause starts to drizzle from the balcony at the end of the first song—a mortal sin among traditional classical aficionados. Respect for the work of art demands that the audience wait until the cycle has ended to applaud. Who came up with this rule and how long ago, I don't know. The truth is that it is broken more often than you might think, and, to be honest, I don't mind. Sometimes it is even refreshingly funny: In Chicago once a few colleagues and I were on tour with Mozart vocal pieces, accompanied by the Freiburg Baroque Orchestra. I was singing Leporello's aria to Donna Elvira from *Don Giovanni.* At the end of the score there is a grand *fermata,* which requires one note to be held at the same pitch for a rather long time. Into this *fermata* someone from the audience yelled "Bravo." Without letting my voice break I yelled back "Too early!" I then continued singing, although the last chords of the piece were not audible, since the audience was doubling over in laughter.

Tonight it doesn't go that far. Nevertheless, it gets better and better because fortunately for us singers, and to the great delight of the audience, Colin Davis has decided to allow all songs written in dialogue to be performed as duets. Though the composer did not intend this, the two editors of the *Wunderhorn*, Clemens Brentano and Achim von Arnim, did. When these poet friends and in-laws presented the first edition of their Old German poem and song collection, it was not pure folk poetry. They had edited the material, smoothed out the rhymes, cut verses, and added entire stanzas at their discretion. Into the "Lied des Verfolgten im Turm" ("Song of the Persecuted in the Tower") a female part was implanted without apology. The seams are visible and audible. The two blocks of lyrics do not add up to a homogeneous whole but are actually two monologues, juxtaposed like parallel action scenes in a movie.

Scene 1 opens in the dungeon. A strip of pale sunlight falls through the bars. The camera zooms onto the emaciated face of a prisoner. He appears composed. He will not eat humble pie. He will resist fate by forsaking all yearning for love and happiness and by conjuring up all the platonic joys of inner immigration. The prisoner rises from his cot, clenches his fists, and sings: "Die Gedanken sind frei, / Wer kann sie erraten? / Sie rauschen vorbei / Wie naechtliche Schatten. / Kein Mensch kann sie wissen, / Kein Jaeger sie schiessen. / Es bleibet dabei, / Die Gedanken sind frei." ("Thoughts are free, / Who can guess them? / They stream past us / like shadows in the night. / No man can know them, / No hunter can shoot them. / It remains thus: / Thoughts are free.")

Scene 2 shows the girl squatting on the stairs in front of the ruins, not willing to have any of it. A tear runs across her little cheek while she imagines the lost togetherness: "Im Sommer ist gut lustig sein, / Auf hohen, wilden Heiden. / Dort findet man gruen Plaetzelein. / Mein herzverleibtes Schaetzelein, / Von dır mag ich nicht scheiden." ("In summer it is good to be merry / on high, wild meadows, / where one finds a green little place; / my heart's beloved treasure, / I do not wish to part from you!")

And thus it continues in alternating counter cuts until the prisoner speaks his final word: "Und weil Du so klagst, / Der Lieb' ich entsage / . . . / es bleibet dabei, / die Gedanken sind frei." ("And because you lament so / I will renounce love, / . . . / For it remains thus: / Thoughts are free!") The camera flies through the dungeon window, leaving the girl below, a pile of misery against the horizon. Cut.

Some wit dubbed the work, a bit glibly but accurately, "a kind of abbreviated *Fidelio* for choral societies." The dramatically scenic is the basis for all *Wunderhorn* songs. In "Des Antonius von Padua Fischpredigt" ("Saint Anthony of Padua's Sermon to the Fish") herring, carp, eel, and pike gather to listen to the words of Saint Anthony, clap fins, but, sermon over, swim away as the murderers and robbers they were; "Der Tamboursg'sell" ("The Drummer Boy") is sitting in his death cell; the "Rheinlegendchen" ("Little Rhine Legend") is being spun during a walk; the "Irdische Leben" ("Earthly Life") and "Verlorne Müh" ("Lost Effort") depict scenes of rural life; in "Trost im Unglück" ("Consolation in Misery") a hussar and a girl are bantering in the night; the "Lob des hohen Verstand" ("In Praise of Higher Understanding") negotiates a singing competition between a cuckoo and a nightingale, decided by the referee, naturally a stupid donkey, in favor of the cuckoo. Everything takes place in front of carefully chosen scenery, with the subject matter giving Mahler the greatest possible breadth of compositional variation on the smallest space. In "Wo die schoenen Trompeten blasen" ("Where the Beautiful Trumpets Blow")

alone—the ballad of the dead soldier who climbs out of his grave
at night to fetch his beloved into his "house of green grass"—he
stuffed: elegiac trumpet fifths, accompanying brute marching
rhythms, a D-major movement in three-four time; a cantilena in
G-flat major; further trumpets in major which in the end dive into
the minor-ish. In other places oddities such as false basses, parallel
sixths between major episodes, tenth leaps over staccato sixteenths
in a dark minor. In "Revelge" ("Reveille"), as Habakuk Traber has
observed, there seemed to be "no more rules about how they had to
stop and go." No wonder that the entire military noise apparatus
comes apart when the fallen drummer drums up the dead bodies of
his comrades, leads them into battle, and proudly lets them stand
at attention at his sweetheart's house. "Des morgen stehen da die
Gebeine / in Reih und Glied, sie stehen wie Leichensteine / Die
Trommel steht voran / Trallali, trallalei, trallalera / Dass sie ihn
sehen kann" ("In the morning there stand the bones / In rank and
file as tombstones. / The drum stands in front / tralali, tralalei,
tralala, / so that she can see him.") Mercifully, the song ends here
with beats of the drum and caustic clusters of trumpets. I certainly do not want to imagine the face his sweetheart made when
she laid eyes on the assembly of zombies. She must have been at
least as stunned as the music writer Ernst Decsey, who once
addressed Mahler in regard to the most effective but "peculiar
shaping and reshaping of a dominant." The composer curtly
replied: "Oh please! Dominant! Take things as naïvely as they are
intended." Which shows that one should not overtheorize things.

Like Mahler, I am over it. After all, musicology can explain
our fascination with the *Wunderhorn Lieder* only to a limited
extent. Let us simply praise Mahler's genius in managing to
imprint a modern *Weltgefuehl,* a sensibility still familiar to us
today, onto the anarchic, naïve, popular texts he was working
with. That hopeless "Thrownness" of the late bourgeois individual, deliberated on for volumes by clever heads like Heidegger

and Derrida, weaves itself through the cycle. Such loneliness, despair, and painful beauty lies in Mahler's music, such fury, stubbornness, and spite in the face of the frighteningly meaningless humming of the world, that it still touches us in our innermost core today.

"It was so wonderful!"

"Unbelievable!"

"Hey, man, great job!"

"That was music; that was sound!"

"You are the best!"

"No, you're the best!"

Backstage has become one great festival of slaps on the back. The two singers are throwing around compliments and the violins are tossing them back. Celli congratulate clarinets, trombones cuddle basses. Everyone has a smile on his face, and the relatives, friends, and acquaintances who have found their way backstage are equally enthused and overflowing with praise for the virtuosity of their loved ones. I find it wonderful. Sweaty, my veins swollen with adrenaline, I give Micha and Renate my first impressions: "Fantastic . . . how Inger sang the coloratura of 'Liedlein' . . . Colin Davis did the triplet part . . . the pianissimo of the Philharmonic . . . super, went fantastically well . . . thirst . . . have got to get something to drink . . . oh, how nice that you are here . . ." I am talking like a waterfall; the floodgates are open. Now everything has got to come out or I will burst. Seven times we left the stage, seven times they clapped us back out, seven times Sir Colin had to receive a standing ovation with British noblesse, meaning with a slightly bent upper body.

Tony, on the other hand, is not so cool and collected. His anxiety about my debut in his hometown probably outweighed Muhammad Ali's before his first world championship fight against

Sonny Liston. Now it is over and Tony is profoundly moved; unlike Ali, he can't find any words. He is waiting for me in my dressing room, and when I return he clasps me firmly to his chest, his eyes moist with emotion. But there isn't much time for sentimentality in this topsy-turvy madhouse. Musicians are coming and going; journalists are piling in; Markus Sievers, a representative of my German agency, is handing out business cards like Chinese restaurant menus; total strangers are baffling me by giving me the thumbs up, then holding out their programs for my signature, and hey, what do you have to do to get a drink in this place? Just in time, Linda Marder and Charles Cumella appear with a humongous gift basket, which I earned not tonight but rather four days ago, on my birthday. The edible contents would feed a polar expedition crew but not the drinks. They are immediately claimed: the beer by Micha, who uses the opportunity to force Charles, a wine drinker, into a debate about the subject of "the global free market and the German law of purity." The champagne is for everyone.

"Somebody open a bottle!" I call out gaily.

Tony does not need any more encouragement. Whistling the triumphal march of *Aida* he shoots the cork against the ceiling and distributes the noble liquid in a super pack of party cups. Then he clicks his heels together, salutes, and raises the plastic goblet: "Cheers!"

I wish it could go on forever, but it can't. There's the "ten-minute smile," the opening-night dinner, and tomorrow another performance. The sponsors are already waiting in the foyer. Inger, Sir Colin, and I emerge to hearty applause and are planted next to the buffet for all to see. There is a short greeting, a few words of thanks to the patrons, and then one beholds the triptych of cultivated society, with its clear distribution of labor: one talks, one chews, the artist smiles. But Linda is right. New Yorkers are as entertaining as they are economical in their small talk.

A librarian manages within ten minutes to cover the Vienna
Court Opera, Shostakovich's *Stalingrad Symphonie*, Kafka's
Amerika, and Bob Dylan's Christian phase. After twenty minutes
more two female doctors have brought me up to date with the
latest on the Lewinsky affair. I know more details of John Carpenter's most recent vampire movie than I ever cared to know,
and every possible anecdote about Jesse Ventura, the former pro
wrestler who just body-slammed the Democrats and the Republi-
cans in the Minnesota governor's election. When the talk comes
around to basketball and the honorable New York Knicks I have
to check out of the conversation. My legs hurt. I can't stand any
longer.

Half an hour later we are sitting in one of the famous China-
town restaurants. "Original Canton and Szechuan cuisine!" the
maître d' enthused, adding, "You have to try our regional specials."

Renate, who once found a dead dog on her plate after a similar
recommendation in Taipei, pleads for chop suey. Starving, I am
not interested in further details and order a sensational sounding
menu translated to me roughly as "thirteen delicacies from the
lotus garden of the seventh concubine of the emperor so and so."
I am not disappointed. Soon there are nimble waiters flitting
about, arranging bowls, pans, and skillets above the can of Sterno.
One brings crab and black beans; another marinated pork, fish,
and beef meatballs; the third brings soy sprouts, carrots, and
leeks with a multicolored dip. Soon we all dig in. Only Sir Colin
does not get to eat. He is sitting next to Tony, and Tony is talking
about his favorite subject, putting Schubert in between the maestro and his sweet and sour chicken, "Schumann . . . Brahms . . .
Wagner . . . the genius of Romantic music. But can you explain
what Schönberg's idea was?" I am unable to make out whether
Colin Davis offers him a satisfying response.

We close down the evening in a smaller circle at Tavern on the Green. The Central Park bar is not exactly a refuge of coziness: the interior is showy and cold, like something right out of *Bonfire of the Vanities*. Nothing but chrome, mirrored walls, and overly bright lights, and the prices are shrill as well. But it's one of the few places you can eat *and* smoke—something the EU fraction of our little group insisted on—and Markus, the guy from my German agency, is simply not to be deterred from playing the big shot tonight: "Come on guys, let's go inside. This is on me."

Well, that was before we got in. After a few rounds his head gleams tomato red at the bar as he digs through his wallet and discusses the bill with the staff, while we at the table discuss whether to bail him out or leave him there to do the dishes. My brother, always one for a bit of wisdom after a few drinks, cites Heiner Müller: "Man is but dirt, his life but a great laughter." He is for washing dishes. We could counter with Kant's categorical imperative, which, as most everyone knows, simply paraphrases the old folk wisdom: "Do unto others as you would have them do unto you." Micha pays up generously, for Renate and for me as well, but he still murmurs in my ear the whole way home: "Reason gives rise to monsters. You hear? Monsters! Nothing good will come of it."

Well, we're all familiar with the dialectic of the Enlightenment. As long as Horkheimer and Adorno stay out of my dreams, anything is fine with me. And tonight the great sandman is conciliatory. No nightmare, no construction crew, no vacuum can wake me up. I sleep deeply and soundly until noon.

Upon waking up I find a greeting from Renate and Micha on my night table: "Checking out museums today. See you later. Have a nice day. PS: You must look at the paper!" I decide to take it slow and have breakfast in the hotel. The hunters and gatherers are already out stalking again, and the restaurant is accordingly empty. Very nice. I make myself comfortable in a corner and order eggs, bacon, toast, lots of coffee, and the morning papers. When my name appears in fat print right under that of Sir Colin my heart pumps *un poco presto*. Alright then. A deep inhalation; then slooowly exhale. All is well. In fact, it couldn't be any better. They praise Colin Davis, they praise the Philharmonic, they bestow highest praise upon the total work of art, but they especially praise "the little German singer with the big voice." Even the *Times*'s incorruptible Mr. Tommasini is delighted. He writes that from now on they'll want to hear my marvelous baritone more often in New York.

The waiter appears and puts a telephone next to the orange juice. It's Linda.

"Good morning, Tommy. Have you already looked at the paper?"

"Just now."

"And? Isn't it fantastic? Everyone is blown away by your voice. Tomorrow you will be a famous singer all over America."

"Great, does that mean I get to go on Jay Leno?"

"That means a lot more. It means you can choose where you want to perform, with whom you want to perform, and what program. Avery Fisher Hall has already called and asked to schedule an evening of German *Liederabend*. Tommy, you have done it. Here we say about New York: if you can make it there, you'll make it anywhere. Whoever comes through New York has nothing to worry about. We will get lots of work."

Linda always means what she says and knows what she's doing. Nevertheless, I want to ask the waiter to pinch me hard, for I can't believe this is really happening. I let myself sink into the banquette pillows with a sigh. The window frames the usual three o'clock performance: joggers grimly stomping across the pavement, chubby schoolkids with sneakers as large as shoe boxes, two homeless people dozing in front of their cardboard caves, businesspeople with fluttering coats striding out of the fine Broadway restaurants into the office towers. A group of black street sweepers strolls laughing into the park, and at the newsstand the cabdrivers are getting bored. Men from Ukraine and Yemen, from Pakistan or Gabon, men who are looking for luck and find it as rarely as a tourist successfully navigates the tangled streets downtown. But luck has never been shy with me. Maybe that's why I often feel as if I am an actor in a movie, a jolly piece but a little surreal, directed not, say, by Billy Wilder but by Luis Buñuel. I like Buñuel, and I like this weightless and slightly insane mood.

This crazy luck was already in the air as we prepared to leave Hamburg: in the next three weeks I would be singing the two most important concerts of my life, on stage in New York and Boston with the best orchestras of the United States. It was exactly what I had always wanted, and I knew I was up to it. Just before we left, the Echo Classic Award 1998 was handed to me in the Hamburg Music Hall. This was like winning the German Grammy for Best Singer. It is a beautiful thing, this achievement, though the trophy itself is heavy and ugly, an old piece of iron we chose to store in my parents' car. My parents were there when I won, sitting proudly in the hall, and they were there to bid good-bye to their America-bound offspring—my mother, as usual, with practical advice:

"Don't get lost, now, no nonsense, and don't have Thomas's dirty laundry washed by the hotel. I'd rather do it myself."

My father with decisive last questions:

"Boys, have you got your passports?"

" 'Course!"

"And your boarding passes?"

"Sure!"

"Better check again. Micha is such an old scatterbrain."

"Don't worry, Papa. It's all there."

"Well, I hope so! Take care then, and call as soon as you've arrived in one piece."

"Otherwise the doctor will call!"

"You are and always will be a clod pole."

"You are the best."

"Okay, enough now. 'Bye my dears."

High above the airfield stretches an azure sheet streaked with cirrus and shot through with sunshine. Golden is the month of October, and the Quasthoff brothers are in a holiday mood. It isn't often that Micha has time to accompany me on a concert trip, and this one is especially nice because almost fourteen free days lie between the appearances in Boston and New York.

I carry those days with me like a precious photo album. There is a rollicking dinner at the end of which Seiji Ozawa asked Micha with a laugh: "Is your brother always this crazy?" And there is the excursion to Cape Cod, the gliding along Highway 93 under a radiant sky, the Indian summer rushing by in psychedelic shades of red and yellow, and our friend Felicitas tooting Loewe ballads through a rolled-up map. There are the colorfully painted wooden houses and cranberry fields of Rhode Island, the marsh lawns and dune strips behind the channel that separate Cape Cod from the mainland, and finally, in Provincetown, the magnificent ocean and lots of wind. Wave after wave rushes towards the beach in foam-crowned Hockney blue while we brace ourselves against the gusts at forty-five-degree angles, like crooked poles. Then there's the bay of Plymouth where the first Pilgrims set foot in 1620. On the left a model of the *Mayflower* is anchored, and crazy Tony jumps around the monumental Rock proclaiming with a grin that this gruesome hunk of granite should actually be a giant doughnut.

Then I see us in New York, worried and incredibly tired at JFK because Renate's flight is four and a half hours delayed. Not three hours after that there we are at the Knitting Factory, beside ourselves with excitement because Steven Bernstein's quintet, Sex Mob Featuring John Medeski is performing "John Barry's Music from James Bond Films." I see us atop the Empire State Building and strolling through Little Odessa, where the blocks of houses almost fall into the ocean. I see us standing rapt before Mark Rothko's fields of color, and I see how Renate snaps a picture of the fraternal couple in front of Carnegie Hall, at which point I hear myself call out like the young Gerd Schröeder, "I want in there!" (in the chancellor's office). But the most beautiful memory picture by far goes back to Birdland. We are celebrating my thirty-ninth birthday. From the stage a thirty-man New York all-star band is peppering us with knife-sharp riffs, while heads and feet are moving ever bolder below in an Afro-Cuban rhythmic frenzy. When midnight strikes, the band pauses and the staff presents me with a bottle of champagne! Renate has conjured up a birthday cake with sparklers and everyone is wishing me well.

Today, of course, the Avery Fisher Hall concerts, so important for my career, have a place of honor in my American album as well. Every time I open it I am reminded of my parents and the fact that this career would never have been possible without their love, their trust, and their support. It means so much to them to see me live a successful, independent, and, most of all, happy life. After all, I wasn't a sure thing when my mother gave birth, on November 9, 1959, in the Bernwards-Hospital of Hildesheim, to one of twelve thousand thalidomide children.

I Got the Blues

Right, left, right, left, right, left: on the bedsheet my head thumps back and forth like a metronome. I lie there half naked, my hips and legs firmly clamped into an elaborate device. Leather straps tether the leg casts to the bed frame on the left and the metal grid on the right. The bed stands in a large room with fifteen other beds, all of them white and empty. It smells of cheap laundry soap, disinfectant, and urine. I don't want to smell it. No, I don't smell it. Right, left, right, left: my head is still going. Has it been an hour? Two hours? I cannot feel my legs nor the sweat-drenched spot where my head rolls across the sheet, nor the ulcers on my sorely chafed buttocks. I don't feel anything. My pupils are leaping: right towards the grate, left to the cross-shaped window frame, right to the grate, left to the window frame. Nice and easy. And into this trancelike lolling nothing can penetrate—nothing but music. It comes from the playground outside in the courtyard, it seeps in from the boarding school's rooms, it issues from a radio in the sisters' station. One, two, one, two, one, two. Happily my child's lips are forming tone sequences, children's songs, shreds of pop songs: "Hytshie boombytshie boomboom, Hytshie boombytshie boomboom."

That's a song by Lolita, strangely enough the name of a very grown-up lady who had a beautiful alto voice and a few hits during the early sixties. My mother loves her records. My mother's name is Brigitte. Two or three times a week she stands behind a thick piece of glass separating the visitors' room from the inside of the clinic. When she comes, a sister pushes my bed to the window and I see Mama's slender, pale face. I see how she puts the palms of her hands against the glass. Sometimes she says something, but I can't make it out. Sometimes she has to cry. Then my father puts an arm around her shoulders, wiping away a tear of his own. Sometimes Micha stands there, too, making faces. He flattens his nose, folding his face with both hands, pulls down an eyelid, and moves his mouth up. He looks spooky. Like Charles Laughton as Quasimodo when he straps the gypsy Esmeralda to his hunchback and screams, "Right of asylum!" In fact, he looks so scary I start screaming. Then Micha gets a slap on the cheek, which causes him to mimic a dying swan. I have to laugh, Micha has to laugh, and Father grins. Even Mama laughs now and gives Micha a kiss. The joys of family!

Half an hour later I am pushed back into the large, barren room, alone again—alone with my yellow teddy bear and the radio in the sisters' room. "Liebeskummer lohnt sich nicht, my Darling. / Schade um die Traenen in der Nacht" ("Being lovesick isn't worth it, my darling / It's such a shame to cry in the night") the blond Siv Malmquist chirps, and I chirp along. And again my head starts rolling—right, left, right, left, right, left.

"You have a very musical child," the sisters tell my mother when she makes her next visit. Mama nods silently and looks at me with big eyes.

"When can the boy finally come home?" asks Father. The sisters' only answer is a shrug.

One and a half years pass like this. For one and a half years I live in the orthopedic rehab center of Hanover's Saint Ann's Diocese, seeing my family only through the glass partition. "Due to the risk of infection, all bodily contact must be avoided," my parents are told. I get everything imaginable anyway: measles, chicken pox, mumps, and, a dozen times, the flu. Actually, I am always sick. The doctors don't mind. I remain in quarantine, or rather: under observation. After all, a thalidomide case is new, medically interesting, and one never knows.

What one does know now is that my mother should never have been prescribed the barbiturate Contergan. When she swallowed the pills ("guaranteed without side effects") in the spring of 1959, rumors of fetal brain and nerve damage, perhaps caused by an ingredient called thalidomide, had already been swirling around the manufacturer Grünenthal for a while. One year later a Hamburg doctor proved the connection between the consumption of Contergan and deformations in newborns. But Grünenthal continued to attack anyone who asserted that Contergan was harmful. By 1962 the evidence had become overwhelming, and there was a trial. Grünenthal had to pull the drug from the market, paying out to the victims low five-figure sums, which the company wrote off at tax time.

With the backing of the pharmaceutical lobby, the company thwarted the federal health ministry's plan to require that future medications be tested for such risks. There was the incredible explanation, in black and white: "We do not believe that recent experience demands a change of the law in this regard." The maneuvering continues until and through the early seventies. When the liberal Social Democratic government tries again to impose stricter standards of testing, the pharmaceutical lobby threatens to devote all its might to quashing these changes. The details are in a dossier held in the Swiss safe-deposit box of FDP man Hans-Otto Scholl, leading manager of the Federal Association of the Pharmaceutical Industry. It contains numbers and a lot of names, many belonging to prominent members of the Bonn government like Alfred Dregger or Martin Bangemann as well as top figures in public health, all of whom received campaign donations or payoffs in exchange for their efforts against the new drug law. Today Contergan is still being distributed, under a different name, in Brazil and the United States.

But the devastating consequences are no different. Contergan, or thalidomide, is especially damaging during the first trimester, when the embryo forms its skeleton and organs. The particular kind of deformation depends on when and for how long the drug is taken. Between the twenty-first and twenty-second days of pregnancy thalidomide leads to brain damage and malformations of the outer ear. Between the twenty-fourth and twenty-ninth days thalidomide causes phocomelia, or "seal extremities," so called because the long bones of arms and legs develop incompletely and the hands and feet grow attached directly at the shoulder and hip, something like fins. From the thirtieth to the thirty-sixth day deformations of the hands arise along with rectal stenosis (abnormal narrowing of the anus and rectum). Close to five thousand thalidomide children, almost half of all those who were affected, died in West Germany alone. Another third suffered lasting brain damage.

After a year and a half the experts at Saint Ann's are certain: little Quasthoff seems to have been lucky. His head works fine, and so does his metabolism. He just looks like a little seal, with crippled hands and feet that arch backwards at a ninety-degree angle instead of facing front. "He'll never be able to walk," says Professor Hauberg, the head of the clinic, "but with a plaster cast we should be able to correct it, at least the way it looks."

I can go home at last. The human bundle they put into my mother's arms is three years old and weighs eleven pounds (actually, ten pounds plus a plaster cast). The unshapely thing comes free of charge, with a lot of advice thrown in for good measure, for instance: "Chin up, even a child like this can bring a lot of joy."

"Adorable," Grandma Else declares.

"What a cutie," Aunt Frida coos.

"But thin as a toothpick!" Grandma Lieschen, heavy and round as an oak barrel, shakes her grey head in dismay. The robust trio leans over his bed to caress his blond hair, and the boy beams happily. A piece of chocolate cake is thrust into his mouth and he grunts cozily, drools, and stammers "choco-load," meaning "refill."

"Clever child!" Grandma Else rejoices.

"Please don't stuff him full of sweets!" my mother pleads.

But Aunt Frida will have none of that. "In the clinic he never got goodies like this."

An hour later I spit my dinner onto Mama's apron, cry, and scream like crazy—not for the first time today, and not for the last time. I have honed this style of protest to a nerve-racking perfection.

"Come on, you little whistle boy." My father deposits his crowing offspring in a corner of the sofa in front of the radio. It's Sunday, and he would have liked to have a peaceful breakfast. The NDR show for seamen, *Between Hamburg and Tahiti*, is on. Gisela from Aurich is greeting Officer Heinz Klüwer at sea near Malaysia on the *Senator II*. Then Freddy Quinn pines away with "Junge, Komm Bald Wieder" ("Come back soon, my boy"). Knowing that one by heart now, I am rolling my head across the sofa cushions: right, left, right, left, right, left. Once the radio plays "Der Lachende Vagabund" ("The Laughing Vagabond"), another hit from those years, the peace is broken—and the song is played all the time.

"They should forbid that song." Mama murmurs this as fervently as Cato the Roman did "I declare that Carthage must be destroyed." For after the refrain the performer, Fred Bertelsmann, laughs so perversely that the number should really be called "The Laughing Fiend." And again I start screaming.

I scream in the morning and I scream at night. I cry because I have spent eighteen months in a plaster cast and am not accustomed to being carried around. When I am once again strapped into the stiff corset I howl because it is so much nicer in Mama's and Papa's arms. I scream and cry when new people crowd into our apartment, when Micha does not give me his red fire truck, and when I have peed into my cast at night. I pee into my cast every night.

Mama accepts it. Mama accepts a lot. Neighbors stare at me in the hallway, as if I were a ghost. People call after her at the supermarket, "Guess you made that one when you were drunk." In the bishop's town of Hildesheim people make the sign of the cross when she takes me for a walk in the park. Mama took the Contergan. Mama tortures herself with accusations: it is her fault that I am handicapped. Father says that is nonsense and Mama knows that he is right. But she scrubs the cast every night without complaints, then carries me to the big marriage bed, puts my head onto her breast, and quietly weeps into her pillow.

At some point Father decides he cannot put up with the misery any longer. One night he stomps across the street to old Bergner, a brawny man with hands like coal shovels and a heart of gold, who operates Hildesheim's only horse slaughterhouse. Both men, being from the country, are used to resolving problems in a rustic, pragmatic way. When Father comes home, he has had a few beers. Across his arm dangles a boiled horse bowel. Mama is horrified: "Hänschen, you're not going to . . ."

"Yes, I am. We dried up my incontinent grandfather the same way." Undeterred he puts the catheter au naturel over my urethra, hangs the other end over a pot on the floor and inspects his work.

"The waters are singing forth from the sleep, from today, from the passed day," he quips cheerfully, "but not today," after which he lies down and sleeps the sleep of the righteous. Mama does too, for the first time in weeks.

That night I dry up and quiet down—a night of great importance for the family. What follows is a weekend during which Micha and I barely see my parents at all. They barricade themselves in the living room. They huddle in the kitchen. They talk. For hours. We are sitting in our room listening anxiously. Things get loud, doors are slammed, and tears are flowing. They fight, they embrace, they fight again. In the end all is well, and it is as if a cloud has lifted from our house. From now on things will look up, or rather: we will move on. My parents have decided to let doctors be doctors and handicaps be handicaps and finally to teach their youngest to walk upright, to take his first step to becoming a complete human being.

To get me into the vertical sphere at least some of the time, they use a variation on the cast: the rail-and-clamp apparatus. As its name suggests, this clumsy prosthesis consists of metal rails running along the hips and legs, fastened with leather straps and steel clamps. The footrest is about twelve inches above the ground, and when I am strapped in I reach an age-appropriate height. That is generally good for my circulatory system, which can finally catch its breath, but sometimes a bit much for someone who has spent his life to date lounging about like Oblomov. In an upright position I often get as dizzy as a land rat moved from the dependable shore to the tipsy mast basket of a brig. But the monstrosity prevents any movement, sparing me most of the symptoms of seasickness. I hang helplessly in my gear and am often leaned against the wall, or put in places where I cannot do too much damage if I fall.

Of course, I fall repeatedly, and since I have no arms and legs to catch myself, I slam down each time like a broomstick. The bumps on my forehead grow as large as eggs.

"A head made of Krupp steel" is Uncle Herbert's approving

comment. Mama's cousin-in-law knows what he's talking about. The old Social Democrat got hit over his bald head with a beer bottle by the SA once. The scars run deep. "No manners, these fascists. That was their recipe for success. The SPD always hit back with decency—with fists, and every once in a while a chair leg. And what good did that do? Nothing!" When this subject comes up, my father knows that only a double Schnaps will keep Uncle from regaling us once again with the story of the workers movement, from Lasalle to the Godesberg Program.

"Herbertchen, think about your heart," Cousin Elsie reprimands with a strict glance at the full glass.

"Don't worry, Mousy, that only beats for you," Herbert says, and he downs the Schnaps.

My father finally solves the problem of my crashing by making a chest-high wooden rack himself. I can hold on to it and am caught by it when I lose my balance. Secured like this it is not far to my next—that is, my first—step. Mama has found out that she can give me a little legroom when she leaves two of the clamps open at hip-height.

The kitchen becomes the scene of my daily exercise: A big plate of sweets sits on the table. Six feet away from it she has set up the wooden rack. Mama lifts me, strapped into the rail and clamp, into it, steps up to the table, and takes a piece of chocolate in her hand.

"Loady!" The scientific subject is beaming.

"Exactly," says Mama, "delicious, sweet milk-orange-chocolate—the best in the world."

The subject begins to salivate, expecting to be fed. But no such thing happens. Instead, Mama puts the delicacy back on the plate, opens her arms, and purrs: "Come, little guy, come. Just put one leg in front of the other and get it."

This trick is based on the famous experiment of the Russian psychologist Ivan Pavlov. In 1904 he held a bowl of food just out of reach of his dogs, rang a bell, and watched mercilessly how they drooled. When Pavlov realized that eventually the reflex functioned even without food, simply in response to the bell, he had discovered classical conditioning and he won his Nobel Prize.

I, on the other hand, get nothing, for now. I do not make a single step. I just don't see why I should. Vaguely sensing that mother and son have reached the Rubicon, and that the basic right to consume milk-orange-chocolate has been denigrated to the point that I must bargain, that the wolfish law of capitalism has thrown its first dark shadows onto the realm of unconditional parental love, my childish self refuses to have any part of this business.

"Mmmmh, tastes good!" Mama is relishing a piece of chocolate, then a cookie. "Just three little steps. Come on. You can do it. It's really easy."

When the next piece of chocolate disappears between her lips, something clicks inside me. Mama reaches for it one more time and looks at me sadly.

"Oh, Tommy, look. Soon it's all gone."

She chews, she swallows, her hand once again circling over the plate. That's it. I put the right leg in front while the hinges of the prosthesis are aching. I pull the left one up. The wooden rack is scratching across the stone floor of the kitchen. Once again the right leg in front, once again the left, and I am there. It really is easy. Mama lights up like a chandelier. She hugs me and kisses me, puts the reward into my mouth and says: "Very good, my sweetheart. Let's do it again."

Thanks to my love of chocolate, I learn quickly. Soon I make it without the supporting wooden rack, and after a week I make it even without chocolate. Mr. Pavlov has undoubtedly earned his

Nobel Prize. We drive to Saint Ann's Hanover to demonstrate our trick to Professor Hauberg. The orthopedist leans against his office window, arms crossed, and chewing his glasses, while I maneuver his rail and clamp apparatus, awkwardly but accident free, around his leather seating arrangement.

"Unbelievable. That is really unbelievable!" Hauberg shakes his head, then turns to my parents: "I never would have thought this possible. Well done." He really is a little bit touched, but he is also an entrepreneurial and helpful human being. He rings a bell, asks for pencil and drawing board, and throws a few quick and precise lines onto the paper. Two months later I have a new, lighter prosthesis—and a new trainer.

Father has taken off his shoes and pulled in his stomach. His hands are pressed against the seams of his pants, and his chin is pointing at the ceiling. He is standing in the bedroom on top of the bed as if waiting for someone to come and pin the Federal Cross of Merit onto his jacket. I am standing in front of him waiting for him to fall over. Father doesn't disappoint.

"Attention!" he calls out. "Watch out!" and his body begins to tilt towards the mattress in a straight line, gaining momentum, faster, faster—but he turns his right arm before impact, thus catching the fall with his shoulder. Unfortunately, the elastic inner spring mattress spoils the otherwise flawless performance. Father loses his balance and lands on the floor with a semiflip. When he scrambles back up he groaningly holds his knee, ignoring my grin, and says: "Forget about the last part, my boy, but the principle is clear, right?"

Then it's my turn. Father attaches my new prosthesis and lifts me on the bed. I am supposed to repeat the exercise. Stand, fall, roll. Stand, fall, roll. Again and again. Half an hour every day.

" 'Til you can do it in your sleep," Father says. When I can do it in my sleep he prescribes the same training exercise without prosthesis. The success is astounding, and on my fourth birthday the plaster cast is solemnly broken. I am whooshing through the apartment like a young badger. Not completely without accidents, but for the most part bump-free!

My turf is clearly defined: three rooms and a kitchen on the second floor of Arnekenstrasse 10, a grey house in the grey town center of Hildesheim. These rooms with their 1960s kidney table, rubber tree, and veneer wall unit are comfortable and never boring.

In this happy space I am happiest of all before the music box in the living room. Our Blaupunkt model has an integrated record player, which can stack ten singles. When a song ends, the arm swings back and the next record falls with a gentle *plop* onto the plate. Once the whole stack has played through, I simply call out the magic words: "Mami, change!" and the good fairy promptly appears, opens the compartment under the radio where the records are neatly, alphabetically organized in green and brown plastic sleeves, and lines up a new stack of singles. She waits, head slightly tilted, hands on her hips, until the needle scratches out the first notes. Then she foxtrots back into the kitchen, whistling cheerfully. During the week, while Father is at the state court and Micha is at school, she and I like to take it easy. The Bert Kaempfert Orchestra plays "Spanish Eyes," Peter Alexander blames "Das Machen Wur Die Beine von Dolores" ("Dolores's Legs") for his presenile dementia, Conny Froboess packs her *Badehose* (swimsuit), and Bruce Low's sonorous bass is a "Wandering Star" across the Arizona desert.

On weekends Father takes control of the programming. Jewels of the classical repertoire join the usual soul balm of the economic miracle years: Josef Metternich sings Verdi, Hans Hotter Beethoven, Josef Greindl the ballads of Carl Loewe, and the powerful voice of Kurt Böhme drones through the comical subject of German opera. Böhme's highlight is the song of Zsupán the pig farmer from Johann Strauss's *Zigeunerbaron (The Gypsy Baron)*.

It is Father's showoff song, too. When the weather allows he stands on the balcony on Sundays, clearing his general's bass and blaring the aria into the morning sky.

Much to the displeasure of Herr and Frau Kurbjuweit from the first floor. Herr Kurbjuweit is an invalid veteran and Frau Kurbjuweit used to be with the Reichsbahn, or German State Railroad Company. Now they ease the boredom of early retirement in a backwater by annoying the house community as guardians of propriety and audio-phobic terror of children. For the Quasthoff kids, Father's performance is huge fun. We especially like the verses that go like this: "Writing and reading my thing's never been / for since the days of childhood with the pigs I've been, / Nor was I ever a poet / Thunder and lightning, paraplui / all I did was breed pigs / poetry was not for me!" In the beginning the *risoluto pomposo* agrarian credo sounds across the backyard as resolutely and pompously as intended. When clanking dishes and muted curses signal that the Kurbjuweits have chosen to take their breakfast al fresco, however, Father adds another layer and turns *molto furioso*. "Yes, my purpose in this life is pigs and ham / my ideal purpose is pigs and ham, is pigs and ham."

At this point comes an artful pause, and Father starts to count slowly. By the time he gets to "three," Kurbjuweit has poked his head, glowing like a lightbulb, over the flower boxes to deliver his rant: "On Sundays this is not just a disturbance of peace but a criminal act!"

The family choir's rejoinder is usually a repetition of the refrain, but with a slight variation: "Listen up and tell us who is such a bore, it's the pig down below on the first floor / Listen up and tell us who is such a bore, it's the pig down below on the first floor."

It isn't the most subtle joke, and Mama is often slightly embarrassed, but those philistines don't deserve any better. Father enjoys his singing, which, to tell the truth, is not only loud but

also rather beautiful. His formal education as a singer was interrupted only because his father, Fritz, died in 1939, and Grandma
Lieschen, like most widows after the war, had the resources of a
church mouse. Whatever she earned in daily drudgery was barely
enough for food; studying music at the Academy in Braunschweig was out of the question. A distant relative who recognized Father's talent offered to cover the expenses, but he died
before he could implement his generous plan. Nevertheless,
Father was polished enough to appear in the vaudevilles and community halls of the Harz foreland, where even stars like Hans
Albers and Ilse Werner silvered up their Ufa-fame at the time. As
singer, emcee, and comedian he could earn a few deutsche marks
or, when the brand-new currency was not available, a round of
black brandy. It was made from sugar beets, and veterans emphasize to this day that its consumption was far more dangerous
than its production.

At one of his performances Father, for the first time, looked
deeply into the eyes of an especially lovely girl named Brigitte
Fellberg. She lived in the neighboring village, worked as a secretary in Hildesheim, and returned his gaze with some interest. It
was the beginning of the end of his young artistic career. Emil
Fellberg, his would-be father-in-law, wasted no time in giving him
an ultimatum: "Choose, son—my daughter or the honky-tonk."

Grandpa Emil was serious. After surviving the ruinous rabid-
ity of Hitlerdom, murder and slaughter on two fronts, a leap from
a Russian prisoner transport train, and a march back through half
of Europe, the no-nonsense Prussian was unwilling to entrust
his daughter to a theatre schlemiel. No, he wanted someone
solid. Father peered into his heart, considered his measly D-mark
salary and the liver-taxing ersatz currency, and concluded that
change would be a good thing. He bid farewell to the arts, high
and low, and embarked on a professional track in law. In 1954,
the year of the Bern miracle, he said yes to Brigitte, and if you

talk to them you will believe that he never regretted it. He also never relapsed—well, okay, almost never. But nobody held that one time against him, because since that day the Quasthoff family has owned a television.

Thank you, Peter Frankenfeld. We got that television in 1964, when the North German Broadcasting Corporation, or NDR, invited father to appear on *Toi, Toi, Toi (Good Luck!)*, a talent show moderated by Frankenfeld, the grand quiz and joke master of the Federal Republic. Micha's godfather, Albert, had secretly given the producers a demo tape featuring his friend Hans. Out of the blue, happy news: Father had three days to get to Hamburg to participate in the live show. At first Father was baffled and angry—at his buddy Albert, at Frankenfeld, and at Mama, who wouldn't mind a little trip to the Hanseatic town. Brigitte Fellberg, of all people! Wasn't she the reason he cut off his promising career, wasn't she the reason he spent his days as a poorly paid administrative inspector in the district court rather than as an idolized star baritone at La Scala? He wasn't complaining—but Father didn't do things haphazardly. Father was a civil servant now, and a civil servant doesn't belong on TV. *Basta.*

"Don't be so stubborn," Mama said.

"No, Puttchen, it's out of the question. We're staying home."

Mama smiled, for when her Hans tenderly called her "Puttchen" it meant the last word has not yet been spoken.

"What are you grinning about? I'm not going to do it."

Two days later they were walking around the Michel church in Hamburg and a TV was delivered in Arneckenstrasse. Grandmother Else, who shelled out the money for this heavy apparatus, directed the deliverymen.

"Careful, gentlemen, there is a shelving unit. Make sure you don't break it. After all, I am only the visiting grandma."

Since seven o'clock in the morning Grandmother Lieschen had been working like a berserker in the kitchen, where she was usually not allowed. Mama didn't want Lieschen in there because she was a professional cook and firmly convinced that her daughter-in-law wasn't up to the job of feeding her family. Mama didn't cook as nutritiously as she ought to, said Grandma—an opinion firmly held despite Mama's virtuous sauce creations, her airy soufflés, and our content little burps. Lieschen had learned her craft at the height of Wilhelminian calorie bomb production. She believed the Quasthoff men to be in constant danger of starvation.

When both women stood at the stove, Lieschen was as liberal with her advice as she wished Mama would be with calories. "Another piece of butter," she would instruct, or, "That needs lard." Or, "That's not a roux, that's water soup."

For years Mama was silent, but one day she exploded and declared her kitchen to be a mother-in-law-free zone. But the day the television arrived the kitchen was unguarded, and Lieschen was in her element. With bare, muscular arms she kneaded Celle-style buttercake, she cured a pork roast, and she whipped up some sausage sandwiches "for in between." On the stove a beef soup gurgled beneath a cozy cap of fat.

"How many people did you invite?" Grandma Else asked with concern.

"Invite? Nobody, but my grandchildren have got to eat properly for once."

By the time Father's show was to begin, the grandmothers had groomed us neatly and dressed themselves festively. A wonderfully fragrant mountain range of fat and carbohydrates had sprung up on the table, but everyone was too excited to eat. Lieschen planted her considerable self before the set a half hour in advance, and Grandma Else, looking for the power button, then her glasses, then the power button again, figured out how to turn it on just in time.

"There's Papa," Micha crowed. Indeed, two tiny men appeared on the screen, and one seemed to be Father. The other seemed to be a salesman for men's checkered clothing.

". . . very nice, you brought your wife. Greetings, Madam." He bowed vaguely in the direction of the audience. "And now of course, we want to know what else you do besides singing."

"I am a judicial officer."

"Oh, a civil servant! So there's a lot of time left for practicing, hahaha! No hard feelings. And what will we be hearing now?"

"Lortzing, *Zar und Zimmermann* (*The Tsar and the Carpenter*). The opening aria of Mayor van Bett: 'Oh, sancta justitia! Ich möchte rasen.' "

"Oh well, let's hope that your head official is not watching. Hahaha! Another little joke. But now let's go *in medias res*, as the old Latin says. Please, Mister Bandmaster. Hans Quasthoff from the beautiful town of Hildesheim with 'Oh, sancta justitia.' Toi, toi, toi."

After the splendid job he did, Father was celebrated like a hero, and not only by the town newspaper. And this television business turned out to be a great thing in general. Besides *Lassie, Rin Tin Tin,* and *Fury,* the box offered me another defining experience with the classical performance arts: Rudolf Schock, the celebrated lyric tenor (and popular heartthrob). He materialized one Sunday on *Zum Blauen Bock (The Blue Horse).* For the younger ones among us, let me say that it was a Hessian Broadcasting Corporation television show. The audience, cajoled by a babblehead named Heinz Schenk; as well as Lia Wöhr, called Frau Wittin ("Mrs. Hostess"); and Reno Nonsens, a sad comedian whose saggy cheeks can be traced back to the cultural wasteland of the Adenauer era, drinks loads of "Äpplewoi" (apple wine) in front of a camera and moves in a sideways rocking motion through the German folk song repertory. This wine-soaked paradise reinforces unified family life up until the early seventies by illustrating a basic tenet of collective life: One must tolerate the circle of loved ones without grumbling. Otherwise there is no sports show or dinner later.

I cowered on the sofa next to Micha, resigned in my fate. We were eating our way through a lemon roll while we watched the aging singer, flanked by Mrs. Hostess, Mr. Schenk, and the slim jokes of Mr. Nonsens, being led with much ado to the Blaue Bock Orchestra to perform Schubert's "Heidenröslein." So far so good. Then, from out of nowhere, came a lesson I would never forget. Schock began heaving the first of four preliminary B's, and his features began to slide eerily. Above the mournfully open mouth the cheeks were pushed up against a mighty bulge laced with red veins. The accordionlike folds on the forehead squeezed the eyes so that they popped out of their sockets. Besides all this, he was twitchy about the ears. Schock's brows swelled and crashed like waves on the high sea, causing his entire hairdo to jump around on his skull as if an invisible paw was massaging his skull from behind. This amazing creature would stare at the head of the orchestra and then into our living room, seemingly directly into my face. I looked around in amazement. Father was calmly smoking his pipe and Mama dipping her cake into tea, and Grandma hadn't dropped a single stitch. Only Micha joined me in noticing that an aesthetic line had been crossed. In horror he jammed his fingers in his ears, though we had not yet heard a single note.

The battle-scarred old fellow brought the song to a passable end and exited to roaring applause. I emphasize this at the request of my dear mother. She likes Schock, and I had to show her the passage above for inspection. She thinks I am exaggerating wildly, that his grimaces were never that bad. Schock just

had an expressive face, she says. But I believe grown-ups don't
see such things, because they don't want to see them. Grown-
ups protect themselves by turning off when everyday insanity
knocks at the door. And that's healthy because there's too much
of it to absorb it every single time it finds you. Children haven't
learned this yet. They look a phenomenon right in the face, and
whatever they see—be it naked beauty or sheer terror—they perceive extremely clearly, as if under a magnifying glass. Whatever
the truth of it, I can tell you that the Quasthoff brothers kept
themselves busy for days mimicking the singer, making wild
faces before a mirror, and doubling over with laughter.

I turned six soon after that. My parents wanted me to start going
to Micha's school, which was only three streets away from our
apartment. I could comfortably reach it by foot. So they made an
appointment with the director and described my case, emphasiz-
ing that I was a completely normal boy, even very bright and
musically talented—just with some physical limitations.

"His brother is around, too, and will take care of him. The two
are one heart and soul."

"Sure, sure," the director smiled. "I understand. Fill out this
form and you will get an answer."

Two days later the answer came in the mail: "Dear Mr.
Quasthoff, I regret to inform you that we cannot accept your son
Thomas at our school. A child with such a great handicap is
bound to put an undue burden on every teacher and the entire
teaching facility."

Mama told Father not to get excited, that maybe this man was
just an extraordinarily obtuse specimen. Obtuse, yes, but unfortunately not alone in his obtuseness, as they realized when
they visited another school director's office. They were politely
but firmly shown the door. They tried different districts, trudg-

ing through the elementary schools of the suburbs. Soon they knew every teacher's room in the district of Hildesheim. Father appealed to the education authority, approaching even the minister of education. The answer was always the same: Cripples are not welcome. Cripples belong in a special school.

For lack of alternatives I ended up back at Saint Ann's, which had no day school, just a boarding school for the disabled, a place for children to live together, learn to read and write, and make new friends. I understood what it all meant—I had to leave home, just like way back when I was in the plaster cast for a year and a half. It didn't sound like such a great idea to me.

"Mama, why can't I stay here?"

"You're a big boy now and have to go to school."

"Micha has to go to school, too."

"Yes, darling, but you are something very special. You are going to a special school."

"To a boarding school!"

"Yes, but you see, it's only five days and on the weekend you're already back home."

"Mama, why am I something special?"

"Oh, Tommy." Mama sighs and squeezes me tight. "Because we are proud of you and love you very much."

"I love you, too."

"I know, my darling. But now you must sleep. We've got to get up early tomorrow."

The next morning Mama took me to Saint Ann's in Hanover. "You'll make it 'til Saturday. Be good and take care of yourself," she said.

As I watched our old Volkswagen roll away, I felt miserable. But I was a special boy, and a big boy. I had to try to behave like one. Before the end of the first week, though, I could tell that it would be harder than I thought, despite my good intentions.

A sister in a blue smock took me to the infirmary and assigned me a room. The scents were all too familiar—cheap laundry soap, disinfectant, urine. Fifteen beds set against the walls, but this time only one was empty.

My new comrades were either thalidomide cases like me, spastically paralyzed, or suffering from muscle atrophy. There were also some demented children, Down syndromes, epileptics, and autistic kids.

The director of the school himself was in a wheelchair. His name was Bläsig, and he gave a speech before lessons began. God, he said, had created disabled and nondisabled humans and assigned each his place in the world. Our place, he said, was here at Saint Ann's, and we should learn to make ourselves useful. He spoke of the joys of usefulness, and of humility and obedience, which alone make it possible to reach those joys, and he spoke of the gratitude we should feel for all the kindnesses and good deeds that would be done for us in the future. A taped chorale was played to establish the appropriate mood. Then we went to our various classes.

In 1B waited Ms. Neddermayer. She was young, friendly, and blessed with kindness and an angelic patience, but it did no good, for she had been given two thalidomide cases, four kids with atrophy, and five spastics—not an easy group to teach. The spastics weren't dumb, but their nerve and speech centers were limited by spastic blocks, slowing them down. Often they were thrown off track by their chronic motor disturbances or an epileptic attack. When she taught at the speed of us thalidomide children, the spastics went crazy at their desks because they couldn't understand a thing. On good days, Ms. Neddermayer attempted to demystify the decimal system as we picked our noses in boredom. On bad days we frolicked as if Ms. Neddermayer were not even present. In other words: class 1B was not a model of pedagogical success.

In the afternoon the freak show continued, but in other rooms and with a larger cast. The spastics would dig around in a pile of Legos, the autistic kids would shake their heads and wander around in their parallel universes, the epileptics would twitch and spew now and then, and the demented kids were unpredictable. Thalidomide and atrophy had to duke it out for supremacy over this bunch. Soon I had armed myself with a big mouth and an indifferent attitude.

Most of my comrades were unfazed by the fact that there was no peace, no place to retreat to, no minute of privacy. They didn't know anything different. Their parents, all endowed with healthy German common sense, had stored their misshapen offspring at Saint Ann's from birth.

A woman called Müller, a decided sadist, was in charge of all of us. Like all sadists she hated people who contradicted her instead of coming crawling. From the first day she couldn't stand my spirit.

"You mustn't do that," I protested when she slapped my bed neighbor Peter because he had knocked over a cup of tea. After all, spastics were constantly knocking something over. It wasn't something they could help.

"I'll show you," she said. She locked me into the storeroom. She took away my tape player because it was too loud, confiscated my sweets because they were unhealthy, and forbade me to phone Mama. "It's no use squealing. Your mother is far away and I will get your contrariness out of you."

She was astonishingly severe, seemingly devoid of feeling. Her disciplinarian's catalogue consisted of nothing but cruelty. Twenty-four hours without food, gargling with saltwater—these were familiar routines. When she really had her eye on someone, she would make sure he got strapped into his bed at night. After that the delinquent would be rolled out of the room and deposited in the bright hallway. If one of the medical directors was scheduled to come by on his rounds, the bed and its occupant would be shoved into the closet where used urine bottles were stored before cleaning. In the winter she'd make sure you were left all alone in the hall—with the lights off. More than once I lay trembling with fear and cold in the darkness, counting every single minute until dawn. So no one could escape the punishment by falling asleep, she instructed sisters, night porters, and cleaning ladies to harass her victims with reproaches and threats. Not everyone would stoop to that level, but Müller could always find someone who was more worried about his job than about being kind. If she had to, she would do the dirty work herself.

Unfortunately, a quiet night was not a guarantee even when I had escaped punishment. Many of the mentally disabled were shaken regularly by screaming fits, and others had trouble making it to the bathroom. Driven by panic attacks they would climb out of their beds to smear themselves and others with feces. The rest of us couldn't alert the staff, since there was no emergency bell—there simply weren't enough staff to respond to one, so none had been installed. That changed only when one of the atrophy children was found lifeless in his bed during early-morning rounds. His name was Tim, and he was my best friend. Müller was called. She gave him a quick and professional look and then pulled a sheet over his head. Two nurses rolled him.

"What happened to Tim?" I was full of irritation.

"He passed." That was all she said. I knew he was very ill, but I had never heard the word "passed."

"Is he getting new medicine?"

"Don't ask stupid questions. Get up and go wash up. Breakfast is in ten minutes."

"Yes, Mrs. Grindtooth."

"You wicked child . . ." Let her rage, I thought. Guess I'll have saltwater instead of cocoa.

After two years of living at the school and sleeping too often in the hallway, I found some relief when my parents threatened Müller with a lawsuit. Ultimately their complaints got us put into four-bed rooms instead of the ward. And they never missed coming to get me for the weekend. At noon on the dot on Saturdays they'd be there standing in front of the school. Father would throw my bag into the trunk and we'd speed down the road to Hildesheim. If the weather played along, we'd visit the public baths or Micha and I would go to the run-down bunker facilities next to the brickyard. Often Mama would pack Tim and Peter or other friends into the car. Those poor kids only got to see their families at Christmas and on birthdays! When my friends came along, Father would treat us to large ice cream cones and movie tickets. We fell back into the balmy darkness, letting ourselves get carried off to those magical places where evil is petty and weak and goodness is noble, clever, and indomitable, where guys like Tarzan live, guys who can talk to elephants, or Ollie and Stan, who can throw pies into their tormentors' faces with no consequences. We went pale when the old fisherman almost threw Pinocchio into the sizzling pan, we laughed about Fuzzy, the dumbest cowboy west of the Pecos, and we twitched in our seats with excitement when Winnetou and Old Shatterhand chased the villainous oil prince through the mountains of Yugoslavia. Back at home, the brave Saint Ann'ers then chased the *comanchero* Micha through the apartment until he capitulated, in his good-natured way. As a reward Mama put hot chocolate and steaming potato salad on the table, and we played Parcheesi. At night the whole gang crawled into the wigwam of chief "Tommy Three Finger," which Father bought with his only (and rather skimpy) lottery winnings.

Naturally the weekends flew by much too quickly. The ride

back to Hanover usually resembled a sad silent movie, and the good-bye a weepy melodrama. When Tim died, Mama said that my friend was now sitting on a soft cloud in heaven and playing with little angels. I said that I, too, would rather die than fight with that dragon Müller week after week. I was fed up, and so were my parents. They would have gotten me out of the boarding school long ago if any normal school would have had me. But they didn't give up. Instead they were with Goethe: "Wir hoffen immer, und in allen Dingen ist besser hoffen als verzweifeln" ("We always hope, and in all things hope is better than despair").

Then comes the year 1967: the summer of love, APO, and the mile-long guitar solo. The grey Neo-Biedermeier of Bonn is being aired out and painted light pink. Habermas demands a "structural change of the public sphere," Marcuse "non-repressive and de-sublimated conditions," and the young are trying hard to cross "the narrow horizon of bourgeois right," as Karl Marx would put it. When this turns out to be more difficult than expected, they simply refuse to visit the haircutter until further notice.

Even arch-Catholic Hildesheim feels the fresh breeze. Among other things it blows right up to the director's seat of the Brauhaus School, Mr. Scholz, who, Father hears, is a free spirit and progressive mind. Father makes an appointment at once, and two hours later he knows that Mr. Scholz also has courage. The Brauhaus School will accept me, becoming one of the first public teaching institutions in Germany to educate a disabled child.

Not everyone greets the news as good. Saint Ann's is strictly opposed to the change and Director Bläsig mounts every possible argument and bureaucratic obstacle he can think of. It is unclear whether he worries about his monopoly on our care or whether he really believes a cripple could not possibly get around in the regular world. I can't say. Maybe a disabled person who has seen and survived the "master race" ideology of the Nazis, and then seen the chutzpah with which Germans once again thrust out their elbows to get ahead in Ludwig Erhard's leveled middle-class society, can only think like that.

Bläsig's contrary resolution cannot shake my parents'. When we enter his office for the last time to pick up my papers, he wishes me luck, then looks at my father and says: "One thing you should know: if it goes badly, we will not take Thomas back."

It did not go badly. I have a lot of catching-up to do at the Brauhaus School, but I'm no dimwit. Besides, I am finally free of that boarding school, and so I feel like Ben Johnson, the hundred-yard man: I am doped up to my hair tips—a natural high! There is so much adrenaline roaring through my veins I don't mind cramming for a while. When things get too difficult Micha and Mama help me with homework, and soon I can manage the fourth-grade curriculum without problems. I also get along with my new classmates. During the first weeks, of course, a dwarf without arms stalking across the schoolyard on stilts is an unusual sight, and it provokes some ugly teasing. My big mouth soon earns me respect. Now we see how right my parents were to treat their little cripple just like big Micha instead of being overly considerate. When I was four they would send us brothers off to the baker, a birthday party, or the haircutter with two marks and good wishes. Silly gawkers were everywhere, and so were mean remarks. They always hurt, but if I came home and complained, Father always cut these bouts of self-pity short:

"Boy, the world is rude and dumb, and most of what stomps around on it is, too. It could be worse for you: you could be blind and mute. But stupid people are worse off yet, for they never realize how much stupidity they've been struck with."

He was right, of course, but sometimes it was hard to be so philosophical in the moment.

For example, on this bright Sunday in August, I am at the

wheel of my tricycle. It is fire engine red, my pride and joy. I round a corner and a boy appears in front of me. It is too late to brake and there is no room to swerve. It can't be avoided: my front wheel and I are rolling across his shoe. The boy, who is rather tall, barks: "Hey, dwarf, watch out!"

It sounds as if something besides his hurt toe is galling him. I mumble an apology, wanting only one thing: to get away. But the boy has other plans for me and blocks my way with his leg, which only puts his other foot in the way of my wheel, which rolls right over it—this time with oomph. Pow! He smacks me across the face.

"Keep that in mind, dwarf," says the big boy. It's a rather dumb remark and I should just ignore it. After all, my father has taught me that dumb people are bad off and deserve pity. On the other hand, there is only one person who can call me "dwarf" and get away with it, and that's my brother. And so I say: "I'm not a dwarf, idiot." Whack! Then another slap lands on my face, and then another. I lose my balance and slam onto the pavement along with my tricycle. The next thing I see is blood, but it's not mine. It belongs to the idiot who is suddenly lying next to me and being worked on by Micha, with both fists. Mama has sent him off at just the right moment to fetch me for dinner. Now he is sitting on top of the idiot, screaming:

"Come on, say it: I am a cowardly ass."

"I am a cowhadly ahf," the idiot is sniffing and spitting two teeth into his handkerchief before running off like a beaten dog.

The Quasthoff brothers are going home in a triumphal march.

"What happened to you?" Mama calls out in horror, inspecting the laceration on my forehead. Micha tells her I fell off the bicycle, which is at least half true. Mama hates fights, and she hates fibs. And it all comes out. We are sitting at the table when the doorbell rings. It is the idiot with his father.

"Look at my son," father idiot gripes. "And look at this." He opens his right hand. My father inspects the two bloody front teeth.

"That's the work of one of your brats. I will sue you and send you a fat bill for damages," the old idiot barks.

"Well, well," Father grumbles, "nice and slow with the young horses." He calls us to the table and asks us to explain, please. I describe the events. Father nods, then scratches his chin and calmly says: "I will not report your son to the authorities. The way things look, he's already gotten what he deserves. But you and your little sausage here should scram, or the matter might not end here."

They basically fly down the stairs.

But the matter, it seems, is not quite wrapped up. Summer vacation ends the next day. Micha is entering fifth grade and now has to go to secondary school, the Gymnasium Andreanum. When he arrives, the idiots, father and son, are already there. One is standing in the courtyard trying to eat a sandwich, his face distorted with pain, the other is introducing himself as the new Latin teacher. Great, Micha thinks, just what I needed. Father says: "Work your butt off. Then he can't touch you." But he can. The old idiot torments Micha every chance he gets.

"*Male partum male dilabuntur*. Nonsense with gravy," Micha is cursing when once again he misses lunch because he has to submit to some punishment. The old guy did not manage to avenge his offspring's beating with D's and F's. Micha was too smart for that. But Latin was never his favorite subject, that's for sure.

Two years later I, too, switch to the Andreanum. The honorable institute—the first documented mention of it dates from the year 1216—is situated in a charmless new concrete building, but it makes up for this with its magnificent location at the Hagen's Gate Wall, high above town.

And indeed, the council sees itself as a bulwark of humanism against the fickle zeitgeist. Intellectual giants reign here. The gentlemen Stolp and Wirschner, philologist and geographer, respectively, have made their names through the practical application of evolutionary theory. Wirschner's fieldwork especially is as spectacular as it is revolutionary. At the beginning of a new school year he bounces into the classroom, inspects the assembly with a grim face, and lays out the game plan: "Bauer, Marschmann, Brunkhorst, I don't want to see you in the last row and I won't see you in the last row."

This so-called principle of unnatural selection functions more often than we like. The mathematician Schaffrath, on the other hand, clings to the erroneous idea that girls cannot count, which is why even the most brilliant of the female interpreters of the rule of three never make it past a C, while we brutes sometimes manage to attain a straight B only by cribbing off our fair friends.

More than a few of our teachers give new meaning to the term "oddball." There is, for example, Dr. Florettiner. A Germanist and experimental poet, he customarily introduces himself with the remark "I am not schizophrenic." Other times he hides for hours behind the *Frankfurter Allgemeine Zeitung* and waits to see what will happen. Florettiner calls it the interactive lesson, but nothing ever happens. Some of us suspect that the interactive lesson is just an excuse and that Florettiner is in fact checking the cultural section of the *FAZ* to see whether one of the dozens of experimental poems he sent to literary critic Reich-Ranicki had finally been printed. But it never happens. Later on he succumbs to his melancholy and gets locked up in a clinic.

It's the other way around with Mr. Schmalbach, who has to live out his depressive phases under medical surveillance. As soon as spring begins and his manic side breaks through, he teaches us ancient languages and does a tip-top job of it—unless his old body has been overly sedated, in which case he puts his head onto the desk and snores all the way to the bell. This never got him promoted, but he did become the most popular graduation exam supervisor in the history of the school.

This zany faculty does not prevent us from picking up some valuable lessons. I sing in the school choir and the associated Michaelis Choir. In sports I have created a new swimming technique somewhere between dolphin and dachshund, which allows me to kick my way to first the beginners', than the advanced swimming badge. In my new class I meet old friends from elementary school and make lots of new ones. In short: in the early seventies the world could not have been more wonderful, or as songwriter Fanny van Dannen will rhyme in nostalgic reminiscence: "Die Welt war jung und Deutschland ein Wort / und Squash war noch gar kein Sport" ("The world was young and Germany a word / and Squash was not yet a sport").

Now the famous TV resides at Göttingstrasse 5, and so do we. The move to Hildesheim South brought me my own room as well as a new place to play in the fresh air. The river Innerste dawdles through our neighborhood. The lush park of its overflow basin serves as Wild West, Amazon Delta, or Treasure Island, depending on our mood. Most often it doubles as the famous soccer arenas of the world: Maracana, Wembley, San Siro, or Anfield Road. On an elevated section there is a field with a handball goal with—what luxury—wooden poles and wire netting.

When Micha and I come home from school at lunchtime, we race through our homework, pump up the ball, and set out for some play. For a good long while our buddies are interested, and we have many playmates, but there comes a time when Kuno suddenly has a different appointment every afternoon, and even

Christian and Uwe appear only sporadically. Why couldn't he make time for some ball kicking? Hemming, hawing, then some muttering about "doing garden work for the Mahlbaums—you know, Moni Mahlbaum who goes to your school in the 7B." My school friends exhibit similar symptoms. My crusaders' castle, usually a continually occupied object of desire, seems to have lost some of its glory. Even Mama's Frankfurter cake does not seem to get anyone out and over to Göttingstrasse. I am at my wits' end until the day I see Bernhard emerge from the ice cream parlor hand in hand with the skinny and much too tall Iris—beanpole Iris! And now it dawns on me why Christian has recently developed an inexplicable interest in Hermann Hesse, begging Regina to read him *Narcissus and Goldmund,* saying he had heard it was "a really amazing read." Why Christian does not mind pushing Suse's broken bicycle home, walking through half of the town, even though his own house is just two blocks from the gym. Girls! They're seeing girls!

I'm happy for them, I guess. Go ahead if you like. But I don't know what to say or do with these capricious creatures. Okay, Mama has given me a rough idea of the kissing and cuddling and having kids, but how does that beat soccer or knightly castles? But more and more I catch myself standing before the tall mirror in the hallway thinking: No girl will ever hold hands with you or go with you to an ice cream parlor. You don't even *have* hands. Nor real legs. You've only got two stumps and they are so short that you cannot look across a bicycle much less push one of those things through town for a girl. You fooled yourself. You are not like the others. You are ugly. You are small. You are a crippled gnome.

I've got the blues. It gets worse every year. In school I no longer look at the blackboard. I am covertly watching the boys and I am watching the girls. They are wearing funny pants now with flares, fur jackets, high-heeled boots, and short skirts that make you kind of antsy. I notice the interested looks and all the small gestures that flit back and forth between benches. I notice how they slink around each other during breaks, seemingly indifferent and immersed in debates about the last student speaker election, the hits of the moment (by T. Rex and Slade), or the newest attacks of the Red Army Fraction, all the while registering every movement of the other sex. I sense the play of hormones, but I feel that I am not included. The worst thing is I cannot even complain. Everyone is nice to Tommy; everyone makes an effort; everyone wants the best for him.

"Hey, Tommy, everything okay?" Sure, with Tommy everything is always okay. Isn't he always joking around? Doesn't everyone fall down laughing when he mimics Wirschner, the cynical old goat? Isn't Tommy indisputably our class clown?

Maybe, but he's got the blues. So does his brother. At least Micha has got the right albums. "I ain't trusting nobody, I'm afraid of myself, / I cannot shun the devil, he stays right by my side, / There is no way to cheat him, I'm so dissatisfied," Peg Leg Howell cries out of his room on rainy afternoons. That's when Micha sits in front of his record player, oblivious to everything around him, copying the sounds on his guitar. I sit on the floor and listen. Though I understand only shreds of the lyrics, Peg Leg's whimpering strikes a chord in my soul. I would like to know whether Micha is going out with a girl, too. But he doesn't talk about it. He is talking much less in general, lately. He refuses to go to the haircutter and has pinned a Che Guevara poster next to the ones of John Fogerty and Eusébio. He now reads books called *The Stranger* and *Iron in the Soul*.

"Somebody has got to get him back down to earth," Father says.

"Leave him. It's puberty," says Mama. She also notices that something is not right with me.

"What's the matter, little one?" she asks me every other day. I can't tell her, though until now I was able to tell her everything. This time I just don't know what to say. I could play her Peg Leg's "Low Down Rounder Blues": "Listen, Mama, I am at least as miserable as the old black man who is singing." I couldn't say it any better. But it would not be any use. Mama doesn't speak any English and she listens to Bert Kaempfert, not Negro music.

My blues make me neglect school. I stop doing my homework. I make huge mistakes on math and chemistry exams while pretending to my parents that I am still the stellar student. Only Micha knows, and he thinks it's not such a big deal: it can happen to anyone, you can tell Mama and Papa. But for me it is bad, it is very bad, for my parents fought so hard for their handicapped child to be able to attend a regular school. For they would surely be disappointed at my having failed and lied. For they might not love me anymore and might take me out of the Andreanum, sticking me into a home for life like other parents did with their crippled children.

"Nonsense with gravy." Micha is tapping his forehead. "You're crazy."

But that doesn't make things any better. I am afraid. I feel guilty. I have no appetite anymore. I don't want to go to school. I don't want to go back to the home. "I got stones in my passway, and my road is dark as night," as bluesman Robert Johnson would say. More than anything, I would like to run away. And so that's what I do.

On a bitterly cold day in November I take advantage of Mama's shopping outing and march off with nothing but a light jacket around my shoulders, since the winter coat is unreachably high on the rack for me. I wander along the big arterial road, then turn into a path going three miles through the Hildesheim forest up to the Blaupunkt factory. A drizzling rain drenches my clothes in just the first few steps and the icy wind goes straight to my bones. When I arrive on top it is pitch-dark. Half frozen, hungry, and dead tired I drag myself down to the village of Neuhof. Shortly before reaching the settlement I weakly sink into the ditch next to the road.

At home all hell has broken loose. Mama is sick with worry, having assumed I was playing soccer with Micha until he came back alone. She calls Father, who drops everything at the office. He tries to calm Mama down, spreads out a map, and makes a plan. Micha should ride his bicycle through town while Father and Mother get into the car and search the area systematically, going in concentric circles. When they get to Neuhof around midnight an ambulance is standing at the side of the road. An old man found me and informed the Red Cross and the police. All I said was, "I am waiting for my mom." Then I passed out.

I am taken to the city hospital. Mama and Father are taken to the police station, where they have to put up with some mean questions: Why did the boy run away? Is he afraid of you? Are you beating him regularly? Have you mistreated the child? Mama has a nervous breakdown and gets an injection. My father says: "If tomorrow in the *Bild-Zeitung* it says 'Cruel Parents Abandon Thalidomide Child' I'm going to hang myself."

Thank God, the head physician who treats me in the municipal hospital knows our family well. He calls the station explaining how absurd such accusations are.

When I come home with a slight cough and fever the next day and Micha tells me what an uproar my excursion has caused, I want to sink into the ground with shame. But no one wants to hear any explanation, and not a single bad word is spoken. On the contrary, Mama cooks my favorite dish—noodle gratin. Micha, himself having caught a bad flu during the search, purposely loses

at checkers, and Father talks about having gotten a few F's himself in school, adding that no one tore off his head because of it.
On top of that, he promises to find me a singing teacher. He
winks at me: "So that our little August is never again so bored
that he will undertake the kind of power walk that will nearly
kill us all."

All the World's a Stage

"All art is utterly useless," wrote Oscar Wilde. I know he didn't mean it—not in any straightforward way, at least—but it shocks me nevertheless to read those words, for the real value of art was revealed to me in my earliest days. Artistic endeavors lend meaning and happiness to the lives of those who undertake them, a lesson I learned when my father acquired an Uher brand tape recorder.

This hi-fi miracle was purchased in celebration of my parents' wedding anniversary in 1965, when I was still boarding at Saint Ann's. On the eve of the big day, my then-still-slender father wrestled a huge, mysterious, and evidently very heavy package up the stairs. With a groan he lowered the carton onto the carpet and wiped the sweat from his forehead. The rest of us were flabbergasted.

"Surprise," Father managed to say. We couldn't get anything else out of him. Grappling with curiosity made it seriously difficult to concentrate on Mr. Ed, the hero of our favorite TV show, which was on that night. Besides being a talking horse, Mr. Ed was a great believer in the usefulness of art. Whenever he met a surprised someone who gasped, "You can talk!" he always replied most beautifully: "Give me a drink and I'll sing, too." (That must have made a mighty impression on me, for I, too, would accept a little something for my belly as compensation for my first public performance, though it wasn't a drink—after all, I was six!)

After breakfast the next day Father managed to install the

apparatus on a wall unit, where it sat shimmering in matte metallic, flanked by Gustav Freytag's *Soll und Haben (Debit and Credit)* and Friedrich Gerstacker's *Die Flusspiraten des Mississippi (The Mississippi River Pirates)*. Micha was somewhat suspicious; he could sense that this machine might require more active participation than he was prepared to offer. Everyone else was thrilled. Mama immediately whipped out her dust cloth to greet the imposing piece of furniture, and Father was not to be approached for the next hour. Sitting cross-legged before his new toy, tugging at cables and fingering buttons, his lips silently reciting the instructions—when all that was over, we stepped up for our first home recording.

"Oh, great," Micha groaned. He had known what was coming.

"Silence, please," Father said, already the crafty producer. "Attention, recording," he announced, donning headphones and thrusting a microphone into Mama's hand. She held it at a distance, with the tips of her fingers, as if it were a dirty diaper.

"Come on, Puttchen, sing something into it!"

"What?"

"How about 'That's Amore.' "

"I'm not Dean Martin."

"I know, darling. I know. Just sing any old thing."

Mama bravely hummed "Drei Chinesen mit dem Kontrabass" ("Three Chinamen with a Double Bass"), a children's nonsense song.

"That was very nice," Father lied with professional tact. "We should try 'Im Frühtau zu Berge' ('In the Morning on the Mountain')—all together!" Father arranged us offspring next to Mama and adjusted the microphone on the table. He pressed the "record" button as we held our breath.

"Take 1. One, two, three, four . . ." Mother whistled away and I was a clean fourth above. Micha grumbled around in the bass as if he had never heard the song before, though he usually sang quite well. The producer could not believe it. He hit the stop button.

"A little more commitment please, my dears. Micha, concentrate! 'Im Frühtau zu Berge,' take 2 . . ." The result was not much better. The producer made a face, Mama suddenly had lots to do in the kitchen, and Micha, fed up, retreated to his room with a shake of the head.

Thus do solo careers begin.

"Just as well," Father muttered. "What does the thing have playback for?"

He fished out the Golden Gate Quartet's *Best of* collection, one of our favorites at that time, and put it on the record player. I knew all the songs by heart, backwards and forwards, and so did Father. We couldn't get enough of the smart vocal arrangements, and in fact had listened the record into a somewhat deteriorated state. With lots of crickling and crackling, "Swing Low, Sweet Chariot" materialized in four exquisite parts as it was transferred onto the first tape track. On the second track Father recorded my solo voice. Once mixed it really sounded as if Tommy was the fifth member of a world-famous black soul and gospel group—a small miracle of the age of mechanical reproduction.

"Papa, that's me," I announced proudly.

"Yes, my son!" Finally the producer had something to beam about. He looked like Berry Gordy after the Supremes' fifth number-one hit.

By the time Mama called us for lunch, we had taped a few more hits and some arias. Father patted my cheek: "That's going to knock the socks off everyone this afternoon!"

For that afternoon the Quasthoffs would be receiving visitors. Mama pulled out the dining table and took the protective sleeves off the three-piece seating suite. Grandma Else and Grandma

Lieschen, our godparents Uncle Herbert and his Mousy, fat Albert and skinny Berthold with their spouses, and a few friends of the family distributed themselves across the sofa, chairs, and fold-out chairs. After coffee and cake, crackers and goldfish, and several bottles of white burgundy followed by Schnaps, the mood was drifting towards pleasantly dim. Father took advantage of the moment to tap a spoon against his glass, asking for attention. But instead of launching into the expected speech, he stepped up to the wall unit and casually turned on the Uher.

A heavy thunderstorm couldn't have had more of an effect. "Ich Liebe Nur Dich Allein," one of Rudolf and Mimi's duets from Puccini's *La Bohème,* blared from the speakers at a deafening volume. Even louder was Father's powerful bass plowing through the tenor part, but two octaves below Rudi. Live and unplugged! After all, it was his wedding anniversary. The guests applauded, Mama's complexion went a sweet pink, and Grandma Lieschen's dentures fell out from the excitement.

"Come on, Hänschen, swing your Puttchen around," Herbert barked, but the living room was far too crowded and the number was soon over. It was replaced by our "Swing Low Remix," issuing from the speakers in five-part harmony. The audience was beside itself.

"Man, I know that voice."

"That's Thomas!"

"I don't believe it."

"Yes, of course, it's him!"

"It is indeed!" Father confirmed. He started to praise the finer points of the Uher two-track system, but he didn't get very far.

"Tommy should sing it for us by himself!"

"A serenade! A serenade, that's good!"

"Oh yeah, well where is the little Caruso?" screeched Aunt Liselotte.

The little one was no longer playing at Caruso but instead had assumed the identity of Buffalo Bill. In the children's room, Fort Laramie had to be defended against Micha's plastic Apaches.

Mama was sent in to negotiate the conditions of a performance. Bad timing—she burst right into a counterattack, and Buffalo Bill was unavailable. An assembly of tipsy grown-ups in need of entertainment was not an emergency, whereas the defense of Fort Laramie was. Walking away and singing would mean capitulating, and Buffalo Bill does not capitulate. Never. He makes others capitulate.

Mama appealed to my vanity. Everyone was totally enthralled by Father's recordings and a song would make them all very happy.

That's when I remembered Mr. Ed, the singing horse, and the three lemon rolls Mama kept in an unreachable kitchen cabinet for moments such as this.

"Tommy will sing if he gets lemon cake!" I offered, Fort Laramie be damned.

A professional is born a professional. I took my position as my audience cheered, and Father began playing Gounod's *Ave Maria*, that wonderful cantata which paraphrases Bach's first C-Major Prelude for well-tempered clavier, a staple of Christian celebration for one hundred and fifty years: *molto animato, molto arioso*, and especially *molto molto mesto*—very animated, very melodious, very, very sad. But none of that mattered to me; I just liked to sing the piece. Apparently my audience liked it, too: as the opening line faded away, everyone's tears were already flowing. My next piece, Jerome Kern's "Ol' Man River," didn't help matters. Uncle Berthold discreetly passed around tissues, and Father chose something more upbeat for my next few songs. The sniffling assembly was no less impressed.

———

After that famous night, I was known as a talented singer. Until then I had always sung for fun, for my parents, or for Grandma's birthday, but now my family's larger social circle learned that Quasthoff's son was, remarkably, not just disabled but a talented vocalist as well. All our visitors wanted exclusive performances, and almost all of them got what they wanted. I didn't have to be begged anymore, so tasty were the applause, approval, and chocolate bars with which my audiences lavished me.

My parents had mixed feelings about my preening in the beginning, but they realized that after a melancholy week at school, I would blossom while performing at home. They decided to let it go on, as long as my freshly won fame did not go to my head. It got to the point that I felt comfortable calling out first to the mailman, then to the chimney sweeper: "I'm Tommy. Shall I sing something for you?"

"Not like that," Mama shushed, turning pink. She asked Father to have a talk with me. Father nodded, dragged me into the children's room, slammed the door shut, and told me that that kind of behavior wouldn't do, wouldn't do at all. But he couldn't keep the grin off his face. Inside he was bursting with pride: his artistic genes had fallen onto fertile ground. He wanted them to take root properly and so allowed me to take the costly Uher recorder to Saint Ann's. I also packed three freshly recorded tapes: one from Mama, with the latest pop and easy-listening hits; the second holding the most precious jewels of classical music; and the third packed with stand-up comedy selected by Micha. I liked it all: Haydn, Mozart, Hans Moser, Herb Alpert, the Beatles, Karl Valentin, or Insterburg & Co. All of it allowed me to dream myself away from the punitive planet Müller.

It didn't take me long to figure out that I could maximize the effects of performances by tailoring my material to my audience.

This I discovered on a warm spring day in the graveyard in Mahlum where Grandfather Emil lies buried. I was sitting in my stroller as Grandma Else kneeled in the flowerbed to do battle with weeds. A gentle breeze blew through the trees as robins and finches chirped. Into my head came a song: "Die Tiroler sind lustig, die Tiroler sind froh" ("The Tyrolean Is Merry, the Tyrolean Is Blithe"). I didn't know how it got there. I only knew that it had to come out, loudly and with gusto.

Grandma didn't find this funny at all: "My dear boy, I always like to hear you sing, but here it's not appropriate. People are sleeping."

"Then I'll sing 'Müde bin ich, geh zur Ruh' ('I am tired, go to sleep')." Outmaneuvered, Grandma took this with amusement.

"Well, then go ahead if you can't keep it shut!"

On our way home, in front of the supermarket, we ran into old farmer Hinke, who was passing time there as he enjoyed, alternately, a beer and a half-liter bottle of Schnaps and hoped for company. He often met Grandma and a couple of other widows for a game of rummy, and he waved to us with his loden cap.

"Ah, Else and her little Thomas. Well, my boy, I haven't seen you in a while," he said. I let his peasant's paw scratch over my cheek.

When Grandma told him the graveyard story, he doubled over with laughter and put a fifty-pfennig piece into my hand, "For your piggy bank." Later on he would reward me even more generously. When my visits to Grandma overlapped with their rummy game, he would ask me to sing the second great Schneider evergreen: "Man müsste nochmal zwanzig sein und so verliebt wie damals" ("One should be twenty again and as in love as then"). Then the rusty charmer would distribute kisses, egg liquor, and compliments, turning the trio of widows into giggling teenagers. I earned a smooth mark piece for my part in the fun.

Mother's tea parties brought me even greater acclaim, thanks to Heintje, the child star singer I think of as Holland's belated revenge for the Schlieffen Plan and Blitzkrieg. The ladies would never disperse without having heard my version of his monster hit "Mama" at least once. In return I was given the choicest cream puffs and began to accumulate a little bacon on my hips. Mama didn't want me to get too heavy, because of my weak hip joints, and besides, she thought the song was rather stupid. But what could she do? Throw her friends out? She only did that once, as far as I can remember, when a certain Mrs. Benedikt expressed her excitement by saying: "Your son sings beautifully. It's just impossible to look at him while he does."

And so Mama suffered until Heintje's voice changed and his star set. But I didn't lose any weight because of it. Three summers in a row we spent our vacation at a lake deep in Bavaria, and my alpine song repertoire was regularly rewarded with lemonade and double portions of dessert. My specialty was the yodeler of Archbishop Johann ("Wo i geh und steh, tuat mir mai herz so weh, jolohodrio, jolohojodrio"), which I once even performed in full costume, accompanied by a zither.

But I also knew rock 'n' roll. Margret, Uncle Herbert's adorable daughter, rewarded me with a big, fat kiss for a smashing rendition of Tom Angelripper's "Marmor, Stein und Eisen bricht" ("Marble, Stone, and Iron Break"). Micha wouldn't talk to me for three days afterward. Mama said I shouldn't be mad at him—he was totally smitten. Indeed, every time the very beautiful Margret spoke to my brother he turned as red as a boiled lobster and knocked over something fragile.

I always liked singing for Heinz Otto Graf, another friend of the family, who played the viola in the orchestra of the North German Broadcasting Corporation. He listened attentively, unlike the singing teachers Father called, who would hang up the phone as soon as my disability was mentioned. When asked for advice on how to foster my talent Graf referred us to a man named Sebastian Peschko. He said that if I introduced myself, an opportunity would surely arise. But he warned us not to rush anything: my voice needed a year to mature.

Professor Sebastian Peschko was already known to Father, for he was already known to all. Before taking over the NDR department of Chamber Music and Song he was a successful pianist and accompanied such greats as Grace Bumbry, Hermann Prey, Nicolai Gedda, and Anneliese Rothenberger. At the end of the year, Father took me to Hanover to ask Peschko for an audition. Peschko would not give us an opportunity, on account of that cursed Heintje. His success had scores of parents dreaming that their own children's golden throats would free them from the bondage of labor and turn them into carefree administrators of a windmill and petting zoo empire.

"Every three days they present a new wunderkind to us," Peschko's secretary said by way of explaining her boss's reserved position. (We would see this phenomenon again in the eighties, when ambitious parents shoved their babies onto tennis courts as soon as they could toddle, hoping that they'd produced another Steffi, another Boris.)

"But my son is really talented," my father insisted. "I will be back."

It was not an empty threat. And after two dozen letters and telephone attacks the professor agreed to give us an appointment. We met him in the small broadcasting room at the station.

Enter Peschko, a stately man with white hair, a high forehead, and dignified features. He carries himself formally. "I have only got five minutes," he repeats for at least ten minutes. Then he spends fifteen minutes describing the troubles of the music industry and aesthetic limitations in the public space.

"All we want is for you to hear our son for five minutes," Mama interrupts him with some irritation, but Peschko does not back off.

"Why do you want to do this to him? Have you ever considered how the public will react to such a severely disabled person?"

"I am just beginning to," Mama says tonelessly. She has turned white as a sheet.

Peschko realizes that Father is about to lose it, too, and finally ends his lecture and becomes sympathetic. "Pardon me, I did not mean to be impolite. I simply wanted you to know what will await your son out there." He gestures vaguely westward, where, behind the soundproof wall, the lake lazily rests in the midday sun. "But now Thomas will show us what he can do."

I have been standing there with my prosthesis long enough and am glad that the preliminaries are finally over. My father lifts me up the four steps onto the stage. I sing Brecht's "Mackie Messer-Song" (famous to English speakers, of course, as "Mack the Knife") through the nose, just like the old threepenny poet himself did on our old Amiga LP. I sing the Gitte hit "Ich will 'nen Cowboy als Mann," and I sing "Ave Maria." Peschko sits motionless in the first row, his eyes closed, his head supported by his right fist. It looks like he's sleeping, but he isn't. After each piece he opens his eyes and says, "That was very good. Just keep going." It seems he does have a little time after all, enough for me to present almost my entire repertoire. I sing opera arias and gospel; I imitate Jüergen von Manger and Theo Lingen; I yodel and present Louis Armstrong, complete with a swinging throat catarrh. By the end all I can think of is Bill Ramsey's "Die Zuckerpuppe aus der Bauchtanztruppe" ("The Sugarbaby from the Belly Dancing Troupe"). An hour has long passed and Peschko lets it be. He shakes my parents' hands: "Forget everything I said earlier. I am very glad you came. The little guy really has a splendid talent. I will think of something and get in touch with you as soon as possible."

Peschko keeps his word. Two weeks later he has arranged my next audition.

It takes place in the village of Arnum near Hanover, in the house of a striving soprano whom Peschko often accompanies at the piano. When Father rings the bell at the garden gate of her bungalow, an attractive young lady appears in the door.

"You must be the Quasthoffs. I am Charlotte Lehmann. Please come in." Behind her stands a hawkish guy with hooked nose, grey beard, and leathery skin. It's her husband, Ernst Huber-Contwig, the conductor of the orchestra in Santiago, Chile, a musicologist, and a card-carrying member of the avant-garde. Inside the house the functional chic of modernism reigns: glass, metal, black leather. The master of the house serves juice; pleasantries and brief biographies are exchanged; and then comes the moment of truth. Frau Lehmann sits at the piano, loosens her fingers, and allows me to take up my position.

"What would you like to sing?"

" 'Una Furtiva Lacrima' from *Liebestrank*."

Huber-Contwig's right eyebrow slides an inch upward. Gaetano Donizetti wrote this sentimental romance, and there are people who consider Donizetti a tacky composer of music for the tasteless masses. To be honest, I would have rather introduced myself with Mozart, but Father would not be deterred. "The aria is fantastic. Pure bel canto, the perfect smoldering platform for your boyish soprano."

It seems he was not totally off. When Frau Lehmann strikes the final chord even the avant-gardist must nod approvingly. But the decisive judgment comes from my accompanist: "There is something about your voice that interests me. I would very much like to work with you."

From then on I go to Arnum once a week. Sometimes Mama drives me, and other times I take a cab. I put twenty marks on the table and get an hour-long lesson plus homework.

Frau Lehmann was an experienced teacher, but it could not have been easy for her to work with me. At fourteen I was rather young for a singing student, still a kid, in fact, and often lacked the necessary seriousness. But she was very sensitive and clever, soon realizing that the precise regimentation and rigorous discipline of music had to be sold to me like a grand playground, an adventure. "He's a stubborn goat," Grandma Lieschen used to say. Frau Lehmann almost never had to think this of me, though, since everything she taught was much too interesting for me to balk. For example, correct breathing, which most people tend to oversimplify.

Im Atemholen sind zweierlei Gnaden:
Die Luft einziehen, sich ihrer entladen,
Jenes bedraengt, dieses erfrischt,
So wunderbar ist das Leben gemischt.
Du danke Gott, wenn er dich presst,
Und danke ihm, wenn er dich wieder entlaesst.

Taking a breath contains two kinds of blessings:
Drawing in air and then releasing it.
One presses upon you, the other refreshes,
Such is the wondrous composite of life.
Be thankful to God when he presses you,
And give thanks once more when He releases you.

I would have agreed with Goethe before, but Frau Lehmann taught me about all the things one can do wrong in breathing.

One's breath can be too short or too restless, too high or too flat, and please, never just from the stomach. It is much healthier to breathe from the diaphragm, though ideally humans, singers especially, should always strive for a combined form of breathing, relaxed and total breathing. Those are the basics. After that, it's all about working towards the so-called support, which depends on the controlled interplay of the lower diaphragm and upper chest musculature. It is the precondition for an elaborate technique without which we cannot transform air into sound and matter into spirit.

"*Piano* singing," Frau Lehmann told me, "does not mean singing at half strength but adjusting the voice, concentrating to achieve finer tone creation."

Before one can sing well, one must learn to speak properly, and that, too, turns out to be an art more subtle than you might suppose. Since our German alphabet has twenty-six letters total plus five *Doppellaute* (double sounds), which should be individually articulated—particularly in the singing arts—a wide field of practice opens up. Beginners are well advised to conduct their training sessions in remote rooms, ideally without any witnesses.

For Micha, whose room is next to mine, my exercises are a trial. Initially Frau Lehmann puts special emphasis on the technical foundations of the art, and so after school I disappear into my hermitage, take up my basic position (*"come una statua"*—like a statue: chest cavity erect, feet slightly apart, but not more than shoulder width), and begin a jerky and increasingly rapid breathing in and out. This exercise is called deep panting. My brother says it sounds like an asthmatic Saint Bernard climbing the Matterhorn. Micha also says he does not see why sound poems of the following type should be hollered through the apartment again and again:

Barrrbarrraraaa sass naaah am Abhannng,
Sprrrach gaaarrr sangbaarrr—zaaaghaft lanngsaaam;
Mannhaft kaaam alsdann am Waldrrrand
Aaabrrraahaaam aa Sanctaaa Claarrraa!

or

Arrrmer mann, ermaaahne Arrrmin:
Wer Macht verrrmeeehrrrt,
Derrr minderrrr' mancherrr Mutteeerrr Müüüh'—
Verrrmeeehrr' verrrrmess'nerrr Männerrrr Muuut!

No less irritating are the speech exercises I must repeat several times a day, fast and loud as a machine gun.

Ta—da—ga / ga—da—ta / da—ta—ga / la—da—la.
Ta—da—ga / ga—da—ta / da—ta—ga / la—da—la.
Ta—da—ga / ga—da—ta / da—ta—ga / la—da—la.

After six months, Micha has devised a counterattack: he starts playing a C-clarinet that he found at the junkyard. It is a shabby old instrument. The claps don't work, the wood is scratched up, and the mouthpiece has been gnawed like an old pipe stem. Nothing much can be coaxed from it but a pitifully thin, painfully piercing cheeping.

"Lord have mercy," Father curses.

"Intolerable," Mama complains.

But Micha doesn't care. He puts on *Live at the Village Vanguard*, holds his instrument in ready-set position, and waits—for the opener, "Naima," for the start of my speech exercises, and for Grandpa Schneiderath, the old Stalingrad veteran who lives in the basement. Our cue is the moment when Pharoah Sanders's saxophone bites into Coltrane's majestically melodic arches with a screeching upper-tone inferno. We are a memorable trio: Micha, cheeping like mad on his found object, me clattering away next door ("Ta—da—ga / ga—da—ta / da—ta—ga / la—da—la"), and furious Schneiderath screaming: "This is not the land of the Hottentots!" He yells this several times, each time higher and more tremulous. We usually notice him only after he has leaned the stump of his arm on the bell for a solid fifteen minutes. Father routinely blames Micha alone for the complaint and rewards his practice with a smack upside the head. The clarinet is locked up for a week, I am allowed to keep singing, and everyone understands that the world is often unfair. But Micha is undeterred. He works double shifts at Bosch-Blaupunkt during vacations until he can afford a saxophone. Four years later we are on stage at the Hanover Jazz Club playing Charlie Parker's "Au Privave" to a content audience, in unison and without mistakes.

But a lot has to happen before that can come to pass. My parents become the proud owners of half a house in Barienrode, a suburb of Hildesheim. Micha and I hide out in the basement, where Father stores his collection of rare brandies and where a small sauna makes a perfect practice space for Micha. My room is on the second floor, and my parents spend most of their time in the living room, on the ground floor. I still marvel at their saintly patience: in their leisure hours they were sandwiched between the free jazz being created downstairs in the sauna and my racy and voluminous scales wafting down from above.

Frau Lehmann's labor is bearing fruit after all. Soon I have mastered difficult jumps across octaves, such as the intricate tritone or effusive fourth and fifth, and the more I learn about what happens physiologically during singing, the closer I am to the day when music truly opens up to me. Since Charlotte Lehmann's heart belongs to singing, I make the acquaintance of the Masters Loewe, Schubert, Schumann, Brahms, and Wolf, with "Nöck" and "Erlkönig," "Mondnacht," "Parole," and "Mignon," with all the wonderful songs and great cycles of Romanticism which have dominated my life as a singer to this day. If it were up to me, I would go on like this forever, but unfortunately it isn't.

At school I am reminded of the fact that art can ennoble bitter realities but cannot dispel them. One day I overhear two girls talking about an upcoming trip, which will take the school choir and orchestra to Finland for two weeks. I am beside myself with excitement. To travel for the first time without my parents— and to the Northern Cape, where the Laplanders chase reindeer beneath the polar light, among the never-ending forests and shimmering lakes.

I hurry to the head of the choir, Herr Rabe, to find out about the details. How much will it cost, and how much pocket money I should ask my parents for, and so on and so forth. He turns dead white while I babble excitedly. After hemming and hawing for a few minutes, he finally says, "We are leaving the day after tomorrow, but there was a problem with your coming along."

"What?"

"It has something to do with the insurance," he says. Then he tucks his Jute bag under his arm and hurries off. I am totally confused, not only by this information but also by the big lump that has formed in my throat. Disturbed, I turn to Herr Jörgensen, the chief of orchestra. He, too, is flabbergasted.

"Insurance? Nonsense. We had discussed whether you might need some help with your luggage or getting dressed. Rabe wanted to discuss the matter with your parents weeks ago. Did he not contact you?"

He did not. Probably he didn't dare. Last I discover that he asked the choir who would help me if the need arose. But among the fifty members there was no one willing to attach himself to a cripple—not even the teacher himself. So he decided to ignore the problem, or rather, to leave it at home. Friendly Herr Jörgensen offers to try to come up with a last-minute solution, but I decline, deeply humiliated. I don't know what hurts more—the cowardice of my teacher, Rabe, who plods across the schoolyard with his shaggy haircut, full beard, and moralizing greasiness like the personification of righteousness but who is really a total fake; or the lack of solidarity among my classmates, many of whom call themselves my friends but who never said a word to me about the trip, and who should know that I manage fairly well on my own with most things. I am especially hard hit because the school choir, in contrast to the sports field or party room, is a place where I have always felt like an equal, where it makes no difference whether someone is tall or short, beautiful or ugly, normal or disabled, where what counts is one's voice.

It takes me a long time to recover from this blow. It spoils my participation in choir and I lose my will to work. My performance in other classes suffers, too, which is nothing new—except that this time I am struggling even in my effortless subjects, German, history, and math. I am compelled to repeat the grade, and my motivation is at an all-time low.

Frau Lehmann and my family are the only things that keep me balanced. Father, like me a choleric person, explodes now and then, but for the most part he and my mother stoically countenance the D's and F's, count their worry lines in the mirror, and search for suitable tutors. Micha, for his part, acts less like a brother than a good friend. We spend our afternoons slouched in the basement chatting about God ("gone missing for a long time, probably dead") and the grown-up world ("needs some serious work") and listening to records. He lends me books by Arno Schmidt, Camus, and Sartre and inoculates me with that degree of existential snobbery that allows a teenager to look *Leviathan* and *Being and Nothingness*—in short, the indolence of one's relationship to society—squarely in the eye. Sometimes I accompany him to his jam sessions with friends and they let me sing a few choruses. Or we walk across the bridge over the Innerste to the Bishop's Mill, where the jazz musicians perform, and we take in a show.

In 1977 that is over. Micha has to start his civil service in the Peine District Hospital. I pass most of the last two years of school in the underground pub Hippetuk. The antiestablishment drinks revoltingly sweet Persico, curses the piggish system, and nods dully when Bob Marley sings "I Shot the Sheriff." The rooms belong to the Bishop of Hildesheim, who rents them out to a well-known anarchist collective. I guess I'm not the only one who got off track. That same year Johnny Rotten screeches "Never mind the bollocks, here's the Sex Pistols" and punk rock sets off on its triumphal procession around the world.

For the most part Hildesheim takes no notice, and neither do the Quasthoffs, who have a different set of worries. The family council convenes to discuss Junior's future. By now my voice has settled at a high enough level to consider a professional singing career, and I don't want to do anything else. But my parents are concerned. What if I lose my voice? What if there's an accident? How will I earn a living? Traditional alternatives such as driving a cab or becoming a mailman are not open to me. And what if people really won't accept an artist with a disability?

"How about a broadcast or opera chorus?" Mama suggests.

"Tommy is already too good for that," Father says. Frau Lehmann feels the same way and recommends the Music Academy in Hanover, where she would be able to continue teaching me.

I complete an application but don't hear anything for weeks. When the deadline for matriculation has almost passed, Father reaches for the phone. He will not be deterred, not by the president's secretary nor by Professor Jacobi. But the head of the academy is an arrogant man who refuses to discuss the matter. He won't even let me audition.

"Dear man, the German academic regulations require command of at least one instrument—the piano—"

"—but I already told you he is a thalidomide child with maimed arms—"

"—and if I understood you correctly, your son is—for whatever reason—not capable of doing so, which is why he will not be accepted here. And I tell you right now he will not be accepted elsewhere either. Good-bye."

Jacobi even sabotages Father's attempt to get me in as a guest student with one of the singing professors. He will not grant me the status of a guest listener. To this day Father is embittered by the arrogance of this music functionary, but Jacobi's conceited pedantry turned out to be basically good luck. My voice was built much more solidly through intensive private study with Frau Lehmann than it would have been in the routine of academia, and I did manage to become a successful professional singer. But back then this refusal meant the death of my life's dream. It was a catastrophe. Though I continued with my lessons, I had to find another way to earn a living.

I choose law. It is a very practical subject, does not require a minimum grade point average in Germany, offers diverse professional possibilities, and can be studied in Hanover, where Micha is majoring in German studies. It reassures both me and my parents to know that my brother and I are in the same town. After all, I have never been on my own, and when I think about what awaits me I feel a little queasy. And as it turns out, the feeling is not wholly unjustified.

The university has assigned me a spot in a dorm called Kirchrode, right next to the medical school. Mama drops me off there with a few belongings. Even before we arrive at our destination, as soon as the view from the car window is of concrete and nothing else, I want to go back home. Once inside I have the same impulse, only more urgent. The rooms are shoe boxes outfitted with some dreary furniture, the hallways have Kafkaesque proportions, and two pale-faced newts stare at me from the kitchen, looking like the sinister hotel staff in *Barton Fink*. For the first few nights I double-check that my door is locked, though by day the pair seems less threatening, more nerdy and awkward. The next day I see one of them in the library and ask him to hand me a book from the upper shelves. He looks at me with amazement and hisses: "You can see that I am working!" My other fellow students are just as polite. In the cafeteria I almost starve because I cannot reach the counter where you pick up the lunch coupons. No one will help me. After a week my social circle has not expanded beyond Micha. During seminars and lectures everyone takes notes and listens in silence, except when the professor asks a question. Afterwards the newts retreat to their holes, emerging only when Teutonia, Saxonia, or another fraternity calls for mass boozing. It takes me all of three weeks to know for a fact that law is not for an artistically inclined person like me. But I still don't know how I am supposed to make a living, so I study on for six semesters, even seriously for four. I still have all those credits. When I drop out, my professors don't understand why I want to stop. But they aren't the ones who have to understand. I know that I've had enough.

I wouldn't say that these three years were lost. Though I don't have a law degree, I got something very valuable: the chance to separate from my parents. I never was a mama's boy. Both my parents made sure of that. But because of my disability we had an almost symbiotic relationship, without which I never would have made it through all the difficulties at Saint Ann's and in school. And because of this I naturally became accustomed to the provision of certain services. In Hanover there is no Mama to console me when I'm down or to put a pot of noodles before me when I am hungry. When I need something I cannot simply call Father but have to take care of it myself. This is strenuous, but it strengthens my self-confidence enormously. I overcome my fear of large groups, throwing myself into the supermarket at rush hour and for the first time daring to go into a pub or cinema by myself. I perform in jazz and rock clubs, often together with Micha but more and more often also without him, meeting musicians and artists of the most diverse genres, thereby decisively expanding my musical horizon. But I will tell about that in more detail later. Suffice it to say that little Quasthoff has grown up a lot by the end of his studies, and he has come to a decision: one day he will earn money as a singer, come what may.

"Then you have to take the profession seriously," Frau Lehmann reprimands upon hearing of my musical adventures. In a stern lecture she warns that these escapades will ruin my voice.

Her husband, Herr Huber-Contwig, blows the same horn. Since the maestro returned from Chile he has been tutoring me in music theory, music psychology, and music sociology, for free. He modestly remarks that this is merely theoretical cement, something to put my singing lessons on a solid foundation.

The first concert offers came in the 1980s. I was well prepared, not at all nervous, but Mama and Father were not so calm. During my premiere in the glass house at Bodenau they sat paralyzed in the back row, waiting for my appearance as though in a court of law. Mama had been ill with excitement all day. She sat at the kitchen table in the morning like a pile of misery and said she wasn't sure she wanted to come along, big tears rolling down her cheeks.

"Mama, why are you crying?"

She embraced me and sobbed, "Oh Tommy, I am so happy for you," but that was only half of the story. She was tortured by the idea that the audience might hiss or jeer or, worst of all, break out in laughter.

"I would have never forgiven myself, never!" she confessed after the performance, beginning to cry again.

But this time they were tears of joy. The audience did in fact whisper and look rather dumbfounded. But that's no surprise— they've never seen anything like me on a concert stage before. A Lilliputian tot without arms, jerking around in front of the podium because his legs are squeezed onto splints. But as soon as my baritone rolled through Carl Loewe's majestic ballad "Prinz Eugen" there was silence in the auditorium. It soon became amazement, and by the end it was sheer enthusiasm. No doubt they felt as if they were watching a bit of magic. No one expects so many rabbits to fit in a top hat. No one expects such a mighty voice to issue from my diminutive frame.

This is one reason why there were, at the beginning of my career, repeated misunderstandings, as in Braunschweig, for example. I entered the concert hall in the company of my parents, and the conductor sailed directly towards Father with flying tails and bared teeth.

"My dear Herr Quasthoff, you cannot imagine how delighted I am that you will be singing the *Elijah* with us today." Father laughed.

"Nope, not me, but my son here." The conductor looked stunned and had to get ahold of himself.

"Ah, the son. Well, well, of course, ahem, delighted just as well, delighted." As he walked off, shaking his head, I could hear him murmur: "The choir, the large orchestra, and then this small person—maybe we should set aside a microphone . . ."

Then there was rehearsal. When my moment came, the conductor waved at me excitedly and called: "Fortissimo, fortissimo."

Well, I gave him what he asked for. I let my voice roar even more than the score demanded, as if it wasn't a piece by Mendelssohn but rather Wagner's *Walküre,* showing Godfather Wotan where Thor's hammer hangs. The good man was so startled he almost dropped his baton.

"Was that okay?" I asked. He nodded silently and did not interfere with my singing part again.

It went that way for years in churches, schools, and community halls throughout Germany, and I can't deny that I frequently cut a funny figure. I forgot the lyrics in Springe and the score in Wolfenbüttel, I was late in Clausthal-Zellerfeld and didn't even make it to Stade, having taken the wrong turn after Hamburg, and I stood in the ice cold wind in front of a locked church in Brake, caught the flu, and had to cancel in Oldenburg. Every musician has such stories, but despite these misadventures the halls where I found myself were, little by little, getting bigger, the fees were getting higher, and the dressing rooms sometimes had working heat. My voice had developed into a smooth baritone that would not capitulate even when it was called to drift into the tenor and bass registers.

Frau Lehmann noted my progress with satisfaction and eventually decided that the time had come for me to assess myself vis-à-vis the competition.

In 1984 I entered the yearly competition of the Union of German Musical Educators and Concert Artists. I sang a Mozart aria and received the Walter Kaminski Memorial Prize, which I was told was "equivalent to" the first prize. But Frau Lehmann wasn't happy. In fact, she was angry.

"Right. Kaminski. You deserved the first prize and would have gotten it if you were officially a music student."

But I didn't care about the intrigues of music teachers and their subtle power games. I posed for the photographers, my chest swollen with pride. Two years later I competed again, but this time I was truly puzzled. Though I was, according to all the jurors, the best, I was given second prize, and first prize was not awarded to anyone.

"Where have you ever seen such a thing," I complained.

But this time Frau Lehmann smiled and said: "That is normal. Just be happy. After all, you've won."

And so I was happy, though the essence of competitions would remain a mystery to me. When I entered the Mozart competition in Würzburg in 1987, I took first prize. But this time there was no second—instead there were several thirds. What madness.

Unfortunately the prize money was always small, and the beautiful certificates bestowed upon me could not be exchanged for food and shelter. Even winners have to live, and so I began an apprenticeship at the Hildesheim bank. The director, an acquaintance of my father's and a lover of classical music, offered me the job. Everyone there treated me with great consideration, though I barely passed the entrance exam and ended up in the advertising department, a jolly bunch that understood more about one-liners than about finance.

I also earned a little pocket money at the NDR, thanks to a cameraman I meet at the Leine-Domizil, Hanover's legendary nightclub. He saw me perform during the notorious *Spontanmukkens*, a kind of jam session in which the big dogs of the scene showed the young talent who's boss. The performances frequently came down to virtuosic improvisation, and I got lucky and got on stage with a great soul band.

During the break the NDR guy addressed me: "Good voice. Have you ever tried voice-over work?"

A week later I was sitting in a small studio at the broadcasting building, reading a sample text.

"Done," said the head producer, Achim Gertz. "Welcome to the team."

In the beginning I was paid by the hour, but later they hired me for a part-time position, allowing me to resign at the bank. We worked around the clock. I was allowed to host music shows and—the high point of my broadcasting career—to act alongside Will Quadflieg and Hans Paetsch in radio plays. On the side I was rounding off my general education, reading scientific texts, poems, and stories from Brecht to Zuckmayer.

Since my broadcasting job was only part-time, I was still able to devote most of my energy to singing. After a lesson in February 1988, Frau Lehmann confirmed that my efforts had been worthwhile. She closed the piano, spun towards me on her stool, and beamed.

"Do you feel like participating in the ARD Competition in September?"

I was speechless. The International Music Competition of the Radio Broadcasting Corporations of the Federal Republic of Germany is one of the most famous forums for young musicians in the world. It is, for young singing talent, the measure of all things. I wanted to go, no question, but I realized that it wasn't possible: vacations had been suspended at work, so there was no way I could take time off.

Thank goodness, then, that I had an understanding boss. Achim Gertz recognized how important this was to me and insisted, "I'll take responsibility. You're going." Promising my eternal gratitude,

I bid him good-bye with the words, "Don't worry, I'll be back in three days."

There was so much to do. Filling out the registration form, sending a check for one hundred marks to Munich, buying new patent leather shoes, and having a black suit made, just in case the impossible happened and I made it to the final round. Most urgent was the composition of my competition program. I had to prepare "eighteen songs, six arias from oratorios or concert arias, or arias from preclassical operas suitable for a concert repertoire," and I had to know them by heart. They had to be from three different style epochs and include at least three different languages. Frau Lehmann suggested that my friend Peter Müller, with whom I have already given several concerts, play the piano for me. Then, of course, it's rehearse, rehearse, rehearse.

Sixty-two vocalists competing for 28,000 marks in prizes, and I the only one who had not had a standard music education. I was not fully taken seriously at first, not by the ten-person jury, not by my fellow competitors. In the end this was the key to my success: Peter and I were so glad just to be able to participate that we didn't feel too much pressure once the competition began.

The early rounds were held in the large Broadcast Hall of the BR. Every participant was accustomed to performing before a fully occupied hall, but this one was practically empty. The few spectators, mostly journalists or the competition, were lost in the large hall, but it was impossible to miss the jurors, a phalanx of expressionless faces. Under those eyes the fifty-meter walk onto the stage was harrowing. By the time a singer reached his mark his knees and vocal cords would both be trembling.

So I did have a *little* stage fright before my first performance, but it was healthy and normal enough. It passed when Peter hugged me and said: "No matter what the outcome is, let's just go in and make beautiful music." Besides, I knew that Frau Lehmann had made a point of being there. Nothing could go wrong.

After my first session I could feel a change in the attitude towards me. All the singers became exceptionally kind, the press took interest in me, and even the members of the jury were smiling encouragingly. Frau Lehmann smiled, too. "You've made a strong impression," she said.

After three weeks (and as many phone calls to the station, pleading for more time off) I had made it through three rounds to become one of the six candidates who would sit for the final exam with an orchestra in the Hercules Hall. The others were the Korean soprano Kyung-Shin Park, the German alto Ursula Kunz, the opera soprano Livia Ághová from Bratislava, and the two tenors Robert Swenson and Martin Rudzinski, from the United States and Poland, respectively.

I sang the aria "Mache dich, mein Herze, rein" from the *Matthäus-Passion* and Mendelssohn-Bartholdy's "Gott, sei mir gnädig." Whoever is in charge up there must have heard me. The audience clapped its hands raw, the jury awarded me the main prize of 12,000 marks, and the critics fell all over themselves. One attested to my performance's "oppressive intensity," adding that rarely is a listener so "mercilessly delivered to an artist." The *Münchner Abendzeitung* quoted Miguel Lerin-Vilardell, a member of the jury: "I consider this man a genius. He has got something rarely found in music: charisma." After the two final concerts for winners, in which I performed Schubert and Mussorgsky songs, even the sober *Süddeutsche Zeitung* was giddy with praise:

> When it came to impressiveness none of the soloists could compare with Thomas Quasthoff. He communicated seriousness

and humor as if singing was the easiest thing in the world. There are no seams there between intelligence, emotion, and vocal ability. One might even say that there has not been a comparable discovery in singing since Jessye Norman.

It was a lot for a small provincial singer to absorb. I had to go underground for a few days with my pianist, and only my old friend Rosi from Munich managed to find us. She simply asked the right man: the porter at our hotel knew what we were up to, and he gave her directions to the pub we had come to think of as our own. "Ven you come aht you make ah left right avay, then ah right, then again ah left, then you oah practically in front of the Augustiner. That's vere they've been sitting for three days, the rascals."

Peter and I were tipsy for more or less a week. My parents, overjoyed, treated us to a lavish meal at the Hotel Rose, the best spot in town. Erwin Schütterle, the concert organizer, host, and Hanover original, threw a big party for us, and suddenly I had a lot of new friends. What could I do but invest a good part of my prize money in free beer for everyone?

I sobered up when the tabloid press from Hildesheim arrived. In just two days they devised all the clichés on which scurrilous publications draw to this day: the business about the handicap ("A young man steps onto the stage, small, misfigured . . ."), the tearjerking ("down in the audience even men covertly reach for their hankies"), and the shocking details about the long-suffering mother ("in her eyes the love of a whole life"). Wild stories began to circulate, the more harmless versions maintaining that I was a trained lifeguard or was practicing to get my driver's license. I also shrank from article to article, finally dwindling down to a mere three feet and nine inches (photo subtitle: "Thomas Quasthoff next to soprano Mechthild Bach. He stands on a box"). *Bunte* beat them all. Under the headline "Thalidomide, case

1600: Singing His Way to the Top of the World," the anonymous author summarized: "He sings as if God wanted to make up for a workman's accident."

When I returned to Munich in November to perform *Winterreise* with Peter in the Hercules Hall, there was a bit of critical backlash. Though the *tz* newspaper still drew a comparison with the big lieder singer of the twenties and thirties, the *Abendzeitung* claimed our performance lacked drama, and Joachim Kaiser, the revered dean of critics from the *Süddeutsche*, landed a painful uppercut. "He lacks power of expression, passion, fierceness" and especially "creative force." The best he could say he said in closing: "Quasthoff does not cheat. He sings in a pleasantly unpretentious, modest way, not wanting to decorate himself with alien feathers. He sings openly and honestly."

I was annoyed at first, but then I have to think: Yesterday I was the Lord's trial, and today I am a target worthy of a great man's criticism. Things could be worse.

All I Need Is Music, Music, Music

On a fall day in the year 1827, Franz Schubert issued an invitation to his friends. "Come over to Schober today. I will sing a round of blood-curdling songs. I am eager to hear what you have to say about them. They have touched me more than any song ever has."

When his guests arrived, the composer sat at the piano and, as reported by Joseph von Spaun, "with a deeply moved voice sang through the entire *Winterreise*." The audience members were not quite sure what to make of what they had heard. "Schober said he only liked one song, 'Der Lindenbaum,'" whereupon Schubert said, "I like these songs more than any others, and you will grow to like them, too."

The twenty-four-part cycle was based on some of the poems in a book called *Poems from the Posthumously Left Papers of a Travelling French Horn Player*, whose author, Wilhelm Müller, was, in fact, not a French horn player but a classicist, a duke's librarian, and a Romantic genius, a correspondent of Goethe, Ludwig Uhland, Justinius Kerner, and Carl Maria von Weber. He once saved the poet Friedrich Rückert from drowning. Müller died at the age of thirty-three in 1827, one year before Schubert, leaving behind his own posthumous papers: five volumes of lyric poetry; countless stories, essays, and reviews; a translation of Marlowe's *Doctor Faustus*; and a ten-volume Library of 17th-Century German Poets, an almost unimaginable accomplishment nowadays. Before he undertook *Die Winterreise*, Schubert had set one of Müller's cycles, *Die schöne Müllerin*, to music.

Both cycles reflect Romantic interest in the lonely wanderer, misunderstood by women, family, and—yes!—all of society, who finds his emotional world reflected in nature. In the *Schöne Müllerin* a bubbling brook carries our lad towards a pretty mill heiress, underscoring first his promises of love, then his gloomy complaints, and finally enabling his suicide. In *Winterreise* a bleak landscape stiff with ice provides the backdrop for the protagonist's hardened inner life. *Die schöne Müllerin* has the structure of a novel. *Winterreise* lacks any real action; it's more of an interior monologue (reader, James Joyce didn't invent it). In the first cycle the stanzaic structure and touchingly simple melody of the *Volkslied* still dominate, but *Winterreise* captivates through its open form and deeply desperate, radical, in fact *modern* means of musical expression. These innovations took the material far beyond what was imaginable at the time.

No wonder Schubert's friends looked rather subdued after the world premiere. But Schubert was right when he said they would come to admire this work. Today *Winterreise* is the unquestioned masterpiece of the genre *Kunstlied*. As such it provides many examples of the difficulties involved in properly performing a cycle of songs. Each part is a masterly and complete miniature. They are connected neither by leitmotifs nor by interludes, so pulling them together can be a challenge. But presented alone, they lose some of their power; only one of the songs, "Der Lindenbaum," resonates with meaning when taken out of context. Certain musical relationships, rhythmic equivalents, and thematic correspondences create a tragic backdrop that subtly connects the whole.

But the somber tones of Schubert's palette can give rise to a wealth of nuanced emotion, a roller-coaster ride of sensations that must be managed by the singer: ironic bite ("Wetterfahne," "The Weather Vane"), condensed despair ("Gefrorne Tränen," "Frozen Tears"), choking passions ("Erstarrung," "Numbness"), and ingenious broken idyll ("Der Lindenbaum," "The Linden Tree," with the premonition of peace that smelled, to Thomas Mann, of the grave). There is nostalgia ("Rückblick," "The Backward Glance") and solemn introspection; there is Impressionist tone painting ("Letzte Hoffnung," "Last Hope") and rage ("Stürmischer Morgen," "Stormy Morning"). Death is established as a central theme ("Der Wegweiser," "The Signpost") long before our weary wanderer wanders into the fangs of the "Leiermann" ("Organ Grinder"), a deranged apparition of ambiguous significance.

Winterreise was the first major work I undertook with Frau Lehmann. I sang it in 1999 when, in the company of Charles Spencer, I made my debut in Lincoln Center, New York. How often have I sung these songs? I cannot say, but one thing I know for sure: I'll never be through with them. They constantly offer new shadings, senses, connections, and sounds; there are always harmonious variants to practice and test for concert-worthiness. Whatever the critics may say, a singer can find dozens of consistent interpretations; there is no one true interpretation for any song.

Schubert instructs us to perform *Winterreise* "strictly in the good measure of time, without heavy expression, lyrically and not dramatically," please. I followed his recommendation in the Hercules Hall of Munich and, as reported, received some harsh criticism for it. Maybe instead of studying scores day in and day out I should have looked at more literature on the subject. After all there is no lack of musicologists eager to tell you how to do a better job with these songs, their writings enticingly titled: *Schubert's Lieder als Gesangsproblem, Prinizipien des Schubertlieds, Franz Schubert oder die Melodie, Les Lieder de Franz Schubert, Auf den Spuren der Schubert-Lieder, Franz Schubert et le Lied, Das Schubertlied und seine Sänger, Schubert's Song Technique* or *Musikalischer Bau und Sprachvertonung in Schubert's Liedern.* *

The most famous, most highly esteemed Schubert scholar, Dietrich Fischer-Dieskau, has written at least three feet of literature on his subject. As regards *Winterreise,* he speaks of "the composer's self-revelation," diagnoses "traits of sensitivity veering into the pathological," and of "madness," as well as Schubert's "obvious tendencies towards self-destruction" *(Franz Schubert und seine Lieder).*

Anxious about these shades of mental instability, I often wondered in my early years: should one, may one, include all this in the act of singing? Today I wonder: is it even true? We know that Schubert was a high-strung fellow and an enthusiastic spirit, and that he often drank much too much. Then again, you could say the same of Hugo Wolf, E. T. A. Hoffmann, Beethoven—in fact, this characterization could be fairly applied to the majority of the versifying and composing guild. Schubert, in addition, was often ill and suffered from depression. But does that really come as a surprise, given that he spent his life in moist and drafty chambers, working to support a family of three, and never making enough money?

The pianist and critic Charles Rosen considers all this psychologizing irrelevant. For him, the main thing is that *Winterreise* must be sung by a tenor. For "only with a tenor," he writes in *Music der Romantik,* "can the cycle unfold its full effect." Even a wonderfully lyrical baritone such as Hermann Prey felt guilty when he put the work onto one of his programs, because

---

* *Schubert's Songs as a Problem in Singing, Principles of the Schubert Song, Franz Schubert or the Melody, The Songs of Franz Schubert, On the Traces of Schubert-Lieder, Franz Schubert and the Lied, The Schubert-Lied and Its Singers, Schubert's Song Technique,* or *Musical Construction and Sound Setting in Schubert's Songs.*

Schubert originally imagined a man's voice reaching "up to the high G-sharp and A." Prey consoled himself with the thought that during Schubert's time instruments were tuned lower than they are today, and he concluded that "the singer may choose the key that best suits his voice."

I have learned that a musician must do his homework, consult secondary literature, compare interpretations, and study the history and context of a work. But when he steps onto the stage he must present his own musical interpretation.

I recorded *Winterreise* in 1998 for BMG, accompanied by Charles Spencer. When I analyze that recording today with an ear to whether my interpretations have fundamentally changed over time, I have to conclude that they have not. Nevertheless, the cycle does sound different. It becomes more substantial as the years pass, as one matures. One experiences life and finds that some wounds heal over and are forgotten, while others stay raw. The pianist's personality and practices affect a lieder recital, as does my emotional disposition at that moment—how I slept and what I dreamt, whether I am newly in love or have just been left, whether I have rinsed my dinner down with two, three, or four beers. Then there is the hall. Is it large? Is it small? Are the acoustics right? Is there a lot of echo or very little? Does it have an orchestra pit? Am I close to the audience when I sing? And what kind of people have spent their money to hear it? Are they distinguished urban swells who consume cultural events as nonchalantly as they do expensive dinners? Or are they loyal subscribers for whom music is a sublime moment away from the daily routine of office, kids, chores, television? Even the weather and the season can play a part. All these factors create an atmosphere that colors the singing.

Some very good, very famous colleagues of mine do not share

this view. They strive each time to present a timelessly valid interpretation of the material, germ-free, so to speak. There's nothing wrong with that as long as striving for the ideal produces artistically convincing results and does not turn into mere musical consecration or—worse yet—artistic handicraft. I, though, am a more intuitive singer. Especially when I am on tour, performing the same material every day, I want to surprise not only my audience but myself. I prefer spontaneous ideas and variable accents to routine. I don't *feel* the same every night, so why should I *sing* the same every night?

For me a performance of *Winterreise* is like visiting a small, familiar museum devoted to the soulful landscapes of Caspar David Friedrich. Like Schubert's wanderer, Friedrich's figures get lost in overwhelming nature, standing before cracked ice walls and mighty rock panoramas, their gazes fixed on eternity or disappearing into shady oak forests, all beneath a ghostly sky. You look at these pictures over and over again and find yourself particularly touched by one detail today, another tomorrow. But taken together they are, every time, an unquestionable declaration of the artist's tragic-romantic attitude towards the world.

To project this attitude believably, to make it work in the present, is, in my view, the chief task of the singer. Technique, reflection, inspiration, and experience must be combined in the right proportions, and technique must not be overvalued. I stand with Karl Valentin: "If one can do it, it's not art, and if one cannot do it, even less so." Technical skill should serve as a springboard for inspiration, but it cannot compensate for a lack of inspiration or become a substitute for art itself. On stage I always realize pretty quickly whether the conditions for a magical performance are present. "Wir machen Musik, da geht euch der Hut hoch, wir machen Musik, da geht euch der Bart ab" ("We're making music so that your hats will go up, we're making music so that your beards will come off"), it says in an old chanson. Maybe that doesn't happen literally, but there's no mistaking this special moment when it occurs.

Of course, every performer is familiar with the opposite scenario, too. The singer hears the first piano notes, opens his mouth, and immediately knows: Oh boy, tonight high art is not in the picture. Tonight there are three wet bathrobes hanging on my vocal cords. But what can you do? You can't turn to a packed hall, smile charmingly, and say: "Sorry guys, it's no good. I'm not in form. So long, farewell, auf Wiedersehen, good-bye. Maybe another time." The concert has got to go on. If this were soccer our out-of-form singer could roll up his sleeves, strap on his shin guards, and hurl himself into it. "Quasthoff seemed to be asleep during the first half, but he found his way into the game after the break by putting up a fight." Unfortunately, a song recital—unlike the team sport of opera—does not permit any sliding tackles, but I do have one thing on my side: sound.

Many a friend of the classics will raise an astonished eyebrow at what I've just written, knowing the term only from the test reports of stereo equipment magazines, where it is usually joined by adjectives such as "brilliant," "mediocre," or "cruel." The term "sound" originated with jazz and later became associated with pop music, referring to the individual sound formation and style of a given artist or band. Proponents of this music hold that *how* one does something is at least as important as *what* one does, a position I share and shall explain.

My voice has certain genetically determined properties, like circumference and force, but it also has a velvety ground coat, which I have worked hard for. This allows me to use what in jazz would be called a "cool" and supple phrasing. I try to find the sound colorations that will show the composition to its advantage, but without losing my own singing style, my personal "sound."

Now he's throwing around platitudes, the reader thinks, but I assure you, he's not.

Let's take as an illustration Goethe's "Erlkönig" ("The Elf King"), the gruesome ballad of the evil spirit sitting on the shoulder of father and child as they ride "thro' the woodland so wild" towards home. First, junior is terrified, and then senior loses his cool, leading him to ride wildly, "Clasping close to his bosom his shuddering child; / He reaches his dwelling in doubt and in dread; / But, clasp'd to his bosom, the infant was dead." There are four parts to work out here: the narrator, the father, the child, and the demon. Many singers, especially those from the dramatically charged field of opera, throw themselves into this bit of horror as though it were a B-movie. The temptation to do your best Vincent Price is great.

Nevertheless, a good singer avoids such mannerisms. He remains "cool" and focuses on connecting the creative variety of the piece with his own personal sound. He tells himself: These four parts lie close together in their keys in the Schubert as well as in the Carl Loewe version. Schubert initially alternates between G-minor and C-minor. The child's panic culminates in B-minor and C-sharp-minor. The elf king's lures are first heard in flattering B-flat-major ("O come and go with me, thou loveliest child") and then more emphatic in C-major ("O come and go with me, no longer delay"). Loewe begins with G-minor and changes as soon as the hairs on the neck of both father and son are standing up, to D-minor and B-minor. His Alder king purrs in G-major, which, right before the deadly touch ("Or else, silly child, I will drag thee away"), tips into G-minor. Naturally, my baritone brings the original tone down. Thus, I have to make each individual voice explicit while ensuring that none sticks out, for in the end, the ballad must remain a formally closed and complete work of art. Whether Loewe's "Erlkönig" requires a more sensationalist coloration or Schubert emphasizes the force of natural powers, false pathos should be avoided. The objectifying distance of method should always be discernible.

With this "coolness" even a not so radiant night can come off to the satisfaction of all. It also enables the singer to interpret noble kitsch like Richard Strauss's "Allerseelen"—"Und lass uns wieder von der Liebe reden, wie einst im Mai" ("And let us talk again of love, like once in May")—a song I recorded in the spring of 2004 for my CD *Romantische Lieder,* with pleasure and good results. For every kind of music, even a piece of kitsch can convey true emotion and insight if the voice has its proper sound. Interpretation must begin with the sound.

Miles Davis counted on this in 1957 when he asked the arranger Gil Evans to stage his soft, vibrato-less trumpet for a big-band recording. Before Evans wrote a single note he replaced the traditional saxophone set with a section of flutes, clarinets, and horns, an alto saxophone and a tuba, thus creating a neoromantic, lyrically cerebral orchestra sound which, according to Evans, hung above the beat "like a cloud." His daring paid off, and the wind instruments enveloped Davis's trumpet sound like a glove. The perfectly swinging arrangements sold like hotcakes, and the *Miles Ahead* recordings soon became classics. Davis and Evans went on to perfect their collaboration on two other albums, the better known being *Sketches of Spain,* based largely on the classic *Concierto de Aranjuez* by Joaquín Rodrigo. The composer refused to recognize the album, leading Davis to say, "Let's wait and see. Maybe he'll like it when the fat royalty checks start coming in." Indeed, not a single complaint was heard from Rodrigo.

A singer of the classics rarely has to explain his interpretive choices to the composers he works with, most of whom are resting in peace. Nevertheless, I am impressed by Davis's chutzpah, by his fearlessness in dealing with musical material. Jazz has its own traditions, though its governing principles are obviously less binding. The only things that count there are creativity, artistic freedom, and individual expression. If that isn't Romantic, I don't know what is.

The ingenious tenor saxophonist Lester Young got the blues when innumerable artists tried to copy his style in the late thirties. At Birdland Young played one night with Paul "Lady Q" Quinichette, a very clever copier. After a few choruses, Young, unnerved, walked off the stage, saying: "I don't know anymore whether to play like myself or like Lady Q, because he plays so much like me." But Quinichette's copies didn't do anything for his own reptuation. Lester Young, Louis Armstrong, Count Basie, Duke Ellington, Coleman Hawkins, Charlie Parker, Bud Powell, and John Coltrane are counted as masters of their trade precisely because they interpreted the standard repertoire in unmistakably personal ways.

These jazz musicians have influenced the way I make music, as have the Beatles and soul singers like Stevie Wonder, Ray Charles, Aretha Franklin, and Al Green. Then of course there are the important interpreters of classical music: Hermann Prey, Fritz Wunderlich, Dietrich Fischer-Dieskau, Hans Hotter, and Peter Schreier. They, too, are great individualists, each immediately identifiable by his own sound.

My godfather Berthold gave me my first jazz album for my confirmation. *Louis Armstrong Memorial* is a double album containing recordings by the legendary Hot Five and Hot Seven with the clarinet player Johnny Dodds and the trombone player Kid Ory, drummer Peanuts Hucko and Earl "Fatha" Hines on the piano. My brother was already ahead of me, collecting the hard boppers Art Blakey, Horace Silver, and Sonny Rollins. At some point he brought the first free-jazz records home, shattering Father's peace for years to come. While Micha's classmates were rebelling in a more or less conventional manner, irritating their parents with hashish consumption, hard rock, and membership in the Communist Collective of West Germany, Micha drank

beer, wrote strange poems, and filled our house with his atonal
saxophone playing, only to win—

("Noise!" Father would moan in agony.

"Hänschen, control yourself!" Mama said.

"I've been controlling myself for years. Still, it's noise.")

—with this noise a first prize at the annual music competition of
the Andreanum, accompanied by his friend and pianist Achim.

"Puttchen, now the teachers have gone completely mad,"
Father exclaimed in bewilderment when my grinning brother
handed him the first-prize certificate. Mama talked him into
checking out a performance by Micha's band, Strange Tune Pictures, in the Bishops Mill. The quintet played its fingers raw in
three sets while our old man leaned against a column, sucking on
his pipe. When the audience hollered for encores, he murmured
into Mama's ear: "The only one working here is the drummer."

Still, Father couldn't help but be a little impressed. He didn't
even object when we announced that I would take part in their
next performance. The band was to make a live cut in the legendary club Onkel Pö in Hamburg. On the appointed night, Hamburg was battered by a raging storm. No one was going out, much
less to the Onkel Pö, and so the joint was empty save for a dozen
friends who had traveled along with us. The mood was down to
zero. Things looked up a bit when, the first set barely over and all
the free beer consumed, the boys decided to exchange their meager night's pay for hard liquor. Of necessity complicated arrangements were abandoned in favor of a wild jam session. I still
remember singing my lungs out during a forty-five-minute-long
version of the Pharoah Sanders number "Karma." We never
determined exactly whose karma was responsible for the failure
of the recording machine or the collapse of the gigantic Onkel Pö
letters above the entrance, which fell and broke into a million
pieces. The answer is probably blowing in the wind, along with
the answer to the question of who ended up paying the bill,

which by the end of the evening was considerably larger than the band's income. Probably nobody, for at three a.m. the owner threw us out with a face that said: "Don't ever come back."

Despite the wildness of that night, I put together my own jazz trio. Oliver Gross played the piano and on the bass was Jürgen Attig, called Jaco by everyone after Jaco Pastorius, the miraculous bassist of the jazz rock group Weather Report. Since Jürgen, like his idol, was a great rock musician himself, we won the first prize at the NDR Hörfest (Listening Festival) on our first go. The victory brought us a small fee, a concert tour through north German jazz clubs, and a few gigs at larger festivals. Among other things we appeared with Miles Davis's drummer Tony Williams during the Hildesheim "Jazz Time." There was even a record producer interested in us. What did we care that he was greasy, fat, smelly, and aesthetically challenged in his choice of suits, appearing altogether unprofessional? We were young, inexperienced, and intoxicated by the idea of fame within reach. At the first sign of a contract, we put our names on the dotted line—neglecting, unfortunately, to read the fine print. We got what we deserved. That villain locked us in the studio for three days and three nights, and we had to play horrible pieces and watch as our names were printed on the ugliest album cover in the world. When we dared to bring up the subject of money at the end, his fat cheeks rippled with a satanic chuckle.

"What money? You guys still owe me a hundred for beer, coffee, and sandwiches."

To make matters worse the product fell into Frau Lehmann's hands. As I mentioned earlier, my music teacher considered this kind of music highly toxic. She spoke firmly to my parents, who then had a firm word with me:

"Dear boy, we live in a free country and you may do as you please, but one thing has got to be clear: if we are to continue paying for your lessons, the jazzing must stop." That was fair enough, but since my law studies were hardly fulfilling and clas-sical concerts were still hard to come by, I did suffer from painful performance withdrawal.

But I didn't suffer for long, for soon art came calling again, as shrill and loud as my telephone. It was Micha, telling me some-thing about "crossover art," "audio-visual media," "referees," "the miracle of Bern," "Francis Ford Coppola," and some kind of museum. I don't understand a thing.

"Doesn't matter. It's a lot of fun. Are you coming?"

Who could say no? Not I.

Later, Andy Hahn, an award-winning experimental filmmaker and, as it happened, Micha's roommate, put a script into my hands. It was titled *Kafka or Tibor (Apoelyps Now—a M(H)ystery Play in Two Half Times)*. The blurb suggested that this was a perfor-mance that "once standing on its baroque feet, will tastefully characterize the blurring and coming together of literary, visual and musical themes in our overstimulated media jungle."

"Are you serious?" I asked.

"No," they chorused. They were overcome by a laughing fit. It turned out they had conceived of this "traumatic spectacle" at a boozy balcony party. After drinking prodigiously they sent it off in the mail, addressed to the "Literanover," a reading event, usu-ally avoided by renowned authors, that was part of some cultural director's misguided attempts to lend a little metropolitan cachet to the capital of Lower Saxony.

"And? Is anyone taking this madness seriously?"

Andy nodded. Micha sighed. Neither of them had expected it. But what are friends for? An ensemble was quickly assembled via telephone and the next morning we held our first rehearsal in the Sprengel Museum in Hanover, where the world premiere would take place.

It went a little something like this. The stage was divided in two: jungle on the right, "another world" on the left. In the jungle

Tibor, a German Tarzan, read his comic adventures to his female companion as she conjured up snakes in an aesthetically pleasing manner. Behind them Coppola's *Apocalypse Now* played on a video monitor. In that other world on the left side of the stage experimental filmmakers and musicians were at work on "the total audio-visual work of art, the only true film music." Franz Kafka also made an appearance, participating in the centennial piece by quoting from his own works. At the end of the first act, a referee blew a whistle. After the intermission an artist called Hiltrud sewed a Swiss flag as Albert Einstein, drawing on his theory of relativity, explained to the audience why the "Miracle of Bern" (Germany was winning the world soccer championship for the first time) was no coincidence. The script then called for a tango, which sweet melody brought all the participants on stage for a finale through the looking glass: Kafka wandered the jungle while Tibor and his playmate discovered visual experiments and free jazz orgies.

That was the plan, and that's pretty much how it came off. To the dismay of the zoology student Heidi, the fire department prohibited the use of real poison snakes. I played Einstein but could not memorize the theory of relativity. Instead, Heidi and I sat in a canoe and hummed the song "Caprifischer." Only Günther, our referee, truly strayed from his written part, which called for him to do nothing but blow his whistle at the performance's beginning, middle, and end and proclaim "a minute of silence for the fathers of the constitution." He was overzealous and yellow-carded spectators who complained. In the second half, two of them got red cards, which as we all know means dismissal from the field. Sure enough, he threw them out of the museum, but what he didn't know was that one of these philistines had a seat on the city council of Hanover. The Christian Democrat raged and made legal threats, but in the end he chickened out. He couldn't press charges against a performance being hailed as a first-rate avant-garde spectacle.

This elaborate joke led me to a new playground: the cabaret. It was the 1980s, and material was everywhere: antinuclear protests, neomysticism, rural Trotskyite communes, health food stores, yoga, Tantra, primal scream classes, feminist tutorials on the clitoris, male bonding. The Federal Republic of Germany seemed to have become a therapy center.

I did a wicked Helmut Kohl in my cabaret act. The rest of my repertoire consisted largely of Karl Valentin sketches and works by Hanns Dieter Hüsch. To rib this part of the '68ers who had turned into yuppies, I did a song called "Sommer der Liebe" ("Summer of Love") that Micha wrote:

> Do you remember how it went back then,
> first a department store started to burn,
> then came Baader and Schleyer died
> and Germany came apart at plain sight.
> German autumn it was later called,
> But it was rather hot back then I recall,
> The Americans threw napalm bombs
> onto the rice of the Vietcong.

It continues with a sequence of chords by the good old Troggs:

> And Jimi Hendrix played "Wild Thing,"
> we stormed off and burnt the *Bild.*
> Then Dutschke was shot at,
> and we ran away flustered
> Usually our brains were full of haze
> From too much Marx and Habermas,
> But comrades, comrades you must admit
> We also had a lot of fun with it.

Refrain:

> That was the summer of love,
> and we were there.
>
> Do you still remember communard Teufel,
> Uschi's breasts and Ho Chi Minh,
> Nowadays every idiot scolds me
> For having been involved with it.
> We only wanted to be free and high,
> To make the world a better place,
> Most of us through free love,
> Only the RAF reached for the grenades.

The final credits are once again made up by the sad Western melody:

> Ensslin went a little too far.
> I knew that wasn't going to work.
> Instead I went through the institutions
> and I have never lost my shape
> I can't complain, it's worked for me.
> Today as then my motto stays:
> Not anvil but hammer be.

I gave performances with the pianist Hubertus Conradi and later with my friend Peter Müller in our pub. The pub wasn't far from the city theatre and one night Pierre Leon, the theatre's director, came in, enjoyed himself, and asked us to perform on his stage. Of course we did it. The show was constantly sold out. After that we were ready for the rest of the world, which in our case lay between Lüneburg and Holzminden. Peter and I moved through the area of Niedersachsen for two years, supplementing our student income with wit, satire, and irony. But after the one hundredth performance we ran out of material. We just could not stand to hear the old jokes any longer. I tried to write lyrics and songs but soon realized that I wasn't cut out for it. We agreed to stay away from cabaret and concentrate on classical music. I am happy to report that the cabaret has managed to get along just fine without us.

But without the music halls and smoky jazz clubs, Tommy Quasthoff would have turned out to be a different (and, I assume, far worse) singer. That kind of life teaches a performer to be relaxed and assertive with his audience. It's hard to rattle someone who has had the experience of standing in the pouring rain at a small-town music festival before five hundred rockers who have been waiting for hours for Peter Maffay, the German Jon Bon Jovi, to appear. When faced with people who have chosen to settle their inheritance dispute at the opera, that seasoned singer will not hesitate to remind them that "it is very impolite to talk during music. After all this is not the Hit Parade." And illness is no excuse for spoiling a concert. When Schumann's *Dichterliebe* threatens to drown in a catarrh of barking coughs I ask "all those with lung ailments to hold their cough until the break when I can cough along with you"—and it gets quiet pretty quickly, unless we're in the middle of a truly terrible citywide case of the flu.

Treat the audience like people, and they'll treat you like a person, too, instead of a trained monkey. Justus "Jussi" Zeyen, my dear friend and the pianist with whom I perform most lieder nights nowadays, is—like me—the soul of punctuality. But at the end of one three-week tour, we were both exhausted and way behind schedule when we arrived in our last stop, Luxembourg. In Mainz we had missed a train. At the hotel we discovered that our suitcases had not arrived. No time to change, no time to freshen up, no time for a snack. A taxi was waiting with its engine running to take us to the concert hall. It wasn't an ideal situation, to say the least, but there was nothing to be done. But when we got to the venue, I caught a glimpse of my drained, sweaty face in my dressing room mirror and knew I could not work like that. So I went out on the stage, explained the situation, and asked for a little patience. Could we have twenty minutes to catch our breath before beginning? The audience had no objection, and when we came back onto the stage we were greeted by roaring applause. The rest of the night turned out to be very enjoyable. In fact, after four encores the Luxembourgers still didn't want to let us leave the stage. We had nothing left, so I said, "You are simply fantastic, but we are knocked out, hungry, and thirsty, and if you don't mind, we will save the rest for next time."

"Promise?" called a man from the first row.

"Word of honor," I said, and we kept it.

Afterwards the *Luxemburger Wort* wrote: "The singer seemed to want to break through the stiff ceremony of the conventional lieder evening," and that was fine with them. "Why does a lieder evening always have to be as serious as the Dawn of the Gods?" It's a fine question. Just a couple of years ago some colleagues reproached me for having dared to announce Schubert's "Forelle" ("The Trout") in Flensburg with the words: "As befits our locale, something fishy is next." Granted, there are no trout in the North Sea, but my quibbling colleagues were not concerned with ichthyological precision. They took objection to my attitude. To their way of thinking, a singer must stand rigid next to the piano like a monument to himself, and if he doesn't, he's an odd bird, a liability for the guild. Nowadays even a guardian of bourgeois etiquette as incorruptible as the newspaper *Frankfurter Allgemeine* knows that it does not hurt to relax Brahms's *Vier ernste Gesänge (Four Serious Songs)* a little bit, writing that it can "provide inter-

mittent relief" for both listener and interpreter "from the pressure to suffer and create."

That artistic pressure is felt, believe me, when Jussi and I
make a crude mistake, something that does happen, however
rarely. I like to relieve such embarrassments with a joke: "We are
serious musicians, really!" I insist, and people laugh. They laugh
because they believe us and because we don't take ourselves any
more seriously than absolutely necessary.

What matters is the art. Whether it is pop or classic, whether
Fritz Wunderlich or Stevie Wonder is on stage, in the end we are
all entertainers.

I believe that every semitalented human being can learn classical
singing, but the German academy does not make it easy for
young people who want to be concert or opera singers. In a heated
moment I once referred to these educational institutes as "breed-
ing grounds for vocal mannerisms." They tend to confuse students with overwrought pedagogy that obstructs the path towards
true artistic sensibility.

Since 1996 I have taught at the Music Academy in Detmold.
The biggest problem is that the course of study is too brief. Five
years are definitely not enough for a voice to mature, but the cur-
ricula are usually designed by bureaucrats who understand little
to nothing about the subject. The academies, for their part, want
as many students as possible to graduate as quickly as possible
because the number of diplomas issued is seen by the supervising
authorities as proof of effective functioning. And it is this false
efficacy, completely estranged from the interests of art, that is
the decisive argument when it comes to the distribution of ever
sparser state funds. Everything is supposed to happen quickly.
Unfortunately, the students, being students, want everything
quickly, too—quick success and difficult parts much too early.

They end up wondering why their vocal cords are ruined before their careers have taken off.

But the path to enlightenment is as arduous as the Buddhist's noble eightfold path. Please follow me now into the song master class of a popular music academy. A student from Korea is preparing to perform in an overflowing "studio." Let us call him Mr. Lee. Mr. Lee has prepared *Vier ernste Gesänge (Four Serious Songs)*, so called for a reason—Brahms wrote the requiem for the deadly ill Clara Schumann, eternal muse and the composer's single great love. He could not sing it to his friends without succumbing to tears. Mr. Lee gives the man on the piano a sign, inhales, and thunders the first lines unto the hall ceiling: "Denn es geht auch dem Menschen wie dem Veeh. Wie dies stilbt, so stilbt er auch." (Roughly: "For man suffers the same fate as cattle. As they die so too does he.")

I interrupt Mr. Lee, asking what he feels when he sings.

"I see a picture with humans and animals."

"Nice," I say. "But try to remember that this is a biblical verse. Brahms did not compose a rural piece. He has set a sermonizing text to music."

But even on the second try Mr. Lee does not become a Solomon. He just gets louder, during his favorite parts, very loud. Notes and vowels and consonants swim together like noodles in an overcooked soup.

"Not *kettle*," I say, "it's *cattle*. A *kettle* is something else."

That's how it goes for another half hour. Then a young lady takes a shot at Schumann's "Nussbaum." *"Duuftig"* and *"luuuftig"* she glides through the romantic floral scenery, her *f* detached from the vowel. Another candidate adorns her very pretty voice with superfluous vowels, not intended by Hugo Wolf. "Heiss(ö) mich(ö) nicht(ä) reden, heiss(ö) mich(ö) schweigen." (Roughly: "Tell(eh) me(eh) not to speak(eh), tell(eh) me to be silent(eh).")

Sometimes, I'm afraid, that's exactly what a weary teacher wants to do.

A philosopher and soccer lover called Sartre once said that one is not a goalie or a striker the same way one is a wage earner. Being an artist of the ball is no ordinary profession; it's a calling. The same thing goes for singing, and that is why I am a very strict teacher. Whoever auditions for my class is being examined down to the bone and often the candidates are rejected. Each time I am deeply sorry, but when I accept students I have to be sure that they can keep up, that their voice can sustain them for thirty, forty years, that they can live off their music. It does no good to give young people false hope only to see them fail on the free market. The offers are few and the competition is brutal. Whoever does not meet the requirements is gone in the blink of an eye. I prefer to judge honestly according to the motto: better a painful ending than pain without end. Life is too precious to waste on impossible dreams, when these young people could instead be discovering the profession that will truly fulfill them.

But I am the last one to proclaim that my way is the only path to success. I advise my students to keep their eyes and ears open, watch what colleagues have to offer, and if they think it will advance their cause to try it. Professors can teach you how to swim, but where you wish to swim to and at what speed is your decision.

After my training with Frau Lehmann I was fortunate enough to find a mentor in Helmuth Rilling, who unites personality, love of art, wisdom of heart, and relaxed joviality in the same matter-of-fact manner in which he combines tea, sugar, and milk. Rilling is the founder and head of the International Bach Academy in Stuttgart, a world-renowned conductor, a formidable teacher, a musicologist, a rediscoverer of Romantic choral music, and, thanks to the composing commissions he regularly hands out, an indefatigable sponsor of contemporary music.

But I knew next to nothing of all this when he invited me to audition in 1987. I had, of course, heard of him, the authority in all matters relating to Johann Sebastian Bach. For me he was an awe-inspiring master, a dispenser of profound statements like: "Music must never be comfortable, never museal and soothing. It should stir people up, reach them on a personal level, and make them think."

On the train on my way to our first meeting, I tried to imagine him. I pictured a large man, ascetic, serious, and strict as a fugue. There was also a chubby version resembling the Thomas cantor, only without the wig. In the event I was greeted in Stuttgart by a small, friendly gentleman with a head of snow-white hair, blinking with alert eyes through his reading glasses, and wearing a mischievous smile. He spoke with a cozy Swabian accent:

"Ah, you must be Mr. Quashthoff. Hello, I'm Helmuth Rilling."

My audition the next day was a moderate catastrophe. Presumably the excitement had affected my stomach. Overnight I was overcome by diarrhea and chills and hardly got any sleep. I felt like a wet and lazy sack but couldn't bear the idea of chickening out. My friend Peter Müller, who had come along to accompany me on the piano, shook his head:

"We are not playing. You cannot sing like this. You're sick and belong in bed." His angel-sweet pleading did no good with me, and so he resigned himself to his fate and heaved me into a cab, direction Bach Academy, so that I could deliver the Bach aria from Händel's *Joshua* oratorio. In the beginning all was well, but I soon noticed that Peter was getting faster and faster. Or was I getting slower? In my feverish state I could not say. I only knew that a major alarm had gone off in my head:

"Oh God, what are we doing? Rilling must think we are out of our minds, amateurs, ne'er-do-wells. The Bach Academy is over and done with for me, once and for all." After that, everything is a blank. I only remember making it back to Hanover in a state of total exhaustion and lying flat for three weeks.

I didn't hear anything from the Bach Academy for a year. Then one day an invitation for a week of cantatas came in the mail. I forget now what I sang; I only remember that this time things went well. There is a deep C in one of the pieces and Helmuth beamed as if he'd won the lottery each time it rolled cleanly from my throat. Shortly after that I went on tour with the Bach Academy. We were performing Händel's *Jephtha* in the former Czech Republic and in Poland. At the end of this journey Helmuth asked me:

"Say, do you feel like recording the *Matthäus-Passion* with me?"

This invitation to perform Bach's key piece was a knightly accolade and another serious push to my career after the ARD competition. Under his conductorship I also sang the Brahms Requiem for the first time, not to mention Mendelssohn's *Elijah*, which is not as lavishly orchestrated as a Bach oratorio but demands much more drama from the singer. I owe a large part of my practical education to Helmuth and the Academy.

Over the years we developed a deep connection, based not only on the love of music. We both know how to appreciate a good red wine and a good soccer game. Helmuth is an ardent supporter of the Stuttgart soccer club and does not miss a home game if he can help it. He also has a soft spot for Cardenal Mendoza cognac and Davidoff cigars, things I am happy to bring him from my travels. Once when I arrived in Santiago de Compostela, where Helmuth was to perform the *Elijah* with the Real Filharmonia, my first stop in the airport was the duty-free shop. Whether due to sheer pleasure addiction or the spiritual atmosphere of the famous pilgrimage destination, the entire stash—which I had planned to last three days—was finished on the first night with the active help of the spouses Rilling and my esteemed baritone colleague Matthias Goerne.

The next day after breakfast I ran into Helmuth in the lobby of our hotel. He skipped "good morning" and simply said, "Tommy, do you feel like going to the airport, too?" We immediately went back to stock up.

In other words, Helmuth is a first-class traveling companion. By now we have covered a good deal of ground together, having toured several times through the Iberian peninsula and having performed the *Matthäus Passion* in Buenos Aires at the Teatro Colón, one of the most beautiful opera houses in the world. Afterwards I taught a master class there. Since Bach tradition in Argentina is still in its infancy, the singers' ability levels were, well, let's just say highly interesting, and there is a lot left to be done. The memory of a certain seven-foot-tall youth with a narrow chest has stayed with me. He wants to sing Hugo Wolf's "Zur Ruh, zur Ruh." I have him do a few breathing exercises and watch as he grows increasingly pale. After the third exercise he looks at me rapturously, rolls his eyes, and faints. When he comes to shortly afterwards he insists on singing again, but once again he turns snow white with the first notes. Concerned, I interrupt him and recommend that he lie down *zur Ruh* (in peace) at home rather than risk totally vanishing "from the realm of earthly pains" ("aus dem Raum der Erdenschmerzen").

Helmuth has also opened doors for me on the North American continent. In 1995 he took me along to Eugene, Oregon, in which idyllic university town he founded the Oregon Bach Festival in 1970. It is one of the most prolific festivals in the United States, and he leads it to this day. I have visited it frequently since, once in 1998, when Helmuth conducted the world premiere of Krysztof Penderecki's *Credo*, a mighty mass for one hundred and ten choral singers, orchestra, and five soloists—at this performance: Julia Borchert, Milagro Vargas, Marietta Simpson, Rolf Romei, and Tommy Quasthoff. The atmosphere was tense. Even Helmuth, usually unfazed, was tearing out his hair. Two days before the performance, Penderecki still had not delivered a complete score. The next morning, the avant-garde composer and his score finally appeared. Penderecki sat in the first row to watch the general rehearsal, but he didn't let us get very far. Again and again Penderecki interrupted, saying he wanted the chorus a little louder over here, a solo voice more distinct over there, and in general a bit more dynamism from the strings. The patient conductor let it be. When we had almost, and with no small relief, completed a run-through, Penderecki leapt up again, screaming:

"Trumpets! Too late! Too late! Too late!"

That's when Helmuth's patience snapped. He yelled back, "Composed! Composed! Composed!"

But the exasperating work did come to something. The *Credo* was frenetically cheered at the festival's climax.

Two other conductors who have greatly influenced my way of making music are Claudio Abbado and Simon Rattle. Compared to Rattle, Abbado is introverted, but in his way he is just as friendly and warm as the Brit. In 1972, for the first time in the history of Milan, Abbado opened La Scala to students and workers, trying to excite this clientele with special programs for the theatre. Abbado has a natural authority driving from his musical and intellectual integrity; he is without tricks or power games. For him it is about the cause alone, about music and about the conductor's interest. When he steps up to the podium one can be sure that he has familiarized himself with the latest and best litcrature and research and that he will present a comprehensive and novel reading of the score, whether it is from the nineteenth-century classic repertoire or the early twentieth century, or the new sound makers Stockhausen, Berio, or Nono. There is hardly a living conductor with a command over such a broad spectrum. No matter what he is working on, Abbado strives intensely for clarity of musical structure and voice direction. With a mimic's talent and body language, he has a fascinating way of conveying in a single look what others attempt to communicate by swinging their batons around as if fencing invisible opponents. I got to know the chief conductor and artistic director of the Berliner Philharmonisches Orchester in 1997 when he invited me to sing with the Chamber Orchestra of Europe during the Berliner Festwochen (Berliner Weeks of Celebration). It was my good fortune only a year later to record Mahler's *Des Knaben Wunderhorn* under his direction; I got to sing with the Berlin Philharmonic and the grand mezzo-soprano Anne Sofie von Otter, and the CD went on to win the Grammy for Best Classical Singing Performance 1999.

I have also given some of my most moving concerts with Abbado. In 2001, ten days after the attacks on the World Trade Center, we were guests at Carnegie Hall, opening the concert season. Our performance became a topic of controversial discussion. Some people thought it impious to think about concerts so soon after the cruel massacre; in Berlin there were concerns regarding security. But when the New Yorkers decided not to be put down by terror, to continue living life as normally as possible, Abbado saw it as a question of solidarity and honor to appear with his musicians. I admit my heart did pound unusually hard during the landing at Kennedy Airport. Smoke was still rising from Ground Zero. I have so many friends in the city and the idea that one of them could have been hit made me both furious and sad.

"We are all New Yorkers," the program said, echoing Kennedy's famous declaration in Berlin, but the orchestra dedicates this concert in particular to the recently deceased Isaac Stern. The eminent virtuoso of the violin saved Carnegie Hall from being torn down and afterwards served as its president for a long time. On this night the metaphysical force of music is palpable. The Philharmonic played Gustav Mahler's "Five Rückert Songs," Beethoven's Symphony No. 3, and the Piano Concerto No. 1, D-Minor Op. 15 by Johannes Brahms. They played as if enraptured. The melody of the *Eroica* unfolds in an iridescent atmosphere, a mixture of vulnerability and consolation, despair and purification. Tears ran down many faces, and in the end the spectators stood as one, enthusiastically applauding the grand orchestra but also themselves, their will to survive and the hope that man is capable of overcoming even the greatest pain.

Simon Rattle, Abbado's successor to the Berlin conductor's throne, loves the spotlight. He is a man of great charisma. When one observes him in the process of conducting one always sees his left hand opened towards the orchestra, a gesture that says: "I am open for everything, and so should you be." With this spirit he tickles energies out of the orchestra that can sweep an audience out of its seats. At the same time Simon is kind, sensitive, highly intelligent, and with all his musical genius one of the funniest men under the sun. I was treated to a sample of his wit the first time we collaborated.

Haydn's *Schöpfung* (*The Creator*) was on the program. There is a point in this piece at which the archangel Raphael is supposed to sing: "Kriecht am Boden das Gewürm" ("on the ground the vermin crawls"). One can let it end on a high or low B-flat, both suiting Papa Haydn. Normally the high B-flat is preferred, by others and by me. After the first piano rehearsal Rattle asked:

"Can you sing it low, too?"

"Sure," I said.

When we made it to the point in question during the orchestra rehearsal I was concentrating so hard on managing my score without mistake that I completely forgot about his request. Once again I sang a high B-flat, and Simon brought the musical machinery to a halt:

"Excuse me, can you sing it low?"

I turned red and apologized, but due to my nervousness I repeated the mistake even at the general rehearsal. I promised myself it wouldn't happen during the concert and indeed, on the decisive day I presented him with a wonderful low B-flat—supersized. The audience was amused. Simon turned to me without interrupting his conducting and through his broad grin murmured,

"Asshole."

But all the kidding around is over when it's time for the actual grinding work of rehearsal. Rattle becomes a manic polisher and rearranger. Never before have I heard such perfect correspondence between instrument groups as when the Berliner Philharmoniker practiced it under his direction, never before such lively swaying of the orchestra apparatus. And once an opus has been renewed from the bottom up it no longer looks like work; even heavyweights such as Mahler or Bruckner symphonies appear playfully easy. When Simon conducts, it is pure magic. One especially notices the freshness of his method when he polishes up stiff oldies like Haydn's *Seasons*, which I performed with Christiane Oelze and the tenor Ian Bostridge in Berlin. With disarming precision and in high spirits the chorus blares through the bucolic scenery while the orchestra conjures up the changing landscape in hyperrealist brilliance, but not without a baroque fullness of expression. No trace any longer of the pomp and pathos of Karajan's time, gone are even the panoramic sound tableaus of the Abbado era. Simon simply did away with the ballast, purging the sound body so that all the score's sparkling details could be seen, displayed like the trophies of a big-game hunter. It is tone painting in a state of perfection, and Karl Raab is absolutely correct when he writes "it is simply wonderful (and almost deliciously entertaining) with what palpable curiosity, precision and finesse his musicians follow this cycle of the year. Simon Rattle is like a child who has not yet forgotten how to be in awe of nature and the music that imagines it."

Simon is a good friend to me and an especially close musical brother, for with all his professionalism he is also a Romantic at heart, and he discovers possibilities in my voice that I would not dare to consider myself. For example, he lets me sing all the bass parts in the *Johannes Passion*. There are five and each has to be sung in a different tone. Jesus must not sound like Pilate, and Pilate must not sound like Judas. That is the high school of character. Simon threw me into it and I succeeded.

In the summer of 2000 we were on the road in England with Beethoven's Ninth Symphony. The former Philharmonia Chorus, founded by Otto Klemperer shortly after the Second World War, had been hired for the choral part. When the dignified gentlemen gathered for the first rehearsal, Simon winked at me and said: "Don't be surprised the chorus sounds deep. It still includes a few of the original members." The last concert took place in the Ely Cathedral, a giant church in East Anglia, England. On the way to the ensuing banquet, Simon held me back and put an arm around my shoulders:

"Tommy, my friend, I believe the time has come. We have to work in opera."

I have received many offers from large houses already and have always declined. I haven't felt mature enough, and it seems an unnecessary display of my disability.

But I trust Simon and I know that he would never push me towards something untenable aesthetically or musically. So this time I said:

"Okay, Simon, what shall we do?"

"Beethoven, *Fidelio*, 2003, at the Festival Hall in Salzburg."

Sympathy Is Free, Envy You Gotta Earn

The large concert hall on the Mönchsberg in Salzburg was once a riding school. Nowadays the bourgeoisie reigns here, and its discreet charm hovers over the Salzburger Festspiele (Salzburg Festival) from July until August and in April infects the Oster-festspiele (Easter Festival), started by Herbert von Karajan in 1967. Discreet or not, there's no mistaking the bourgeois prices in the neighborhood and the dark limousines circling the block before the premieres. I see it in the well-honed boos lofted at the director Nikolaus Lehnhoff, who insists on presenting his Easter *Fidelio* not as historicized Singspiel but as an abstract, sparely decorated drama of ideas. Perhaps he can take consolation in the fact that the original performance did not fare much better.

I know that in terms of my voice I can manage the part, for in 1996 I recorded *Fidelio* with the Symphony Orchestra of the Bavarian Broadcasting Corporation under the direction of Sir Colin Davis. But when I watch the first rehearsals in Salzburg I must ask myself whether I really have enough acting talent and physical presence for it, for despite Simon's encouragement the fear of exposing myself to ridicule still gnaws at me. After all, I am to play the respectable Minister Don Fernando.

"What's the big deal?" says Tony, amiably trying to erase my concerns. He is sitting in my hotel room, dragging on a bag of Afghan Black with visible enjoyment. "All those fat old tenors stalking young girls like Aida or Desdemona? That's the real ugly stuff. Not you, little big man."

He can talk, not yet having seen me in the tailcoat the stylist gave me that morning. The thing is snow white and at least two sizes too big. Instead of dignified tails I drag two rags of fabric behind me like giant insect wings. By noon I feel like Gregor Samsa and by night like the cleaning woman because the stage is wiped sparkly clean in my wake. But even when they get me a properly fitting coat, my stage fright does not dissolve, especially when I witness the professional devotion with which Angela Denoke (Leonore/Fidelio) ensnares Jon Villars (Florestan) and with what erotic verve colleague Juliane Banse (Marzelline) sings the joys of love. But with time it gets better.

Director Nikolaus Lehnhoff is very pleased with my work and Simon Rattle has no complaints. After the general rehearsal he slaps me on the shoulder and says: "Tommy, the rehearsal was *wunderbar.* Don't be afraid. If something goes wrong, shake it off. Then you just go on with your concerts."

I tell myself that this is a man who is seldom wrong, and I am very calm indeed on the day of the premiere. Since my big entrance does not come until the second act I watch the performance up close from behind the stage. The direction has cut all explanatory dialogue, and the opening motif demonstrates Simon's willingness to make his orchestra the primary interpreter of the action. He leads the Berliner Philharmoniker through the overture, avoiding empty heroism and pathos. His tempi are slow and his metri flowing, lending expressiveness and suppleness to the arias.

To establish the setting, a Spanish prison near Seville, three shining steel walls suffice. The stage displays a pair of old shoes and a mound of earth. A steep staircase stands out in the background. The young prison guard Jaquino (Rainer Trost) declares his love to Marzelline ("Jetzt Schätzchen, jetzt sind wir allein,"

"Now darling, now we are alone"). She sings: "Oh, wär ich doch
schon mit Dir vereint" ("If only I were already united with you"),
meaning not poor Jaquino but Fidelio—that is, Leonore dressed
up as a man. Marzelline's father, an old guard called Rocco (Laszlo
Polgar), blesses the union. When Fidelio/Leonore goes down the
stairs upon her cue, the steps are glowing in the morning sunlight
and the view from the claustrophobic bunker opens up to the
wild dangerous vastness where the villainous governor Don
Pizarro (Alan Held) is spinning his yarn. When Leonore raises her
voice this business of romance is over at once, and the music
begins to gather Beethovenian force. "How large is the danger?"
are the young woman's first words upon sneaking into the prison
with death-defying bravery. Her heart belongs to her one and
only, her husband, Florestan, fighter for freedom and justice as
well as sole witness to the misdeeds of Don Pizarro, who, precisely for this reason, has had him thrown into the deepest hole
of the dungeon.

And already the bastard is standing on the steps to silence Florestan for good, for news has come from the capital: Minister
Don Fernando, an old friend of Florestan, is planning to inspect
the prison in the near future. But my moment has not yet arrived.
First the simpleton Rocco must be convinced to help the murderer ("Dem Staate liegt daran," "in the interest of the state"),
only to be told by Leonore, who overheard everything, that there
is nothing more urgent for him to do than to open up the cells.
Rocco does her the favor of giving the choir of captives an opportunity to intone a moving song ("Oh, welche Lust," "Oh what
pleasure"). But the joy does not last long. When Pizarro finds out
about the unauthorized amnesty he is frothing with anger and
orders the delinquents locked away again. Before the intermission we will see Leonore and Rocco descend into the dungeon's
depths, he in order to dig Florestan's grave and she to free her
husband.

The second act brings the dramatically underscored lovers' reunion, a political statement by Florestan ("Wahrheit wagt' ich kühn zu sagen / Und die Ketten sind mein Lohn," "Boldly I dared to speak the truth / and chains were my reward"), Pizarro's attempted murder, and—before the worst can take place—the turning of the opera towards the utopian and miraculous. A trumpet signal causes the hand with the traitor's blade to freeze. Don Pizarro has lost, the minister approaches, and Quasthoff has his work cut out for him.

Nikolaus Lehnhoff has thought of something spectacular for my appearance. While the prisoners in the form of the Arnold Schönberg Choir come together to form a wall of mistreated souls, I sneak in through the side entrance behind the human chain. Then it recedes and I step—Bloch's principle of hope on two short legs—out of the circle of disenfranchised towards the front, releasing Don Fernando's famous credo:

"Nicht länger kniet sklavisch nieder! / Tyrannenstrenge sei mir fern. / Es sucht der Brüder seine Brüder / und kann er helfen, hilft er gern" ("No longer kneel in slavish fashion! / Tyranny is far from me. / Brother looks after brother / and if he can help, he gladly will").

The lovers sink into each other's arms and all is well. Almost. The *Süddeutsche* criticizes a "smooth designer-Beethoven," the Viennese critic Volker Boser states that "the audience reacted politely but was not beside itself." On the other hand, the *Kölner Stadtanzeiger* reports that Simon Rattle was celebrated with calls of "Bravo," attesting a "grandiose debut as new leader of the Osterfestspiele." The *Welt*, too, lauds a "purged Fidelio," saying it "functions splendidly." Even the *Süddeutsche* makes room for Quasthoff in its otherwise derisive piece, saying that I "communicated the message of brotherhood with intelligence and great sincerity." Sybille Mahlke, the reviewer of the Berliner *Tages-*

spiegel, likes it even better. She writes I should "confidently treat myself to more theatre in the future."

And so I did. Almost a year later the announcement was made:

Vienna (dpa)—The celebrated baritone Thomas Quasthoff is giving his debut at the State Opera in Vienna. The Grammy winner will sing the suffering King Amfortas in the new staging of Richard Wagner's *Parsifal* (Direction: Christine Mielitz). Johan Botha sings the title role and Angela Denoke will appear as Kundry. Opera director Ioan Holender announced to the press before the premiere: "It will not be a smooth evening, but we have to do what we think is right."

Mielitz wants to put Wagner's last opera on stage as "a merciles farewell to utopias." Quasthoff, who won his fame as a singer of songs, débuted on stage in April 2003 at the Salzburger Osterfestspiele under Simon Rattle. Hitherto he had avoided appearances in opera, not wishing his disability to be used as a stage effect. The forty-four-year-old singer commented on his debut at the renowned house at Ringstrasse in the Viennese paper *Kurier* on Tuesday: "Thank God there are more important things than me singing Amfortas. It isn't about me. It is about the beautiful music existing on this planet."

I must confess that for a long time the world of Wagner was as far away from me as Jupiter. Although my theory tutor Ernst Huber-Contwig had introduced me to the basics, the goings-on up in the hills of Bayreuth had always seemed rather suspect to me: the cult around the performances, the annual parading of the Federal Republic's wannabes, Wagner's anti-Semitism, the old Bakunin friend's sucking up to Ludwig II, his political ruminating, leaning first towards anarchism then German nationalism, only to finally propagate the salvation of socialism with the help of "veg-

ctarians," "animal rightists," and "the cultivation of modera-
tion" through religion and art *(Über Religion und Kunst).* The
entire clan's undeniable sympathy for Nazi ideology has always
repelled me. When Simon offered me the role of Amfortas in *Par-*
sifal I could not pass up the opportunity to grapple with Wagner
on a more intensive level, and in less than four weeks Saul had
turned into Paul. I accepted Thomas Mann's judgment that Wagner's oeuvre "is one of the most complex and fascinating phe-
nomenons of the creative world." If nothing else, it is hard to find
another work in which the madness, achievements, and woes
of the nineteenth century come together so seamlessly. And
so I learned how wonderful his music sounds at the Festival of
Bayreuth.

Tony, himself a glowing Wagnerian and regular guest at the
festival, procured for me one of the rare tickets for the *Meis-*
tersinger. Christian Thielemann was conducting and I was enthralled by the almost transparent sound of the orchestra, the
Shakespearean jolliness of the songs and choruses. The next day
Tony's veteran status got us an invitation to tea with Wolfgang
Wagner, the grey old head of the heritage society. I would like to
offer you an anecdote, but the old man does not speak much. If he
does say something he mumbles in an old Frankish dialect while
moving pastry from one cheek to the other. Apart from that he
does not hear very well any longer, something I noticed when
Tony launched into his standard lecture in music history. Wolfgang Wagner gazed out the window, dipping cookies into his tea
with an unearthly smile on his face and mechanically jerking his
head every other minute. When Tony reached his destination ("I
don't know what this Schönberg wanted!") our host just said,
"Ya, ya, it is beautiful, but we don't call it a mountain, rather
a hill."

I gladly accepted Simon's offer after Bayreuth. *Parsifal* considered the least operatic of Wagner's large works, which made it

easier for me to agree. It might even be thought of as an "oratorio with costumes." I liked the part of Amfortas right away because of its singable character, very unlike Verdi's crippled Rigoletto, for example, which I had been offered frequently but which I did not want to sing.

On the other hand, I had no idea how demanding a Wagner part, even a lyrical one, would be. After one month of rehearsals and six performances I had almost come to agree with Schopenhauer, who referred to opera as "a gathering for the purpose of self-flagellation." The five-hour staging demanded that I draw on undreamed of energy reserves, and not only because I am small—even the three-hundred-pound Johan Botha singing the part of Parsifal looks rather fatigued in his armor at the end. After all, it is not only the length of Wagner's operas that takes strength. Standing beneath the stagelights is unimaginably grueling. Each individual spotlight burns with 1,000 watts, and they make you sweat as well as any sauna. And in this condition one is supposed to concentrate on Wagner's highly dramatic singing voices and act as if the Gloria Swanson Memorial Prize were at stake!

For me all this is especially hard because my mother, unexpectedly, has to undergo a complicated heart surgery after having collapsed during my parents' move to Hanover and being suspended between life and death for a week. Father is in a desolate state. Though I know that Micha has left everything in order to take care of them I am so worried I can hardly work. I would like to go home, and when I confide in the director Christine Mielitz she does not hesitate for a moment:

"I understand it well. If you think you can't do it, go home. You don't have to be considerate about *Parsifal* and even less about me." The tomboyish East Berliner has a big heart and is movingly concerned about me. The same is true for the fantastic colleagues who are wrapping me in cotton during rehearsals. Micha, who sends a daily medical bulletin by phone, advises me to remain in Vienna as long as Mama's condition is stable. Tony also thinks I should not rush anything. Torn, I finally decide to continue rehearsing at first, but I am no great support to the conductor Donald Runnicles or to the director. Three days after the surgery Micha finally lets me know that Mama woke up and is through the worst. An entire mountain range drops from my shoulders and I approach Amfortas with new élan. Christine Mielitz had already hinted at his special significance in her directorial plan but has not yet revealed any details.

"First, I've got to know what you can do!"

"Sing, I guess!"

"I know, man. But I mean whether you can run with your disability, whether you can act on stage, or whether we've got to roll Amfortas from the mattress right into his coffin."

"No worries, I'm a veritable jock."

I should not have said so, for now the King of the Holy Grail will go through miles instead of cultivating the wound inflicted by Klingsor on soft pillows and getting carried around by his attendants on a sedan chair. At least that's what it says in the libretto, but Ms. Mielitz has prescribed some exercise for Amfortas.

In the third act the sedan chair is taken away from me—by then nearly dead—altogether. Instead an elevator is built for me which will transport the King of the Holy Grail onto the stage from the space below. One can reach the vehicle only via a steep staircase behind the stage wall. It is a tight and dark place and the first time I attempt to climb it I nearly fall into the scenery.

"Put a lamp up here," I scream. "I thought they always say Amfortas must not die."

"If you keep yelling like that I'm gonna have to reconsider that," the director calls out. When the elevator after much jolting and jerking gets stuck ten feet above the ground I worry she might be serious.

"Don't get excited," Mielitz calms me down. "Coming down is always easy."

"Yeah, but in what condition is the question. Probably Amfortas will never have to go to the makeup room again."

As you can see the tone is rough but friendly. Everyone appreciates this, and they follow Christine Mielitz, who pushes the ensemble around like a general in order to illustrate properly the projected farewell to utopia. After the general rehearsal she surveys the scenery with contentment.

"Well, that all looked good." Opera house director Ioan Holender nods in agreement and gears up for opening night. Little does he know what awaits him.

The Viennese State Opera community are not dissimilar from the Knights of the Holy Grail. On the night of April 8 they sit in their seats projecting their determination to carry out an aesthetic ritual and to punish any desecration of a twenty-five-year-old performance tradition, August Everding's staging of *Parsifal*.

Donald Runnicles lets the A-flat major motif of the grail proclaiming heavenly love and strength rise from the depth of the strings and get branded onto the walls of the Castle of Montsalvat, which is decorated like a cross between a public swimming hall and a deteriorated fin de siècle salon. Two attendants are lugging Amfortas in. A piece of linen drenched in chicken blood is lying across the king's shoulders. I am accepting Kundry's healing balm and am already carried off again.

In this way at least the king does not have to watch the walls crumble down. When I appear again it has begun to dawn on the audience that the population is doomed. The knights are not the blessed elite of the Western World but a decadent power club, an assembly of dimwits who have quite a few skeletons in the closet, having kidnapped small children, conducted shady business deals, and stalked women. As Keepers of the Grail they are finished, and along with them the overarching ideological constructs, assembled by Wagner from Christian Salvation teachings, Germanhood, Persian music, and Schopenhauer for the "Stage Consecration Festival" to present Germans with the *Gesamtkunstwerk*, or total work of art, as a substitute for religion and politics. Consequently, the formerly proud warriors are mutating into petty bourgeois types filled with self-pity. Parsifal is a more dumb than proper fellow, and Klingsor a bordello owner who forces Kundry and the flower girls to succumb to the knights' will. Master of ceremonies Gurnemanz executes the meaningless regimentation with bureaucratic rigidity, and my Amfortas turns out to be a rueful sinner who knows no longer whether to suffer due to the unholy doings of the world or his own imperfection. He even hesitates in undertaking the necessary revelation of the grail, a procedure which ensures his survival as well as that of his accomplices. And so Father Titurel (Walter Fink), muttering about in his grave and alive due to the grace of God, has to step in before his son can execute the sacred act himself. With trembling hands Amfortas fiddles around on the relic doing irreparable damage to it in the process. Parsifal watches it in awe, forgetting to pose the decisive question of compassion and thus ringing in the first intermission.

The next act takes place in the red-light district of the Godfather Klingsor. The mega-gangster and media tsar is in firm control of all the players, not only the naïve Parsifal, whom he attempts to seduce with the help of beautiful Kundry. Contrary to what Wagner had intended, she really does get him to have sex with her, but instead of climaxing, the youth, with the help of Doctor Freud, comes to realize that the greatest satisfaction derives not from drive relief but from sublimation, and it is sublimation that now commands him to free the "grail from guilty hands."

Since there is not much for me to do in the second (and rather long) act, I am sitting behind the scenery with a good book. However, it remains unopened even in the sixth scene, since I cannot tear my ears from the Philharmonic, who, under Runnicles's subtle guidance, are staging the erotic showdown between Kundry and Parsifal in masterly fashion.

In the third act, following the intermezzo of the Good Friday Meadow, Mielitz sends me out on stage all by myself. Like Lear gone mad, Amfortas drags himself across the heath, accompanied only by a funeral march and weighed down by a gigantic grail crown. The procession with Titurel's body approaches. The son is guilty of the titan's death because he has declined to reveal the grail for the second time. Whimpering, Amfortas crawls into the father's coffin blaring out his lamenting song ("Mein Vater, mein Vater, Hochgesegneter der Helden," "My father, my father, most blessed of heroes"). All that remains is to ask the knights to put an end to my ruined existence, but Parsifal, who meantime has been elected King of the Holy Grail, heals my wound with a touch of the sacred lance. Once more the orchestra whips through the final scene with dramatic grandeur before Runnicles lets the transfigured grail motif roll from A-flat major to D-flat major and back. Parsifal's lance glows like a Jedi sword. That truly is a miracle of higher healing—deliverance is near, but the spotlights circle above the audience as if wanting to ask: "Deliverance for whom? Deliverance from what? Deliverance? Why and what for?"

At least a third of the audience seems to find this question well worth thinking about and applauds enthusiastically, but it clearly offends the sensibilities of the Wagner community. Mean calls of "boo," "outrageous," "unbelievable," and "scandalous" are being yelled from the expensive rows. Christine Mielitz takes it in, relaxed as ever, standing at the ramp and smiling happily about the unanimous cheering for the singers. "Phenomenal singing, interesting interpretation" the *Wiener Kurier* decides the next day. Other papers also speak of a "superb ensemble of singers," and "world-class casting," and my colleagues, above all Angela Denoke and Johan Botha, really deserve it. I myself have never been so tired and so happy.

I am especially pleased that Joachim Kaiser finds my Amfortas thoroughly believable, writing: "As spectator one quickly accepted the seriously wounded, suffering King of the Grail to be just as Quasthoff personified him. The artist played the part with authority, highly musical in his phrasing, with captivating clarity in diction and tone quality. He combined Schubert-melos with well-placed musical-dramatic emphasis." I can understand that he ultimately missed the "sapping Wagnerian quality, the arch, the mad, suicidal ecstasy," but it is a matter of taste. Holender, the director, could obviously have given the part to a true Wagnerian baritone, but he explicitly wanted a lyric singer.

That is also how Eleonore Büning of the *Frankfurter Allgemeine* saw it: "Neither the direction nor Quasthoff left the slightest room for sensationalist effects. He sang his narration of crime, punishment and deliverance like a lied singer capable of packing the entire world's suffering into a few notes. . . . Parsifal heard the call of the heart and had to cry, and it was the same for all those who listened." Of course, there were exceptions, like the man from the Associated Press succinctly stating that "his voice, while pleasant, was occasionally not up to Wagnerian demands of sonority."

If there is one thing one learns in twenty-five years of professional life, it is not to get excited about reviews, though it is sometimes difficult to maintain a calm distance from the critics. "Whoever reads these lines has come too close": the Bavarian genius Herbert Achternbusch once confessed to an interviewer that he would like to write this line at the end of his books. Aperçus such as "the critique is the psychogram of the critic,"

which the German actor Will Quadflieg would have liked to tat-
too onto the forehead of his tormentors, may be true, but who
does this help? Without critics the enterprise falls apart. Everyone offering his art on the free market knows that. Wherever the
guild of reviewers is rationalized away, the PR agencies of the
entertainment corporations take over. The outcome of that has
been apparent for some time and can be seen in regional newspapers as well as on private radio stations and the TV establishment: a hollow imitation of culture, impertinently tarted up
with the unrevised press release jargon.

Most critics work very hard. At the ARD I was able to look
over the shoulder of Joachim Kaiser of the *Süddeutsche* as he
wrote his review. The way he did it was impressive. Grey head
drooping onto his chest, arms wrapped around his shoulders as if
he had to stop his shirt from sliding down, Kaiser strode through
the office chewing on the rim of his glasses and oblivious to
his surroundings. First it was three steps to the right, then four to
the left, then back again and so on. During each right turn he
would halt in front of a carefully placed mirror, peeking into it
to observe his own strong profile, only to emerge from reverie
visibly strengthened, though silent, and return to his train of
thought. After another five miles Mr. Kaiser did indeed give birth
to an adjective, accompanied by much growling and grumbling. It
was, I believe, "brittle." A jolly clicking promptly began: past a
rubber tree and three degrees west at a desk sat the secretary,
eagerly tapping out those seven hard-won letters. Does not this
scene suggest a righteous man wrestling with the gods of music?

Where vanity starts, the mind stops, a saying goes—but it isn't
true. For the bustling, juggling, and self-promotion are not separate from the cultural enterprise; they are part of it, whether in
front of, behind, or on stage. Anyone can observe this in the foyer

of a theatre. When the spectators step out for intermission, relaxing their gluteus maximus through discrete muscle contractions, they begin to resemble Mr. Kaiser. The men put a hand in their pockets, wrap the other around a beer, and then they begin to circumambulate. The double chin slides down towards the necktie, the forehead crinkles, and after much pondering a first judgment is made, usually a hoarse "oh, well," which can mean anything, and it should. First, we have got to wait until (a) the wife, mistress, or best friend of the same, having organized the evening, sips her champagne, and resolutely decides: "It is wonderful," or (b) a first judgment blows over from the critics' table, or (c) one runs into the honorable director who greets us with the jovial "Well, Krause, how is it going?" He may also add "What do you say about this theatre director's nonsense?" One soon tires of the posing.

The hard-won judgment of the amateur visitor does not lack in decisiveness, but it rarely reaches the splendidly heated style of professional criticism, in which "Verdi's Cantabile passages" are coming along "like dark-red bubbling Chianti," romantic songs satisfy like "succulent fast food" and Thomas Quasthoff is a "master chef," and orchestras find "unerring ways into their audience's viscera." In Schubert's tender "Frühlingstraum" "the third part of both verses detonated" while Quasthoff "horrified purists with the all too common African-American spiritual 'Swing Low, Sweet Chariot' " and also "at times falls like a bland leaf onto the autumn ground." What an insane effect! Even more wacky is a singer who "breaks over the audience like an emotional wave, leaving it almost anaesthetized in its seats" or, differently: "whoever arrives unprepared finds himself confronted with the unexpected." Some even hear "enticing voices from a different world." The interpreter is either "an island in the concert business from which one does not want to be rescued" or he labors on "dimness in the register break area." If he is really unlucky that

Viennese critic is in the house who once publicly executed an alto with the following judgment: "Her voice sounded like an ass hair—rough and unclean."

The writers bring out the big guns when they want to connect my singing with my unorthodox appearance. "He did not let himself be disabled" is one of the more subtle lines, "Disability is no obstacle" or "Disabled takes all hurdles," and "Disabled with superb voice." The unsurpassed classics remain: "The handicapped dwarf Quasthoff limped across the stage and illuminated Paulus" and the one I already mentioned, "He sang as if God wanted to correct a shop accident."

Classical music has always been big business, just like the visual arts, TV, or rock and pop, and there is nothing wrong with that—after all, people need to earn a living. The agents ensure that the artist receives his fair share of the cake. They keep the sordid details of business away from us and are compensated for it with a portion of the proceeds.

It takes me a while to realize that this is a fair deal. In the beginning I am dealing only with small, regional concert bureaus and a lot goes wrong. Sometimes there is a confusion of dates, other times I have to wait months for my meager fees. Therefore, I am quite happy after the ARD Competition not to be tied to an agency. Having done roughly fifty performances a year before it, I can now do two hundred at once. A crafty agent surely would have sent me through the entire Federal Republic to take advantage of this, but instead I am able to calmly consider the offers and pick the best ones. My old teachers were helping me out.

That works until Huber-Contwig gets it into his head to become professor at the Musikhochschule Hanover (Hanover Music Academy). The problem is that the newspapers write about my musical development in each town in which I appear, never forgetting to mention with what disdainful manner Jacobi, the head of the academy, had rejected the talent in his time. Now Jacobi looks like a big joke across the republic, which serves him right. On the other hand, it does not exactly increase Huber-Contwig's chances for a well-endowed official position. He reproaches me severely for the press articles, but it is not my fault. The facts are out in the world and the journalists love pulling them out of the archive each time, thinking it makes a great story. I don't push it on anyone but also see no cause to deny it when it comes up.

Huber-Contwig does not want to accept that and seems increasingly embittered. I can accept that he presents himself as my great discoverer and sponsor, since it does not seem to bother Frau Lehmann, who really deserves this title. But the fact that he circulates ridiculous stories about me—along the lines that I was lazy, arrogant, and ungrateful—is not funny. I tell him so and I tell Frau Lehmann who seems upset by it but also somewhat helpless. After seventeen years of close collaboration the situation feels as muddled as an overstressed marriage. I have a hard time with it. On one hand, I cannot tolerate such behavior, but on the other hand, I don't want to lose my teacher. Then comes a bizarre situation during a vacation in Lugano. I had previously worked with Huber-Contwig on *Entsorgt,* a solo piece written for me by the avant-garde composer Aribert Reimann, with lyrics by Nicolas Born. Still under the impact of the Chernobyl catastrophe he dissects the Western world's blind faith in progress with apocalyptic images. The composition is as difficult as it is fantastic, and I am looking forward to opening night, but first I need a week to unwind. On my fourth day of vacation I am sitting on the hotel terrace with Mama and Father when Huber-Contwig rushes in—in his luggage two pairs of underwear and the score. He does not say hello but rattles off the rehearsal plans he has worked out for me. *Entsorgt* was so important for the world of music that one couldn't just take off into the fresh air of summer. On top of everything, he expresses all this in such high volume that half of Lugano can listen in. My first reflex is to send him to hell. Then I look at my parents. Their facial expression tells me he could be right and so, to preserve the peace I spend the rest of my vacation in a hotel room blaring Born's verses towards the ceiling.

But after the premiere I decide to part ways with the spouses Lehmann–Huber-Contwig. The time has come for me to make my way by myself.

In the late eighties the air smells of change in any case: the coming down of the Wall, the collapse of communism, the end of the Cold War, world history, the first Easterners in the center of Hanover. Unfortunately, it is the same for me as for the brothers and sisters in the newly added territories: after the rush of freedom comes the hangover. Though I work regularly with the Bach Academy, give song recitals, and get invited for recordings by Leopold Hager and Peter Schreier (Haydn's *Orpheus and Eurydice*, Mozart's *Krönungsmesse [Coronation Mass]*), I soon realize that negotiating with organizers by day and performing by night takes a lot out of me. At some point I have to rehearse, after all, and a little more sleep wouldn't hurt. Someone has to be found to take care of business, and quickly. That is when the offer from a Munich agency comes, just in time. The boss—let's call him Hinterseher—tries hard to make the contract attractive. Shreds of a promotional spot are flurrying through my head: Bavaria is beautiful, its landscapes typical and its solidity world famous, or was it the buildings? The *Weissbier*? In any case Hinterseher promises me that I'll be world famous in no time. All I want is to sing, and so I sign. Afterwards Hinterseher shakes me down for five hundred marks—an entry fee into the world class of singing, I think, and am baffled when he explains that this amount is due each month.

"Those are the usual fees," Hinterseher tells Mr. Greenhorn. Then I don't see him for a long time. Instead, a young lady steps into my life. Her first name is Christel and her last name is "personal manager." She is charming, new with the agency, and not exactly a dimwit. We have long phone conversations, go out to eat, and walk through the English Garden, pleasantly chatting. I do less public singing, for as it turns out, this businesswoman understands even less about the concert business than I do. Somehow I had imagined my life as one of Hinterseher's exclusive artists differently. A glance at my bank account tells me that I can no longer afford this man.

Upon the advice of colleagues I switch to a concert bureau in Vienna. Here I am not taken advantage of. Here I am simply unlucky. The agent assigned to me is as infatuated with singers privately as she is professionally. Her favorite of the moment is a baritone whose name is right next to mine in the Rolodex. It takes a while for me to catch on to this. In the meantime I wonder why I don't get any good jobs. I am constantly addressed by colleagues who have seen this or that concert—everything being very nice, only the baritone had not been well cast. When I put it all together, I go to visit the head of the agency in a rage.

In his mild Viennese singsong, he says, "My dear young friend, don't get excited. Have a seat and have a cup of coffee."

"I am not thirsty. I am fed up with this kind of cronyism. I want your office to get me decent performances!"

"You're right. We'll make it up to you." The old fox. Two days later another agent is looking after me. Things are improved, if not ideal.

Nowadays I work with the Schmid agency in Hanover, and there I have found my luck. Of course, even here there has been one or another minor problem, but with Cornelia Schmid, the head of the agency, this is usually cleared up with a friendly lunch. It is not the least of her feats that she found Linda Marder for me in New York.

But even under the auspices of the Schmid agency I'll run into a snag every now and then as I ply my trade. In the summer of 1997 the Berlin Philharmonic asked me to perform Mahler's *Des Knaben Wunderhorn* with Claudio Abbado and mezzo-soprano Anne Sofie von Otter. It is a much coveted assignment, and I looked forward to it all year. A week before rehearsals began, Cornelia Schmid found out that an agent from Wiesbaden was trying to knock me out of the contract and put up one of his artists instead. No one should ask how he did it, but it worked. My competitor took to the stage, but he didn't last long. Seems he was less than ideal for the part. When Claudio Abbado did the piece three weeks later for EMI, he let me sing, helping me win my first Grammy.

It was about this time that I cast off the burden of sympathy I had lugged around my whole life like a backpack full of rocks. But a new burden was in store: the envy and ill will of people who believed I got things only because I was different. When I took that first Grammy, a disqualified colleague bitterly hissed, "You owe this victory to your disability, nothing else."

This person's career went nowhere fast, and I cannot say I am sorry about that, but I do understand his bitterness. The music business is grueling and selective. Singers invest a lot of time and energy struggling to reach the level at which they can live off their art, and there's no guarantee that their struggles will pay off. When success and recognition are not forthcoming, it can be very humiliating. I myself have had a lot to chew on with this talk of a "cripple bonus"—until I realized that it just is not true. The disability is without doubt a part of my personality and it influences the way in which people perceive me on stage, but it isn't the reason I find myself on stage in the first place.

My friend and good colleague Juliane Banse put it like this: "Thomas's gestalt automatically turns the attention towards the music." I believe there is something to that.

I cannot wear a chic tailcoat on stage, I don't make a splash, my body is small and unimpressive, lacking the extremities for the most impressive gestures. Most of the time the spotlight illuminates nothing but my sweaty skull and the big mouth, out of which the sound rolls. What matters is how it rolls out. Someone who looks like the hunchback of Notre Dame may pass for a season as a curiosity, but in the long run the audience will accept an artist only if he has quality and has something to communicate.

In the meantime I tell myself: Compassion is free, but envy must be earned. So I try to see the music business like a big game in which competition, envy, and intrigue are unavoidable. The art is not to get thrown off track by the trade's highs and lows. By now I am rather good at it. A journalist once asked me: "What does excellence mean to you?"

I answered: "More than anything lack of space on the shelves."

A Golden Camera, two Echo Prizes, and two Grammys rub elbows with my books. Of course I love it, since being honored is important for one's reputation, but when I have three beers and a Schnaps I still get drunk and I still have an aching head the next morning to bring me back down to earth. How I wish I could have been present at one of the Grammy Awards, even just for the chance to shake hands with icons like Prince. Unfortunately, it never worked out because on the decisive day there was always a concert to which I had to attend. Maybe I didn't miss anything, though; maybe the entire spectacle looks more impressive on television than it does in reality. This is usually the case with award shows, at least in my experience.

And I've not lacked for brushes with fame and power. The G8 meeting in 1999 was very entertaining. After all, it isn't every day one mingles with the forces that govern the world. Chancellor Gerhard Schröder invited me to sing the *Four Serious Songs* in the Cologne Philharmonic for the heads of state. Naturally the event was "security level 1" and a sea of police and federal agents was patrolling all around the Philharmonic. The American contingency especially was something right out of a movie, with the Secret Service men looking like a phalanx of Terminators: buzzed hair, features cut like Mount Rushmore, and intimidating muscles. They wore Ray-Bans and large-caliber revolvers, so obvious beneath their jackets that the guests all turned as stiff as boards when walking past, each one with the same thought: a sudden movement now could be my last movement! At the reception after the concert everybody's heart skipped a beat when the bodyguards suddenly began screaming into their walkie-talkies. All I can make out is "Potus and Flotus. Potus and Flotus coming." Were two wild elephants about to come storming into the hall?

"That only means the Clintons are approaching," my friend Uwe Carsten Heye soothed me. "POTUS means President of the United States. FLOTUS is the abbreviation for Hillary, First Lady of the United States." Uwe's wife, Sabine, tells me with a chuckle that the night before the Secret Service had occupied an entire county because the Schröders and the Clintons dined in a famous restaurant. Outside men in fighting gear guarded the spot, and plainclothes guys monitored the restaurant from within. The host almost had a heart attack when his antique beams were drilled into and stuffed with bugging devices. When the agents approached his oak barrels to check whether an attacker might be lurking in the Riesling, it was too much. He threw himself at them in death-defying manner, calling: "Only over my dead body."

For Bill Clinton, of course, these security measures were nothing new. At the after party he thanked me for the concert and promised to attend the next time I sang in Washington. It didn't work out after all, but he did send a telegram expressing his regret in kind words—unavoidable government affairs had detained him. Without doubt the man has style and charisma. In Cologne he was the undisputed cock of the walk. While Chirac, Blair, and the other VIPs politely sipped their drinks, the American president was flirting with ladies, slapping men on the back as if he were each one's best buddy, and telling jokes to everyone.

(Only Gerhard Schröder was similarly frolicsome. I often ran into him in Hanover and even Mama has met him. When he came to our table, he greeted my mother like an old friend and asked me to call him by his first name. He even scored lots of points with Father, who otherwise considers Social Democrats to be the downfall of the Occidental world.)

My parents accompanied me to Berlin when I was awarded the Golden Camera by *Hörzu* magazine. The other winners were Suzanne von Borsody, Kate Winslet, Sir Peter Ustinov, Ricky Martin, Sasha, Günther Jauch, as well as Dieter Pfaff and Dirk Bach. I wanted to exchange a few words with Sir Peter but feared it would not happen. The Springer publishing house had forwarded the schedule a few months in advance, and it looked as strict and demanding as that of the G8.

10:00–12:00 a.m.	Individual arrival, pickup by *Hörzu* staff member with Mercedes limousine. Hotel Vier Jahreszeiten.
12:15 p.m.	Blocking rehearsal with camera
3:30 p.m.	Get-together of award winners, VIPs, jury, and *Hörzu* editor in chief at Axel Springer House
6:45 p.m.	Reception for award winners at the Four Sea-

	sons Hotel, Salon "Langhans" with Friede Springer and CEO August A. Fischer
7:30 p.m.	Warmup with hostess Désirée Nosbusch
7:45 p.m.	Makeup check, start of ZDF recording
8:00 p.m.	Awards

Those arriving a day early had further opportunities:

9:30 p.m.	Dinner party at the Foyer Concert house, Hotel Adlon bar and Paris Bar open
midnight	Opening Golden Dance Club at the Foyer, then everyone to Harry's New York Bar

Later I received a second letter from the Springer publishing house. The *Hörzu* editorial office wanted to know whether I could imagine singing a short piece, accompanied by a piano. "Please take into consideration that the piece should be no more than 1.5 minutes long."

I reached for the phone to say that while I was capable of imagining almost anything, "at 1.5 minutes all I can think of is 'Good Golly Miss Molly' or something by Fats Domino. And I don't imagine that is—"

"Sorry, but it isn't actually 1.5 minutes," my interlocutor interrupted. "The director has rearranged the on-air schedule. You now have exactly forty-five seconds."

"Get out of here," I said. "In that time I could whistle the first four bars of 'La Paloma.' Would you like that?"

"Is that a joke?"

"That's just what I wanted to ask you. I think we'd better forget about it."

I decided not to throw myself into the entire program of

events, appearing only at the reception for the award winners. Peter Ustinov was there, too, and we had a good chat about movies, music, and the meaning of the term "small talk."

It must be related to "small print," Sir Peter thought: "One easily overlooks it, often with dire consequences." He closed one eye and peered at the crowd with the other.

Thank goodness I met him early. Later that night conversation became impossible, since such masses were pushing through and around us that it took ten minutes to advance three feet. Everyone who had ever put his face in front of a camera for money was present. When the official part of the evening began, the seating arrangement established a clear pecking order. Guests were sorted by A, B, C, and D levels of prominence and distributed onto the seven floors. Backstage we award winners were awaiting our moment. Each honoree was to be introduced by a previous winner. For me *Hörzu* originally envisioned Claudio Abbado or Daniel Barenboim, much to my delight, but unfortunately neither maestro was able to come. The editor's office sent me a list of alternative candidates: Herbert Grönemeyer, Nina Hagen, the actress Meret Becker, José Carreras, and Plácido Domingo. Why in the end not one of them but the philosopher and then German minister for cultural and media affairs Julian Nida-Rümelin appeared is a total mystery to me. Maybe some image consultant was urging him to get on TV again, for he seemed to have very little interest in dealing with me as a person. His office ordered the presentation speech—from my brother. He should really have read it, too. Five minutes before our appearance I saw Nida-Rümelin wandering around backstage, staring at a piece of paper. As a polite person does, I introduced myself and thanked him for giving my award speech. The learned moral philosopher glanced at me, nodded, and walked away. Rude? Weird? I'm still not sure. Soon he was on stage, where he failed to read his few lines without mistake. Then Nida-Rümelin was done. He stuffed the paper in his pocket and waited for the moderator to call: "A Golden Camera for Thomas Quasthoff."

They had given us instructions for this moment as well. "The award winner steps out to the right through a pyramid gate and walks to the moderator's podium, where he is handed the Golden Camera by the presenter. The winner thanks him or her—you may also use the auto cues for this. Award winner and presenter then walk off stage and back to their seats in the parquet."

That's where Mama and Father—*Hörzu* readers since the first hour—were sitting, beaming. Shortly afterwards the battle at the buffet began. I don't even want to know how it ended, but it couldn't have been pretty. When my parents grew tired I fled to the Paris Bar, where a few others had already taken refuge, including the comedian Hella von Sinnen. This hilarious person and I connected right away, and we gabbed until four o'clock in the morning.

The Echo Prize is the music industry's equivalent of the Golden Camera—part celebration of achievement, part marketing scheme, and part high school reunion. In the Hamburg Music Hall, where the Echo Classic Awards presentation ceremony is held, everything is a little bit smaller than it is at the Golden Cameras—the buffet as well as the number of guests and VIPs. Since the show airs on television, they try to hide the small scale by filling at least the first ten rows with well-known faces. When I was nominated in 1998 in the category of Best Singer my parents were seated next to Inge Meysel, Germany's "Television Mother of the Nation." But since she nodded off right away, my parents were never shown on camera. It wasn't the fault of the emcees, Senta Berger and Roger Willemsen. Meysel's snoring began even before the event.

Berger and Willemsen give their best to show each artist's

works as well as they can—not an easy task. The spectrum reaches from classic to jazz, from chanson to tango. Curiously prominent are the many hybrid tunes, polished down until every edge is gone and every cross-grain has been effaced. They are ear candy sound designed to please several diverse consumer groups. In marketing departments this musical soup is called "crossover culture," which sounds trendy but is really just the latest anchor thrown out by the entertainment companies to save the horrendous profit gaps of the last years.

What does this get us? Mass products like André Rieu, Andrea Bocelli, or the "wet T-shirt," elfin Vanessa-Mae, who compensates for her rather modest talents on the violin with physical appeal. It's okay, of course, since there is room for all kinds of rubbish in the world, but these entertainers should not be mistaken for artists. They are craftsmen and -women, and if they are sold on the classical shelves, it is a labeling scam that deprives serious artists of the chance to be noticed according to their abilities.

It all began with the Wagner heldentenor Peter Hofmann. Faced with the end of his career, he decided to turn a new page— by arranging the songs of Joe Cocker in what turned out to be the style of a hotel pianist. Another much more tragic case was David Helfgott, the pianist whose life inspired the movie *Shine*. A mediocre pianist with a severe psychological illness, he was urged on by unscrupulous managers, leading to his collapse during Rachmaninoff's Piano Concerto No. 3 on a profitable world tour. Helfgott never recovered.

The "Three Tenors"—Plácido Domingo, José Carreras, and Luciano Pavarotti—represent another variant of this corporate strategy. I don't want to say anything about the artistic quality of their performances—I have always been a great fan of all three— but I am bothered by the fact that such spectacles have become a fashion, which means that they eat up sponsorships and advertising budgets, leaving quieter and more ambitious projects without resources. If effortless millions can be made off such carelessly warbled songs, glitzy arias, and soft rock tearjerkers, why should money-hungry companies invest in young, unknown but serious interpreters, who may or may not bring in a profit after years of patient waiting?

This development was waiting in the wings when I made my first wobbly steps toward the singing profession. Luckily for me, Helmuth Rilling referred me to the Hänssler Publishing House, which specializes in sacred music. There I was able quietly to record CDs while maturing as an artist, but at first it did not benefit me as an interpreter of songs. I sang several Loewe ballads (with Norman Shetler) for EMI, with BMG producing: Schubert's *Winterreise,* his Goethe Lieder, and the Schumann CD *Dichterliebe / Liederkreis (The Loves of a Poet / Song Cycle)* (with Roberto Szidon). Then they put me on a back burner. BMG canceled confirmed performances again and again and failed to release finished material, supposedly because my CDs weren't selling. Among them was a collection of Brahms lieder I later sang again for Deutsche Grammophon, which suddenly sold like hotcakes. The simple truth is that BMG lacked either the distribution, the motivation, or the know-how to take the CDs to the people. When I performed, organizers complained about not being able to find my recordings on the retail market. It took me a while to understand that they just were not being delivered. You'll see it in lots of industries: fixated on a few eminently marketable top acts, management loses interest in small stuff. The backlash has come now that MP3s and illegal downloading threaten the industry's monopoly. With so many options, people are no longer quite as eager to spend their pennies on the 576th new recording of Beethoven's *Eroica.* Deutsche Grammophon has always shown the kind of imagination every recording company will need to cope with these new challenges. When the first mixes of Claudio Abbado's *Wunderhorn* were heard, Deutsche Grammophon immediately offered me a long-term contract. They didn't know it would be so successful—they just liked the singer. When first sales figures were published, BMG suddenly signaled great interest in an exclusive contract with me. But, hey, you snooze, you lose.

Another mantra of the marketing strategists is that classical lied singing isn't popular enough. They should tell that to my colleagues Matthias Goerne and Andreas Schmidt, who, with their constantly sold-out concerts, will scratch their heads in puzzlement. It's rare for me to encounter empty rows of seats, too. The three of us are, of course, true lied singers. If the genre has suffered a bad reputation from time to time it is due to the so-called star system and to those opera celebrities who believe they can casually roar away *Dichterliebe* in between two *Magic Flute*s, simply because television has rolled out the red carpet for them. The great baritone Hans Hotter, a master at both subjects, knew better:

> Even if he has average technique and is an average performer, an opera singer can be successful as long as he has a truly beautiful voice. The voice is decisive, and a singer who knows how to make use of it can become a so-called top singer without being otherwise distinguished. The lied singer, on the other hand, must be a musician. The technique is the same but must be used in a more differentiated manner—the sense of fantasy, taste, and the understanding for meaning as well as the positioning of the word—all that is incredibly important, as is the text's quality. It is often incomprehensible with opera singers. As an opera singer

one cannot worry about the quality of the libretto—no one would expect that. But with the lied the singer has to consider such questions and judge whether a mediocre poem might not perhaps gain a higher standing through the composer's genius.

And so here and now I predict the renaissance of the lied. At some point the marketing departments will realize that the genre is not just about musical quality (although it is); its entertainment value is definitely competitive. A lied can tell an entire story, while an aria always tells a mere portion of the events. In effect, every lied contains a small opera. And what's more, a lied singer delivers an average ten of these mini-operas for the price of one *Rosenkavalier,* and on a dizzying spectrum of themes. Even Hollywood can't beat it. The typical lied program I play with Jussi begins with five ballads by Carl Loewe: "Odin's Meeresritt" ("Odin's Sea Ride"), "Herr Oluf," the "Nöck" ("The Merman"), "Edward," and "Prinz Eugen," offering everything a movie fan could ask for: horror, shock, war, patricide, love, madness, and fairy-tale magic. Three narrative ballads by Schubert follow: "Der Sänger" ("The Singer"), "Szene aus *Faust*" ("Scene from *Faust*"), and "Liedesend" ("The End of the Song"). They revolve around classic film noir subjects like alcohol, psychoterror, and artistic misery. Brahms's *Four Serious Songs* finally lead one into deeply existentialist territory: no exit. The songs are based on the Old Testament and deal with the vanity of human existence ("Denn es geht dem Menschen wie dem Vieh," roughly: "For man suffers the same fate as cattle / or beast"), the vileness of the world ("Ich wandte mich um und sah alle an, die Unrecht leiden unter der Sonne," "I turned around and looked at all who suffered injustice under the sun"), transience ("Oh Tod, wie bitter bist du," "Oh death, how bitter are you"); and last things ("Wenn ich mit Menschen—und mit Engelszungen redete," "If I spoke with men's and angels' tongues"). If encores are requested we play

Schubert's "Heidenröslein" ("The Heath Rose"), his "Forelle" ("The Trout"), and the "Sapphische Ode" ("Sapphic Ode") by Brahms, rounding everything up with the defilement of nature, spoiled innocence, and the miracle of female beauty.

Since I've already gone out on a limb here in matters of the lied I might as well add my plea for live singing. Unlike literature and painting, music is a highly social phenomenon. If I had the choice of listening to the same program on CD or in a concert hall I would always prefer the concert hall, no matter how fancy my stereo equipment. Even among my successful studio recordings I can't think of one that wouldn't have gone better in a live performance. I have already discussed the various factors that create a singular atmosphere for every recital. It is very difficult to achieve this inspiring feeling in the studio.

Studio work is a very exact, almost mathematical affair because one has the option to polish every single note. When a musician enters this sober realm stuffed with technical equipment for the first time he is tempted to make use of every trick that helps perfect the recording. It is hard for the layman to imagine how far that can go nowadays. It is no problem at all for the computer to alter any note that has been sung, whether in pitch or note value, and without changing the character of the voice. Theoretically, it would be possible to separate Wagner's *Ring* into its parts and reassemble it digitally. Of course, no one wants to do that. It's too much work and with classical music this procedure is used only rarely. The sound engineer knows that it takes more than clean notes to bring a work to life. A recording needs that certain something, and that's exactly what gets lost when one monkeys around too much. My pianist Justus and I have always placed great emphasis on designing our playing in a very purist way. We record a cycle like Schubert's *Schwanengesang* in two or three run-throughs, making smaller corrections afterwards if necessary, not digitally but by repeating the particular parts. The new bits are simply inserted via computer, and now we get by without too many cuts.

I adopt the same method with recorded opera productions. I would never participate in an *Aida* in which King Amonasro tapes his recording in a London studio and sends it on to Amneris in Chicago who forwards it to Berlin where Radames lives. When I did the *Meistersinger* with Christian Thielemann and the baritone Bryn Terfel, an American colleague wanted to set up her part in this way. Both Thielemann and Deutsche Grammophon categorically rejected that idea. It might work for a pop song, but if the parts are supposed to interact with one another, there has to be eye contact.

I also want to be able to look at my pianist during recordings and therefore hate soundproof walls and enclosed sound booths. I simply need the live feeling. After all, a good lied pianist must not only have first-class technique but also be a great listener and know what will happen even before I sing the note. Anticipation is the magic word. Presence of mind is another, as Michael Raucheisen, one of the great accompanists of the last century, illustrates in an anecdote: "Once Erika Morini gave an evening of violin in Berlin and succumbed to a lapse of memory. I whispered to my page-turner, good old Burghard who has turned pages over for me for forty years: 'Turn five pages!' I found the spot as if in a trance and we were connected again."

This quasi-somnambular understanding presumes a high degree of trust. In any case, I can only make music with people whose style of playing I love and whom I like on a personal level. That is as true for famous pianists like Daniel Barenboim, Wolfram Rieger, András Schiff, Charles Spencer, Julius Drake, or Graham Johnson as it is for those who have yet to become famous.

I have tried many pianists but have always had the luck of

running into the right people at the right time, top-notch people who have seen me through thick and thin. The first was Norman Shetler, who saw me through the churches and community halls of Lower Saxony and with whom I recorded my first lieder CD. I met Peter Müller through Frau Lehmann and we became close at various student parties and on pub benches where themes like God, the world, and the mystery of women were at least as important as music. Peter and I made music for many years and had more fun than I can say. I owe him a lot because he is so multifaceted, being just as able to play from a score as to improvise, that we worked up a broad repertoire. Over the years we established different priorities. Peter was drawn to theatre, where he got pretty far in a short time, even going to Cairo to stage Brecht and Weill's *Threepenny Opera* as musical director. When Peter moved on I had to search a long time for an adequate substitute. Thank goodness, I got to know and appreciate Charles Spencer. He is a professor of lied interpretation at the Music Academy in Vienna, a fine person and phenomenal pianist. I'm not the only singer who would like to appear with him. He has accompanied Gundula Janowitz and worked with such greats as Jessye Norman, Marjana Wald, and Thomas Hampson as well as having been the permanent lied accompanist of Christa Ludwig. We record CDs and play together whenever it works out, but I also need someone with whom I can work continuously. I found that person at a lieder recital at the Richard Wagner Foundation in Hanover in the fall of 1998. The singer was mediocre, but the person sitting at the piano was a true artist. His name was Justus Zeyen, and I immediately asked him whether he would like to appear with me and the Russian violinist Gidon Kremer at the Lockenhaus Festival. He said yes, thank goodness, and we have been inseparable ever since, which means that he sees his wife and children less than he sees me, for we have circled the globe at least twice. But more about that in the next chapter.

On the Road Again

At the end of one of R.E.M.'s exhausting tours a curse escaped Michael Stipe: "I hate my audience." He had bad luck. The reporters heard him. Later Stipe insisted he didn't mean it like that and that he was terribly sorry for everything. Theatre folk aren't as diplomatic. The actor Klaus Kinski always meant what he said and he was never sorry for anything, especially not for the paying audience, which he considered incurably ignorant. His indignation turned to pure hatred in the late fifties when he decided to recite the New Testament on the stages of German city theatres. The audiences screamed with laughter. By the fifth day of the tour—if I remember correctly, it was in my hometown, Hildesheim—Kinski had begun to throw one-pound Bibles at the audience, a performance that cemented his reputation as an enfant terrible and ultimately made him an international film star *(Aguirre, der Zorn Gottes; Aguirre: The Wrath of God)*. In general, though, it's a good idea to treat your audience with some consideration, especially when you're performing in a foreign country.

The famous tenor Leo Slezak was not spared this realization. In the mid-1920s he toured the United States with Verdi's *Otello* for the Metropolitan Opera. Everything went smoothly until the production came to Georgia, where the Ku Klux Klan still enjoyed considerable power and popularity. In Atlanta, Slezak reports, the mayor begged them to cancel the opera or at least to perform the Moor "in whiteface," since the artists might not be safe otherwise. It was known that Mr. Slezak interpreted the role

of the Moor in a particularly brutal manner, and the mayor sus-
pected that locals would take it rather badly if a black man, even
a fake one, were to kiss a white woman and then twist her neck.
But the manager would not change the production, and when the
curtain rose, Slezak, blackened according to script, did what he
had to do and managed to bring the performance to a quick end.
They asked him to leave the theatre before he had even taken off
his makeup. When he tried to sit down for dinner at his hotel,
Slezak was met with hateful hisses: "There ain't no room for col-
ored people here."

I am happy to say that the world has learned a lot since then,
and I have never had such an ugly experience in the United
States. In fact, some of the most delightful moments of my professional life have happened there, perhaps most memorably at
the Oregon Bach Festival.

I first appeared in Eugene, Oregon, in 1995. There I befriended
Jeffrey Kahane, the head of the Los Angeles Chamber Orchestra.
Jeffrey is also a virtuoso on the piano, and he shares my love of
jazz. After performances we have often jammed through the Tin
Pan Alley repertoire deep into the night. The idea for a regular
jazz night was born at the farewell party in 1999. When all the
drinks were gone and most of our colleagues had turned in, Jeffrey was still sitting at the piano, rolling out "One for My Baby
(and One More for the Road)" onto the keys, Frank Sinatra's hom-
age to the very last drink. I had spread my tired body across two
chairs, guzzling a white wine spritzer and bathing in the casual
harmonies.

"It's a perfect song."

"It's an American classic," Jeffrey said, letting the piece taper
off with a tasteful seventh chord.

"If that's so, we should play the song again next year, but as
part of the festival program."

Jeffrey laughed and nodded. "Okay. I will suggest it to Mr. Saltzman and Helmuth Rilling. Cheers."

We treated ourselves to "one for whatever" before trotting off to bed. I had to get up in three hours to make my plane. When I landed in Hanover a headache had obliterated the episode from my memory, but Jeffrey had not forgotten. Two months later I got his call.

"Hi, Tommy! I'm preparing our jazz concert. The title is 'American Songbook.' I need a list of all the songs you want to sing."

This knocked my socks off. Though America is the land of opportunity, I could hardly believe Jeffrey was able to get this approved by the organizers. It was like asking the head of the Salzburg Festival to hire B.B. King for the final concert. But Jeffrey had no such reservations.

"Keep cool, my friend. Just send me your list."

No problem.

For the next months versions of the program went back and forth across the Atlantic. I asked Micha to help me select material, and he got even more fired up than I was. Soon he was unstoppable, forwarding me endless song lists every day. My own ideas were slightly muddled by his fanatic enthusiasm.

"No Ray Charles title? Ten times Sinatra and not one number by Dr. John? You can't be serious. That's nonsense with gravy— absolutely no way!"

"Yes, I am," I wrote back, a bit miffed.

But he was not to be deterred. Soon my phone started ringing: "Call the police, hurry, hurry!" he howls, "'cause the guy has stolen my girl from me."

"What is it?"

"That is Nat 'King' Cole!"

"Yes, Micha, but you don't have to scream like that. I know the song. It's on every other tape you've got in your car."

"And why is that? Because it is fantastic. An American Songbook without Nat 'King' Cole, that's impossible!" After a few weeks he had sung the entire works of Aaron Neville for me, compiled ten CDs of "genius" underground soul, and reimagined country legend Willie Nelson as a jazz musician. Finally I had to explain to him that the first-ever jazz night of the Bach Festival would require a certain measure of stylistic finesse. After all, Jeffrey had to sell the program to Mr. Saltzman, a professor of classical choral music, and while Saltzman may be a gentleman of the most tolerant sort, he is no soul brother. Together with Jeffrey we finally agreed on a rather conservative selection, one we could offer to the festival audience in good conscience, including five songs from Leonard Bernstein's *West Side Story*, the Sinatra hits "New York, New York" and "My Way," Jerome Kern's "Ol' Man River," movie songs such as "They Can't Take That Away from Me," written by George and Ira Gershwin for *Shall We Dance*, Henry Mancini's "Moon River" from *Breakfast at Tiffany's*, a few pieces by the duo Rodgers and Hart, and gospel classics such as "Swing Low, Sweet Chariot."

It must have hit the right note, for at the end of the year Jeffrey announced that the festival had accepted our American Songbook. But the real trouble was only just beginning. For *West Side Story* a large orchestra was needed, but a big band had been planned for the rest of the program. We had an orchestra at our disposal but were told ix-nay on the big band, and there was no money to shop around for orchestra arrangements for the jazz numbers. Luckily Jeffrey was able to call on James Taylor, the composer and singer of such fantastic hits as "Fire and Rain" and "Country Road," with whom he had worked on several occasions. To be more exact, he had conducted the orchestra for Taylor when he needed string instruments in the studio or for a live appearance. Now the songwriter returned the favor by putting a few arrangements at our disposal at no cost, among them "Our Love Is Here to Stay," "The Way You Look Tonight," and "Fascinating Rhythm," which we gratefully included in the program. We decided to play the rest with quintet instrumentation.

When the big day arrived the Hult Center in downtown Eugene was totally booked. Jeffrey, just as nervous as I was, compulsively ran his hand through his hair, sparse as it is on his mostly bald pate. As Mr. Saltzman greeted the audience and thanked the sponsors, Jeffrey and I shared a skinny joint. Strictly taboo, of course, but the night called for blue notes. It was "jazz time," with all that that entails.

"Ahhh," and soon the smoke was caressing our central nervous systems. I spat across Jeffrey's right shoulder.

"Good luck." Jeffrey spat back, took a deep breath, and stepped out into the unknown. For a long time we had agonized over whether to go from the small instrumentation allegro con brio to the grand orchestra finale, or to choose the knock 'em dead technique, that is, to light up Bernstein's fireworks of sound right at the start. We chose the latter, which turned out to be the right move, since the highly effective numbers from *West Side Story*, pulling all the registers from jazz over opera and symphony, catapulted the audience to the right operational temperature. When we followed up the street hits "New York, New York" and "My Way" with first-class Taylor arrangements, we were sent into the intermission with roaring applause. After the first part, the orchestra podium could be taken down. Backstage my friend Rick Todd was waiting and warming up to support our quintet with his horn. I already mentioned that Rick can let this heavy instrument swing as light-footedly as a cornet, but on this night he outdid himself. One moment he whipped out a Dizzy Gillespie style, the next he made funky twists and turns, then took on "Moon

River," blowing his solo into the microphone as bittersweet as a young Chet Baker. If you don't believe it, you can borrow the accompanying track of the concert. After two hours and five encores, three thousand people were literally standing on their chairs. They still hadn't gotten enough.

I looked at Rick and Jeffrey: "The last waltz?" They grinned.

" 'One for My Baby (and One More for the Road),' " said Rick. A good choice. After that everyone knew there would be no more freebies, even Mr. Saltzman, who had rushed backstage to congratulate us.

"Wonderful," he murmurs, "fantastic," patting Jeffrey on the back, but we were in a hurry now. I changed out of my sweaty T-shirt and made a dash for the stage door where Tony was awaiting me with his engine running. "Fasten your seat belt, sweetheart!"

We roared through the starry night along the banks of the Willamette and into the hills outside of town, where John and Kazi Steinmetz had set up camp. My fellow musicians and a hearty barbecue were waiting for us in a cozy wooden house. Such private after-show parties are a much cultivated festival ritual. Just the day before, my friend Stevie, who plays violin in the festival orchestra, had grilled some tuna, and the night before that, when Sybilla Rubens, pianist Jussi Zeyen, and I performed Wolf's *Italienisches Liederbuch (Italian Songbook)*, juicy hamburgers were on the barbecue at the Todds' house. Only Jussi and I are real spongers. Since it is not worth it for us to rent a whole house during the festival, we stay at the Valley River Inn. The name fits: whoever stays in the west wing can spit from his room into the river, but grilling is strictly forbidden. So we hosted our friends for bathing fun, doughnuts, and soft drinks, served by two coattailed waiters at the pool.

The reader will have noticed that this town of 100,000 souls called Eugene is an oasis of sociability, and that warmth does not come at the expense of its high musical standards. The foundation for the Bach summit was laid thirty years ago in Swabia. At the request of the University of Oregon, Royce Saltzman was looking after a group of American music students who had come to Ludwigsburg for the year. One of the lecturers was Helmuth Rilling, and Saltzman asked whether Helmuth might like to teach some courses at his university. That was 1970. By the next year a small festival had grown out of this first workshop for choir conductors. In the meantime the organization had turned into a "musical enterprise," which as noted by the *Los Angeles Times*, does not have a peer in America. I would say that there's nothing quite comparable to it in the whole world.

Nobody comes here for the money. While they do not work for free, the festival surely would be done for if it had to pay the orchestra musicians the going rate—twenty-five concerts in seventeen days would not come cheap. Most of these instrumentalists are in high demand and could get along just fine without the festival. Rick, for example, is part of the well-endowed group of professionals who make music for Hollywood studios. Our real compensation is the wonderful concerts, the familiar atmosphere, and the magnificent surroundings. Since soloists do not have quite so much to do, I am in the privileged position of being able to explore the area. Eugene lies in the middle of the Willamette Valley, an alluvial plain bordered by the Klamath Mountains to the south and the Cascades to the northwest. Mount Hood, the Three Sisters, and Mount McLoughlin tower above the wooded slopes of the mountain range, piercing the sky like the Dolomites. It is not far from here to one of my favorite spots: on the high plains behind the Willamette Pass, surrounded by eternal snow, sits Crater Lake, an extinguished volcano that has been storing ancient waters for a million years within its cone. When the clouds move across its surface, changing the color of the water from deep blue to emerald green, it's easy to understand why Crater Lake is holy territory for Native Americans.

Renate and Micha visited me in Oregon in 2000 and trotted through the woods on horseback. I, on the other hand, have a horse allergy and am a lazybones in general, working up a sweat by lying on the hotel terrace and waving to the group of Kenyan runners who zip along the Willamette every morning. The sinewy men were staying on my floor and training for the Prefontaine Classic. Anyone of rank or name appears here. I saw aces like Carl Lewis, Marion Jones, Tim Montgomery, the former world champion in the hundred meters, and the long-distance Olympic champion Gabriela Szabo.

Just as much fun is a visit to the ballpark of the Fighting Ducks with Stevie. He has tried and failed for years now to explain the rules of baseball to me, but it doesn't matter. In this game nothing happens for the first three hours anyway, and accordingly the scene resembles a folk festival with people stretching out in the sun, chatting, and drinking beer while the smell of grilled sausage and fresh popcorn wafts through the innings. Then, everyone suddenly gasps as if struck by lightning and stares at the playing field. You can hear the grass grow in the stadium, though to the untutored observer nothing appears to have changed. The pitcher throws, the hitter hits or doesn't hit, but all hell breaks loose in the ranks and one team has won. It's rather confusing, but all in all rather relaxing, too. Even more relaxing is golf. In the States this sport is very democratically organized, not just a privilege of high earners. There are public courses everywhere and anyone can play a few rounds for little money. When we try it, the Quasthoff brothers beat the duo Renate and Jussi right away—thanks to a superior team strategy that has Micha lofting the balls onto the green and me putting them in. This calls for a celebration, especially since it is the last vacation day for Renate and Micha. I stay on and treat myself to a week of camping in the dunes of the Pacific with the Steinmetz family, Jussi, Rick, his wife Marder, and his little daughter Haley, my adorable godchild.

On the evening before departure Jussi, Juliane Banse, and I gave another recital, singing lieder by Debussy and Mozart arias. It must have been a memorable event, at least that's what the reviewer of the local paper thinks. Under the heading "The Banse-Quasthoff-Zeyen Trio Makes History" he summarized it like this:

> On Thursday Juliane Banse, bass baritone Thomas Quasthoff, and pianist Justus Zeyen delivered an Oregon Bach concert that the audiences will remember for a long time to come. How good was it? After two encores and true standing ovations (not one of these pop-up-while-the-guy-next-to-you-is-getting-up-anyway applauses) the audience began a kind of rhythmic Eastern Europe style clapping reminiscent of political rallies in totalitarian states.

I mention this not for reasons of self-aggrandizement but by way of a (semi)elegant transition. Here it is: in eastern Europe people really do clap differently than in the West, and even the fall of the iron curtain has not changed that. I have personally experienced it in Saint Petersburg, where I appeared with the violinist Vladimir Spivakov. At the end of the performance there was suffocating silence. I walked off stage and asked Spivakov with some concern:

"Vladimir, what is going on? The people are not clapping. Were we that bad, did we do something wrong?"

But Spivakov was ever so calm, and grumbled in his bass,

marked by the inhalation of thousands of Papyrossis cigarettes, "Just wait a moment. They will clap their hands off!"

And so it was. As if answering some secret command, applause materialized and resounded evenly through the hall like a Russian regiment in marching step, holding the volume at an even level for twenty minutes straight.

"Now," grumbled Spivakov, pulling me towards the ramp to watch the cheering masses.

This uniform collective clapping is also heard in Hungary and Chechnya, though there the volume rises and falls rather like a sinus curve. The phenomenon is unknown in Poland, where the applause essentially does not differ from that in middle and northwestern European countries. No matter on what level of excitement one operates, the superego always claps along, the only exception being the Viennese, who are capable of great enthusiasm in both the positive and the negative regards, and who, on top of that, like to explain to the singer what he or she has just sung. People from Latin cultures would never think of such a thing. They view the arts much like soccer and love. There is only hop or top—either you are booed out or borne away on the crowd's shoulders. Thank God, I have only experienced the latter so far. At a guest performance in the Teatro Colón of Buenos Aires it even rained roses—first on stage and later at the stage door, where the Argentinians were waiting to bombard us with pounds and pounds of the thorny merchandise.

"You see," says Helmuth, "now you, too, can feel like Maradona."

The Japanese, of course, are another story altogether. They are unpredictable, either applauding demurely as a group of house-wives from Lower Saxony or getting out of control. When they go nuts, they really go nuts, as if they had just heard Oasis instead of the Saint Matthew Passion. This behavior is even more astounding in a traditional Kabuki theatre. Attending Kabuki is a classy social event, very expensive, calling for the most festive attire. Initially the feeling is one of reverent communion, the audience watching motionless as fantastically outfitted protagonists perform ancient and well-known pieces in highly stylized form. But as soon as the action approaches its dramatic climax, the place suddenly turns into a wrestling tent. Men and women jump up, shaking their fists and yelling at the protagonists: "Give it to him," "Knock him down," or "Finish her off."

I have been to Japan four times but am certain that it will remain a mystery to me forever. I always get sick there, something I do not wish to blame the Japanese for, by any means, but rather my overly sensitive stomach and my ignorance of the language. Many travelers to Japan assume that they will be able to get along fine in English, but this is a mistake. The Japanese speak and primarily understand Japanese, while the alien visitor understands primarily nothing. This can lead to high confusion. One night in Osaka, an emaciated figure stormed into my dressing room. He was wearing a worn-out black suit. He bowed and began talking to me in an urgent manner. All I was able to make out was some talk of *"kane,"* *"shinyo,"* and *"bijinesu."*

"That means money, trust, and business," Miss Noriko, the local organizer's press woman, explained. She has studied music in Germany and I was very glad she was standing next to me. Noriko obviously knew what to do, giving the sinister figure a short, sharp response. The thin man stared at us grimly for a moment, then bared his teeth for a crooked smile, bowed again, and left. Did I notice, Noriko asked, that he was missing two fingers on his left hand? "He is a Yakuza, a gangster, and he wanted to know whether Quasthoff-san needed a manager."

"Oh God, and what did you tell him?"

"No need."

"And he just accepted that."

"Yes, of course."

I was speechless. As I said, a foreigner does not understand anything there. The Japanese are well aware of that, and I think they feel a little pity, which is why even gangsters treat the long-nosed Gaijin with great courtesy. This courtesy is all well and good, but it doesn't make ordering food any easier, even something as simple as a hard-boiled egg. You can say *"tamago"* (egg) and *"yuderu"* (boil) but it doesn't work. No doubt my pronunciation is as shaky as the questionable English of hotel receptionists worldwide. The bilingual menu, that pillar of international gastronomy, is a precious rarity, even in large cities like Osaka. Instead, Japanese chefs display plastic versions of their creations in the window, leaving diners to point as they ponder the name and taste of the dishes they are meant to represent.

"Of course, we could just go to an Italian restaurant," my brother suggested one night when I was plagued by hunger in Tokyo.

"I'm there!" My friend the wonderful tenor Jimmy Taylor rubbed his hands. He had already eaten lavishly before the concert, but this Pavarotti-shaped singer always has room for more. We called a taxi. The driver had white gloves, like all Japanese cabdrivers, and he had decorated his vehicle with white doilies. His driving style, though, was less *gemütlich* than the decor. In order to avoid the permanent traffic jam on the main roads, he shot through lively residential and business areas like a kamikaze, barely squeezing through the narrow sidewalks. After watching pedestrians dive right and left into doorways to avoid us, we were relieved to arrive without bloodshed at an establishment with the inviting name Via Veneto. Unfortunately, the *ristorante* was just about to close. It was only half past ten, but the waiter who greeted us shrugged and said that restaurants generally close at this time. Oh boy! Micha and the eternally thirsty guys from the Prague Philharmonic would have to take their nightcap at one of the omnipresent vending machine centers that offer everything the heart could possibly desire, from a pint-size bottle of Sapporo to women's underwear—already worn, if you please. But it was our lucky night. Two streets farther down music could be heard from a Japanese restaurant, and since I was really very hungry now, I decided I had to risk an upset stomach.

"Come on, guys, let's go in. It's our last chance for today." Indeed, even here they were starting to clean up. We took our shoes off and were led into the guest room. Two dozen businessmen were sitting in lotus position at small tables, having abandoned their jackets and ties. Their heads, heated by the swift delivery of beer and sake, were glowing and sitting visibly heavy on top of their shoulders. Some were even asleep. A waiter brought us the menu. In English Jimmy ordered chicken with rice. The waiter bowed and served him a pork cutlet with marinated carrots. Micha and I ordered noodles, and we got them: cold and as green as their seaweed, cucumber, and wasabi garnish. Micha thought it wasn't half bad. I went to bed hungry.

Please don't get me wrong. I have eaten very well in Japan, especially in the many restaurants in train and subway stations that serve the kind of earthy soups and quick meat and fish dishes people can enjoy as they hurry to and fro, for the Japanese are always in a hurry, either on the way to work or on the way home. Pity the person who cannot reach his work by train, for endless traffic jams spill across concrete levels stacked two and three layers on top of each other and tangled like a bowl of spaghetti. The Japanese face this grim reality with heroic discipline, though there isn't any guarantee they'll reach their destination: narrow parking bays allow these unhappy drivers to park their cars and spend the night wherever they may find themselves. The next morning they will turn around and the whole thing starts all over again. The traffic chaos seems to be the reason why concert and theatre performances, as well as movies and other entertainment in Japan, start right after work, and why the nightlife ends at eleven p.m. There is simply no time to lose.

One of the most popular postwork activities is karaoke, whether in any old bar or at one of the monumental karaoke palaces. Their façades are adorned with dragons and samurais or fantasy creatures from pop culture. Within is a hive of tiny sound-proof booths, each of which is equipped with a CD player, a TV, and someone practicing his singing for the next social event. The Pachinko halls are just as serious but infinitely louder. From the outside the fancy buildings are easily mistaken for banks, but they contain nothing but hundreds of clanking gambling machines. People really seem to enjoy the noise.

The Japanese appreciate noise, but they love silence. Before coming here I did not know that one can stage contemplation so perfectly. Teahouses, artistic gardens, expansive parks, and temple facilities all find their places among the capitalists' fortresses. Maybe they aren't so different after all. Before the monks come out with a soothsaying or lucky oracle, one must pay, and those who would like to address the gods directly have got to pay up as well. In Tokyo I always preferred carrying my coins to a Shinto shrine on the territory of the Asakusa-Kannon temple, where three fantastically tall badgers stand at attention on their wooden hind legs. The trio has the same mysterious grin on their faces as the Cheshire cat who makes the following statement to Alice in Wonderland:

"We're all mad here. I'm mad. You're mad."

"How do you know I'm mad?" said Alice.

"You must be," said the Cat, "or you wouldn't have come here."

It helps me see Tokyo with different eyes. One must respect a people who transcend the demands of modernity in such a surreal and ultimately highly comical way.

If what I have written so far suggests that globe trotting allows my kind to live it up, I must correct that impression. Everyday life on tour is no day at the beach; it is exhausting and marked by unnerving redundancy, just as it is for professional athletes. Jussi and I get on a train or plane somewhere in the morning, arrive exhausted somewhere in the afternoon, and are dropped at a hotel to relax a little bit. Often the rooms are not ready yet, in which case we hang around the lobby or trot through the evermore-similar shopping malls. When there is finally a clean pillow available for a weary head, the first rehearsal is scheduled to start. So I quickly check whether everything is as my agency has requested: Are there towels? Is the sink low enough for me? If not, is there a foot bench? Can I get into the shower without help? If I'm unlucky, I have to switch rooms, and because negotiations take awhile I usually have to rush off to rehearsals in a state. Afterwards we eat something and go—no, not out on the town—to sleep. We have to perform the next day and so smoky rooms and alcohol would not be the right thing at all. After the concert, there is the reward of a glass of wine, and then it's off to bed—because the voice has to regenerate, because we have to get up early and get to the train station or airport to get to some other place, put the luggage in the hotel, check the room, leave for rehearsals—the same old thing all over again.

If you stumble even a bit you'll pay for it soon enough. In Madrid Peter and I really did get smashed once. When we got back to the hotel Peter staggered into his room, mumbling "Good night." I could hear him lock the door, toss the key on the table, and flop onto the bed before it dawned on me—

"You idiot," I shouted, "you've locked me out!" for to save money we have taken a double room. But Peter wouldn't stir. I knew I had the second key, but where was it? I went through my pockets once, twice, three times. Nothing.

It can't be, a key cannot just dissolve into thin air, the thought goes through my drowsy head. Rioja disappears, tapas can disappear, and cognac, but things? Things can get lost, but they cannot disappear in the sense of not existing any longer.

And so I paced the length of the hallway five times, searching all the corners and inspecting every carpet tile. I checked the door lock again: had I put the key in after all? No, I'm not that drunk. Then I realized: Peter must have taken the second one in with him. Reinvigorated, I knocked at the door, kicked it with my shoe, and screamed his name. In vain. The only thing coming out of the room was Peter's blissful snoring. I had no choice but to go down to reception and ask the night porter for a third key. I stepped into the elevator and reached for the control panel. Thank God, I was able to make it—just barely. The cabin began moving, traveling eight floors without problem, but then there was a sickening jerk and the lift stopped. I was suspended somewhere between the first and second floors. At least that's what I thought, since the door did not open and the display showed the number 2. My acute panic sobered me right up. As I've said, I am not very fond of elevators in general. All the buttons that allow passengers to communicate during an elevator malfunction are pretty much out of my reach. So I had two options: wait until some early riser noticed the problem or make a racket. My claustrophobia nullified the first option, and so I took a deep breath and started yelling. After ten minutes those years of vocal exercises paid off. The porter's voice came through the speaker promising immediate help. Our definitions of "immediate" turned out not to coincide, and I fell into a rage. When the elevator was finally repaired two hours later I was a mental and vocal wreck. When I got back to our room, I had just a bit of voice left to ruin. Peter, having emerged from his coma, listened to my tirade. Thankfully, he barely remembers my outburst. Sometimes a hangover has its advantages. But we barely managed that second concert in Madrid. We still got great reviews because the journalists were all there on the first day. But we felt rather guilty and made a solemn vow to leave escapades of this kind to rock bands.

I owe one of my most memorable rock band experiences to my brother and his former girlfriend, Sabine Haack. Sabine worked at the press office of the Lower-Saxon State Chancellery, home to Gerhard Schröder. Early in 1992 she had to deal with the World's Fair taking place in Seville the following summer. Chancellor Kohl decreed that each German state would control the German program for one week. Since Sabine had other things to do, she hired Micha, who was at the listings section of his newspaper and knew many prominent people on the cultural scene.

With the help of the EXPO budget Micha resorted to a worldly and simpatico nepotism. I was the first one hired, and the second was his buddy Thomas Haug who headed Frec-Frec, a performance group with six musicians from three federal states. His drinking buddy Thomas Kuhlenbeck, along with the two lovely ladies Antonia Jacobsen and Katja Schmiedeskamp, would represent the visual arts. International short films would come from the avant-garde director Ecki Kähne in Hanover, who would finally be able to settle up his drinking debts with Micha, thanks to the stipend. And the blues band Crayfish issued from the rat catcher town of Hamelin, just like one of Sabine's colleagues.

But hold it! Honored reader, of course, all this is only a joke and not true at all. Only artists officially acknowledged by various awards and cultural newspaper sections qualified for the EXPO, and Micha was lucky enough to be on a first-name basis with more than a few such creative types.

The Scorpions were traveling with us to Seville—not thanks to Micha's maneuvering but on the goodwill ticket of Gerhard Schröder. No one else wanted to take them along, not Micha, not Sabine, not I, and not the speaker of the government Uwe Heye, who was ultimately responsible for the program. It wasn't primarily a matter of taste: the theatre in the German Pavilion held only two hundred spectators and simply could not accommodate a heavy metal concert. The Scorpions had just landed a global monster hit with the Glasnost song "Wind of Change," and everybody could imagine what would happen when news of their concert got out: the onslaught of fans would be uncontrollable, and the Spanish would rightly ask why the Lower Saxons were dumb enough to try to stuff their stars into this much too small pavilion. Gerhard Schröder, however, did not see it this way; his final pronouncement: "Enough! The Scorpions are coming." The band promised him to travel lightly and perform unplugged. On top of that, Sabine and Micha tried to talk the management into not publicizing the appearance too much, especially not on the Iberian peninsula. Management agreed but in the end didn't give a damn.

Hanover's colorful cultural group landed in Malaga at the end of August. My opening concert almost got aborted because Lufthansa sent two-thirds of our instruments, among them a Bechstein piano, to Istanbul. Luckily the Dutch Pavilion was kind enough to lend us a piano.

For the Scorpions these logistical snafus were without consequence. They were flown in on a privately chartered plane shortly before their appearance. Things brightened for the rest of us when we saw our quarters. The spacious bungalow facilities with swimming pool, bar, and restaurant left nothing to be desired. I moved into one of the white boxes with my girlfriend Eva. I had been been totally smitten with this blond creature for the past six months and vice versa. She is not only the most beautiful woman in the world, she is simply perfect: apart from being in the master class for piano at the Music Academy in Hanover, she regularly reads *Kicker*, Germany's most popular soccer magazine—and she likes to kick, too. When we were not offering Italian arias in amphitheatres, we were organizing a game with the guys from Frec-Frec or walking hand in hand through the old part of Seville, directly across from the EXPO district at the foot of the mighty Guadalquivir. That is very practical as one can find shelter from the sweltering heat in the shady alleys, coming across bodegas hung with grapes at every corner where a siesta can be had in splendid fashion with a glass of port. At night after work we would stroll across the EXPO plaza. Once the pavilions shut down, the Spaniards turn the premises into a party zone for young and old. The veterans sip port out of basket bottles and watch the flamenco groups in connoisseurlike fashion. Seville's youth dances in front of the salsa stage, on which two magnificent Cuban bands are grooving, until the morning hours. Or the young couple would sit billing and cooing in the hotel garden, and watching how its comrades-in-arms were handling the gigantic portions of Osborne sherry offered cheaply and poured generously by the hotel.

The only ones who were not enjoying the excursion were Sabine and Micha. The two were everyone's host and hostess, suggestion box, and general information center, distributing aspirin, making sure that everybody was on stage on time, taking care of the journalists.

The Scorpions arrived one day after the president, and from then on all bets were off in the German Pavilion. Roadies were piling tons of equipment onto the stage and did not allow themselves to be deterred even by my Verdi arias. After the third piece

I was fed up and stopped. Uli Orth also refused to appear while
the heavy metal quintet was sitting in Auer's restaurant and getting celebrated. The girls were in lederhosen and leopard bras
with bursting bosoms, the men were showing off their midriffs,
looking like the late Udo Lindenberg—without the hat.

Two hours later the first fans were standing in front of our doors.
By the afternoon there were hundreds, and by evening thousands
occupied the pavilion. A crisis meeting was called in the office of
the German Pavilion. To bring order into the chaos there was no
choice but to ask the EXPO management to call the police, but
they did not arrive. Instead the Guardia Civil was coming. The
paramilitary troop was not exactly considered squeamish, and it
lived up to its reputation. With their batons drawn they cleaned
up the premises, surrounded the building, and counted exactly
four hundred persons who were allowed to reenter. The hard
rockers were unfazed by all this. They barricaded themselves in
their dressing rooms and polished their act. The group thought of
something unheard of: "The Scorpions Meet Elvis Presley," a
journey through the works of the King of Rock 'n' Roll. The effort
required for the "unplugged" simulation of the three-chord hits
was unbelievable. The crew erected an entire percussion park in
front of the amplifiers with twenty-five guitars, so that the virtu-
osos would not err on the fingerboard if the key changed for the
next song. It was of no use, for what took place on stage once
Klaus Meine crowed his pithy "Hello, Seville. We are the Scorpions from Lower Saxony. Hope you feel good" into the evening
sky is hard to describe. I will try anyway.

The honored reader should please imagine the original version
of "Hound Dog," recorded in 1956 for the Sun label—the angrily
vibrating but ever smooth organ of the King, D. J. Fontana's driving drum set, Scotty Moore's rousing, shuffling rhythm guitar,

which he underlines with elegant single notes. Got it? "You ain't
nothin' but a hound dog"—dub dabdoodoo dub—"Cryin' all the
time"—dub dabdoodoo dab . . . Now, one should imagine how the
piece sounded when the Scorpion front man actuated his castrato
falsetto, Rudolf Schenker's acoustic guitar sounding as though it
was not about *the* rhythm and blues classic but the 1970 British
hit "Neanderthal Man" by Hotlegs (soon to evolve into 10cc),
and drummer Herman Rarebell following the actually bone-dry
groove on two bongos. Highpoint of the performance was the guitar solo by Mr. Matthias Jabs, who seemed to have forgotten that
a blues scheme has only twelve bars. The Scorpions kept forcing
themselves ahead and on to "Jailhouse Rock," "Love Me Tender," "Don't Be Cruel," and fifteen other gems by the King. One
could literally hear Elvis the Pelvis turn over in his grave.

At least Gerhard Schröder was enthused, because "In the
Ghetto" always reminds him of his hard youth, back in Mossen-
berg, when "we had to eat the cement out of the window frames,"
as the chancellor likes to recall in sentimental moments. One
has to excuse him—he is not too much into music, he collects
art. The Lower Saxon delegation at least could exhale when the
spook show was over and the Scorpions were packing up the next
day. The amphitheatre was returned to us for the next five days.
Then the Thuringians arrived.

The good-byes were even more sad than usual, not just because
the Spaniards were great hosts, but because a standing engage-
ment is always much nicer than a regular tour, with its constant,
disorienting, exhausting movement. But I don't want to complain. Life is a journey; parts of it are uphill and parts of it down.
Some assignments are almost pure pleasure, like cruising on the
Mermoz, a ship I have truly grown fond of since I first went
aboard in 2000.

What sets the *Mermoz* apart from the other ships? It can't be seen or explained; you just have to feel it. For me the *Mermoz* is like Eugene at sea. I do not make it every year, but whenever I go aboard I meet dear old friends and fantastic new colleagues like the cellist Boris Pergamenschikov, the soprano Andrea Rost, the pianist Byron Janis, or the famous jazz vocalist Maria João. The pay is not bad at all, and on top of that there is sun, exquisite food, and as many drinks as my stomach can handle. The man who makes all this possible is a Hungarian concert organizer named André Borosc. I first met him in Paris in the home of the art patron Marc Smeja. Smeja regularly organizes house concerts, and when I performed there in 1993 Borosc was among the guests. He told me that he owned a small but comfortable ship that offered just enough space for a handful of clients with deep pockets to cruise the Mediterranean. Could this be something for me and the *Winterreise*? At first I was skeptical—playing clown on a cruise ship? Isn't that the last stop of an entertainment career, worse than resort tours or singing at a bank president's sixtieth-birthday party? Borosc, a sophisticated man with a worldly impresario's charm, sensed my concerns.

"Pleease Mistar Quaahsthoff, you doo not know me yaht, but I am a vahry serious man. Ask your friend Vlady."

He pointed to the famous violinist Vladimir Spivakov, standing all by himself next to the punch and looking around in a melancholy manner. Impressed, I listened up and was fully convinced once Borosc spelled out the conditions of the contract. It didn't hurt when he casually mentioned that, should I decide to accept his offer, I would be on the same boat as the god of cello Rostropovich and his wife, the exceptional soprano Galina Vishnevskaya. In the same boat as Rostropovich, literally! And she is one of the three artists for whom Benjamin Britten wrote his great pacifist work *War Requiem*, though the Soviet government kept her from the Coventry Cathedral premiere in 1962. Being a big fan of Vishnevskaya I gladly promised Borosc I would be there when his ship "set sail" in May. That night I called Charles Spencer, full of excitement. I needed to ensure that the piano, at least, would be world class.

The *Mermoz* was docked in Marseille. Charles and I arrived one radiant spring morning, never imagining that only two days later I would be familiarly calling Rostropovich "Slava." After my first concert the couple hugged, tears in their eyes, and Rostropovich said:

"Young man, we have to do some work together!"

At first that meant drinking together—vodka out of water glasses, to be exact—five ounces a shot. My stomach contracted and my hands got clammy but Rostropovich gave me an encouraging slap on the shoulders.

"Choo have to drink these. This is Russian mentahlity, and now call me Slava."

He then let his glass clank against mine and bolted the contents in a single gulp.

"I am Tommy," I murmured in awe. What could I do but defy death by emptying my own glass? After all, one does not want to be embarrassed in front of a genius. My new friend poured again. I have no idea what happened after the third glass. The next day I was woken up by a stormy sea, nausea, and a pounding headache. When I saw my pale face in the mirror I was sure it was all a dream, but as soon as I slithered back on deck I found Rostropovich standing at the railing, bright as a button, his chiseled profile facing the wind.

"Aaaah, goot morning Tommy. You sleep too long. I see you need another lesson in Russian style." I tried to smother the urge to vomit with a smile, but it wasn't powerful enough, and the railing was too high for me to lean over. I turned without issuing a greeting and barely made it back to my cabin before experiencing the previous night coming back to visit me with redoubled fury.

But later I managed to sit with Slava and his wife in the salon. They were drinking Campari, and I stuck to peppermint tea. Galina Vishnevskaya told a story about what kind of stuff the ship's owner is made of. André Borosc actually never had anything to do with Christian seafaring and only entered the cruise business when his friend Rostropovich emigrated from Russia and had to make a new life for himself. Borosc knew that the musical sea trips would be a lucrative business, and sure enough, they were a success. It wasn't just profitable; there were musical benefits to be gained as well. Slava was as good as his word. Even after all the fun we had that first week, I didn't truly believe that he was serious in his offer to make music with me in the near future. But when I had been home for barely a week, the phone rang.

"Here is Rostropovich," the caller announced. I assumed it was one of my friends playing a joke on me, for I had already told them all about the cruise in vivid detail, and so I answered: "Yes, and this is the Queen of Sheba. What can I do for you?"

"Really, here is Slava," the voice gurgled once again.

"I know, and this is the Queen of Sheba speaking."

"Thomas, don't be ridiculous," the sound at the other end was slightly exasperated now, and I realized that it was in fact him. Slava invited me to sing the baritone part in *War Requiem*, which he was to conduct in Tokyo.

Now we are old friends, thanks to the *Mermoz*, and I must say that with Slava it is never boring. His better half is prone to frenzied bouts of shopping, driving even the generous Slava to the brink of despair and amusing everyone else. When the *Mermoz* dropped anchor at Casablanca, a shore leave was on the program. Slava and I sat in two lounge chairs on the upper deck and ate ice cream, since it was much too hot for anything else. Galina, on the other hand, had already ordered a cab and wheedled a bundle of cash from her husband. Twenty minutes later she was back on deck asking for another bundle. Grumbling, he pulled a handful from his pocket. Vishnevskaya returned after an hour in the taxi—now towing a trailer. Slava shook his head.

"I don't like the looks of this."

"Oh, darling, it's not for me, it's for the walls of your office." In hopes of delighting her Slava, she had bought exactly nine hundred feet of costly damask, for his office in Saint Petersburg. Having lost his appetite for ice cream, he disappeared in the direction of the bar. Later that night he was still there, having consumed six Irish coffees in the meantime, not without a certain effect on his attitude. When I asked how he was doing, he said, "Oh, very gutt. My wife is sleeping and can't buy anything."

When I went ashore in Marrakech, I would usually end up in a coffeehouse, exhausted by heat, dust, and the swarming bazaar. Jussi would often sit with me, since he shares my dislike of rambling and crowds. One of the reasons we like to go to Marrakech is that the Mamudiah is there, one of the five best hotels in the world and a very pleasant place to sit. We climbed out of the bus, walked through the lobby into the magnificent garden, and settled down under palm trees. After a refreshment we went swimming; true luxury is the pool of the Mamudiah. Each time we paddled to the edge we encountered a waiter who wanted to know what he could do for us. We sampled everything the alcohol-free menu had to offer. Only when the call of the muezzin came through the speaker did we order beer—a German's duty.

In 1996 the young piano genius Evgeny Kissin was added to the *Mermoz* concert schedule. He was a good kid but didn't get a lot of opportunities to show it, since his mother and harsh piano teacher shadowed his every move. This two-headed Cerberus kept its protégé from getting too close to life's temptations, that is, wine, women, and unchaste song. The violinist Shlomo Mintz, the viola player Yuri Bashmet, and I watched this for four days and finally felt too sorry for him to stand it anymore. That night Evgeny got kidnapped, snatched away from his grim protectors. Taking our catch with us we fled to the restaurant through a side entrance. The watchdogs lost the scent and we ordered a round of beer to celebrate our successful mission. The taste seemed to agree with Evgeny. Indeed, he drank his second one with visible enjoyment. We ended up talking until five o'clock in the morning, dancing around the discotheque, and, of course, drinking more beer. The next morning Cerberus stomped toward us across the deck while giving us the evil eye. Evgeny appeared only hours later, walking in slow motion, shielded by big sunglasses.

"Well, how do you feel?" Shlomo asked with a laugh. Evgeny beamed.

"Terrible, but it was a great night."

The following year Yuri and I noted with some satisfaction that he had managed to ditch his watchdogs for good.

I could write a whole book about my old friend Yuri Bashmet. The man is a musical character, an original, and a bon vivant, not to mention one of the most lovable and generous human beings I know. Experts count Yuri among the best viola players in the world, and there are those who maintain that the beauty of his playing is unearthly, which is why envious souls can be heard to murmur that he sold his soul to the devil. Indeed, there is something demonic, or Paganini-like, about Yuri's overall appearance—his raven hair, dark eyes, eagle's profile, and challenging, imperious demeanor. This rumor is not discouraged by the fact that Yuri plays piano and violin as well as the viola. I personally witnessed the conductor Bashmet telling a well-known violin virtuoso off when the man could not manage a few difficult chords—I think it was Bartók's Violin Concerto in C—in the way Yuri had imagined it. He tried again and again until Yuri had enough of it, tore the instrument away from him, and fiddled the treacherous part right then and there with unbeatable grandeur. The humiliated violinist's jaw dropped wide open and Yuri, black eyes flashing, handed him the violin and bowed, murmuring contemptuously:

"You have to do it in this way."

Yuri could make millions as a soloist but instead supports an entire gang of musicians in Saint Petersburg, with whom he goes about the world as head of orchestra. I have visited Yuri and his family a few times and have seen what his commitment means for his colleagues. The town is full of wonderful musicians, but since the collapse of the Soviet Union most live in conditions that no one in the West would tolerate. Many of the once famous broadcast and state orchestras have been disbanded, wrapped up by a new time that has no money or need for the blessings of culture. There is no work because there is no audience, and so Yuri offers them a rare opportunity to continue to play and to live with dignity.

When I asked him why he would choose this stressful way instead of taking some agent's lucrative offer to travel the world as a celebrated star, he shrugged.

"Tell me what is a star. A star is so far from all human beings, a cold glittering light in the universe. I want to stay on the bottom."

Nicely said, but even Yuri's touching earthiness must contend with an artist's moody nature. Tortured by the unbearable aspects of being in general and the music business in particular, he will fall into a white rage or black melancholy for days at a time. For example, when rehearsals are to be organized, appointments to be taken seriously, or his amorphous orchestra body to be kept in balance—inside the concert hall and outside of it.

When I met Yuri and his orchestra again at the Elmau Castle he was in the middle of a melancholy phase, which he was nursing with plenty of alcohol—so the Petersburg Ensemble made for a fine contrast with the cheerful group of guests who had descended on the hotel for the New Year. Elmau, much like Eugene, is a town with personality. The name Elmau designates not only the castle but an entire high valley lying tucked away between the limestone walls of the Karwendel and Wetterstein mountains near Mittenwald.

The traveling minister Johannes Müller was the founder of the friendly lodge. Around 1900 he tramped through this part of southern Germany fishing for human souls—a popular sport at the time among a bourgeoisie deeply unsettled by industrialization. But unlike most of his competitors, Müller had lasting success, thanks to his queer but well-meaning mixture of "back to nature" appeals and individualist biblical interpretations, especially with the ladies. When he discovered the quiet Elmau Valley, he decided it was the right place to establish his reformed community. One of his more solvent admirers, the Countess Waldersee, built a castlelike main house next to the brook, and in time Elmau became a place for therapeutic encounters which, luckily for the clientele in need of recuperation, were limited to Müller's general credo "life is more than work, and being is more important than doing."

However, even during Müller's days not everyone could afford such a sensual credo, and so an illustrious mix of artists, ministers, and big earners of all stripes was cultivated to ensure that over time that special essence would develop that still permeates the air today—a kind of grand bourgeois sensibility spiced up with wellness, light esotericism, readings, roundtables about the state of the world, and—last but not least—a first-class music program whose heart lies somewhere between classic and modern jazz. I sang at Elmau Castle for the first time shortly after winning the ARD Competition. Since then I have spent every other New Year's here. Each time it is like a big family outing.

Jussi arrives with his wife and three children, I bring Mama and Father along. Sometimes even Micha and Renate are able to make it. The two of them tramp down to the Partnach Gorge or up through the snow to the mountain cottage built by Ludwig II in order to daydream undisturbed by any Bavarians. I prefer to stay in the fireplace room and watch live socialites, some of whom are always there: the comedian Loriot, the deeply simpatico actor Achim Rohde, or the Social Democratic politician Peter Glotz. In 2002, Glotz was simply impossible to overlook. The heavy thinker was wandering about for days, his forehead crinkled, gaze fixed on the floor as though looking for a lost button, a mighty folder tucked under his arm. I knew it contained a manuscript only because Glotz frequently left it casually but temptingly open as he continued wandering and searching for buttons. Once I had to peek in and was rewarded with phrases like "portray a European problem in a new way," "national traditions," "Sudeten-German problem," and "swimming against the stream."

"Oh boy," Micha sighed when I told him about it, "I guess we can get ready for something by next fall's book season." Indeed, a few weeks later the comrade announced that he was heading up a movement whose central idea was to erect a memorial for the expelled Germans right next to the Holocaust memorial. It was as if he wanted to throw German-Polish relations back to 1945.

The next day the poet Hilde Domin held court in a much more becoming manner. She has style and nothing left to prove to herself or anyone else, and she read accordingly. Reading? Actually it was more of a performance, one of the best I have ever seen. When Domin tiptoes onto the stage I immediately say to myself: Tommy, watch out. There is something to be learned here. Her posture—spine and silver chignon form a straight line—is as exemplary as the tone of voice she uses in opening her performance, putting the audience on guard but without giving offense: obliging but firm, racy but with precise articulation of each word. Ms. Domin is in control of the situation at all times.

"I am now reading my first published poem," she begins.

"I will read it twice. I always read everything twice. Whoever has heard me before knows that."

She reads nothing at first but talks about some personal things.

"I am a witness of the time period," Domin says. "This is permitted to me."

She then talks about how her colleague Marie Luise Kaschnitz at times came up with some rather wild rhymes. When Kaschnitz wrote that "two lions were running through the room" she had asked her,

"Luise, is that true?"

"No."

"You see."

Her own poems always came flying to her. Whoever dealt with lyricism would know that, and for the rest she really would now read one of her poems in order to demonstrate.

"Or two. Well, okay, two—one from the year 1947, my first published poem, the other from the year 1958. Or rather I will read the first one twice, then the second one twice."

For one should know that she, Domin, would read everything twice.

"... and never longer than fifty-nine minutes. Could someone tell me what time it is?"

"Quarter to five," somebody calls out.

"Oh, then we have got to hurry. I will now read two short poems. They are dedicated to Virginia Woolf—a suicide."

But even here Hilde Domin cannot resist another anecdote, and so it goes on and on. It was great. Unfortunately, Jussi picked me up for rehearsal before I found out whether she managed to end her reading without reading a single poem.

I was glad in any case to see her sitting near the front that night during my recital of Wolf's *Italian Songbook* with Sybilla Rubens and Jussi. Sybilla is not only one of my oldest companions on the music path, she also has one of the most beautiful soprano voices I know. She is the ideal partner for the *Liederbuch* because, like me, she enjoys adding a bit of mimicry to this sweet and sour relationship. In any case we get a lot of laughs. Even Yuri's mood barometer creeps towards sunny. Our evening of arias was a lovely event because once again the Petersburgers were in grand form. Afterwards Yuri, my parents, and I sat together for a long time—I could afford it, since my work was done. Then it was time for a little fun, which in Elmau usually means listening to the jazz musicians. That year the Swedish pianist Esbjörn Svensson was a guest. I had seen him last season with the trombone player Nils Landgren, who sings in a captivatingly laconic style. Sometimes the jazz musicians also come to the classical concerts, or one jams and meets in the bar afterwards. There is a real festival atmosphere all week long, but the high point is without question New Year's Eve. If he is not on tour or lying on a southern beach, Klaus Doldinger, Germany's best-known jazz musician and film score composer, stops in. He lives close by and always has his saxophone on him. Then the New Year is rung in with a wild session.

The relaxed way we interpreters of classical get along with the jazz musicians confirms yet again that the German way of rigorously categorizing any and everything is neither necessary nor even useful. All that really exists is good music and bad music, and what one learns as a traveling singer is that good music of any kind touches people in their innermost being. It forges connections, whether in Berlin, Moscow, Tokyo, Houston, Johannesburg, or Timbuktu.

This is how it was at the most controversial concert I have ever participated in. On May 7, 2000, the anniversary of the liberation of the Mauthausen concentration camp, Simon Rattle and the Vienna Philharmonic were to play Beethoven's Ninth Symphony and its "Ode an die Freude" ("Ode to Joy") in the quarry right below the "Death Stairs." For many people, the idea of hearing this music in a place where 105,000 people were murdered was unbearable. Even the renowned jazz musician Joe Zawinul, who was to play a piece of his own, registered his concern.

"I think the Philharmonic should play something new and not Beethoven, since that is also what the Nazis played." He was supported by the historian Niklas Perzi: "Zawinul has dealt intensely with Mauthausen on a musical level, but the Philharmonic just wants to superimpose Beethoven on the concentration camp."

Simon pointed out that Beethoven and Schiller were not Nazis. It was a difficult decision for me, but in the end I was convinced by Simon's view of music as "remembrance, redemption, and respect capable of healing." After all, music has helped me survive so many of the unpleasant things in my life.

Dietrich Fischer-Dieskau watched it all on television and described his impressions in the *Frankfurter Allgemeine Zeitung:*

The Vienna Philharmonic was fantastic and television really was able to convey the atmosphere. One saw the quarry in which humans had been tortured, and at the end one saw people sitting there without applause, after all that jubilation. Everyone sat still, each with a candle on his or her lap, in complete and

absolute silence—several thousands—and millions watched.
That really is shocking. After all the Ninth is still a hairy piece
for a choir and for soloists too, but to carry such an event into all
the homes really is something special. It works better than any
memorial the experts are fighting about, shaking up everyone it
reaches.

I have often experienced the quasi-magical, cathartic powers of
music. The most intense memory is of an occasion that took
place ten years ago in Israel when I was on the road with Karl-
Friedrich Beringer and the Windsbach Boys Choir. After three
concerts in Tel Aviv we want to perform the *Matthäus Passion* on
the Lake of Gennesaret. Bach's work is very controversial here,
since certain lines clearly accuse the Jews of having killed Jesus.
Ultrareligious fanatics take it all literally and threaten us with
demonstrations and worse, but Beringer is not to be deterred—we
perform the piece. After the concert an older man steps into my
dressing room. He is wearing a short-sleeved shirt and I can see a
faded blue number tattooed onto his right arm—the identifica-
tion number of concentration camp inmates. In broken German
the man tells me that he, too, is a musician, and that he was
interned at Bergen-Belsen. Tears run down his face. He takes my
hand, squeezing it for minutes, and says:
"Today, after fifty years, I have cried for the first time. I thank
Bach for that and I thank you!"
Five weeks later I saw him again at one of my lieder recitals in
Munich. He came especially from Israel in order to hear me
again. This time it was me who could barely hold back the tears,
but the old man didn't want things to get too sentimental.
Instead he told me a nice musician's joke: "An Israeli conductor
goes for a walk on the beach and finds a closed bottle. He opens it
and a genie comes out. He says, 'You have freed me from this bottle after three hundred years. Now you may make a wish.' The

conductor thinks for a long time and then pulls a map out of his pocket, opening it up on the beach.

" 'Look here, this is Israel and here is Palestine, here Syria and there is Egypt. For decades violence and conflict have reigned here. If you could manage to finally make peace I would be happy.'

"The genie pensively rubs his chin.

" 'Hm, a very difficult assignment. I have only been out of the bottle for a minute or so and am still a little bit out of practice. Do you perhaps have another wish?'

"The conductor thinks about it: 'I lead an orchestra and, like all conductors, I have a problem with the viola players. They are always late, demand the most breaks and the highest pay, but cannot play their instrument correctly. If that could stop I would be grateful.'

"The genie scratches his chin and says: 'Better show me that map again.' "

Life Is a Total Work of Art

"In Detmold there is a position open on the singing faculty that is tailor made for you." Hilde Kronstein-Uhrmacher looked at me searchingly as she said this, but the jolly woman from the Rhineland should have had her eyes on the road instead. Her Mercedes was drifting disconcertingly close to the shoulder.

"Watch out, the car—" I squeezed my eyes shut, gripped the door, and tried to ignore the panicky sweat running down my neck. Hilde had no trouble ignoring my unease.

"Calm down, just listen. Apply and we'll be colleagues by next year."

Again the Mercedes veered off course, this time actually scraping the green divider on the right. Hilde simply cannot drive straight.

"Apply. Don't forget." I would promise her anything at this point, quietly sweating as I concentrated on calming my stomach. That's how it went, all the way from Hamburg to Hanover. When we arrived I emerged from the car completely exhausted.

"Bye, Tommy, see you later." She stuck her head out the window. "And don't forget Detmold!"

"Yes, Hildchen." How could I after that trip? I gratefully took refuge in the dressing room of the Theater am Aegi where Hilde's husband, Mr. Kronstein, the superintendent, had organized a lieder recital for me and Jussi. I have held Hilde Kronstein-Uhrmacher in high esteem since we met at a boring conference of singing teachers in the late eighties. Once we were colleagues she would often chauffeur me through the curvy Weser Mountain land to the Lippe area. I have had to learn to live with her driving style, for it takes almost two and a half hours by train, with two changes for connections.

I have always loved teaching. After the ARD Competition many young singers asked me whether I could help them. I happily took on the talented ones, and though it was hard for me to make time to teach in between trips, I did seem to have a talent for it. My first student, Katharina Petz, soon became a member of the ensemble at the Zurich Opera. But even under the threat of Hilde's driving, I wasn't going to apply to the Music Academy in Detmold without considering it seriously first. I had just gotten used to my life as a nomadic lied singer, and the little I knew of Detmold did not exactly make attractive the idea of moving into the Teutoburg Forest.

This small town of Detmold boasts Germany's largest open-air museum, which features historic farm cottages and attractions like the Lippe Goose and the Bentheim Black Pied, a rare domestic pig breed. The Federal Institute for Grain, Potato, and Fat Research is another jewel. Aside from that the city guide lists several furniture manufacturers and breweries, a theatre, a late-Gothic church, the sixteenth-century castle of the Counts zu Lippe, and 72,600 citizens, the majority of whom are civil servants.

Johannes Brahms came to town during Pentecost 1857, for he had accepted the position of choir conductor and pianist in the castle. It was meant to last three years, according to the contract, but in reality the young man fled to Göttingen as often as his duties allowed. In Göttingen, after a wavering and consequently unsuccessful attempt to woo Clara Schumann, he found consolation with a professor's daughter, Agathe von Siebold. That consolation was to come to an end when her father mentioned marriage, inspiring Brahms to flee. Now he had time for frequent

walks and two serenades (op. 11 and 16), his First Piano Concerto, and several romantic songs, the most romantic of which is
"Unter Blüten des Mais spielt' ich mit ihrer Hand," dedicated to
beautiful Agathe. When he dumped the maiden, Clara Schumann
moaned: "Oh dear Johannes, you shouldn't have let it go so far."

But Brahms told his still-adored Clara that he loved "only
music": "I think of you only and of other things when music
embellishes it for me." It is a noble deed that he immortalizes the
almost-fiancée in his String Sextet in G-Major—the side theme of
the first movement revealing the motif A-G-A-B-E.

Even less inspiring than Brahms's Detmold experience was
Christian Dietrich Grabbe's. When lack of funds forced Detmold's greatest son, Germany's most important poet next to
Heine, to leave Berlin and return to the shores of the Werra and
Berlebeck, Grabbe complained to a friend he felt banished to a
"dreary nest," "where an educated man was taken for less than
an ox," "the name of which I can barely stand to write out." In
"this Detmold, where I am cut off from all literature, fantasy,
friends, and reason—whispering into your ear—I find myself at
the brink of despair." He abhorred the profession of military
judge almost as much as his wife, Louise, and consequently spent
his days and nights in the Posthaus Pub or the drinking cave Zur
Stadt Frankfurt. In 1836, shortly after the completion of his
drama *Hermannsschlacht*, Grabbe died from a broken heart and a
ruined liver.

So you will understand why my feelings were mixed when
Hilde and I finally turned off the Bielefeld exit and rolled into the
town of Detmold. Hilde had wisely agreed to introduce me to the
nicer parts of the town—and it went well, actually. I was relieved
to realize that quite a few things had improved over the course
of the last one hundred and sixty years or so. The polished half-
timbered houses looked homey, the people were friendly and
open-minded, and there was plenty of green in and around Det-

mold. The Music Academy, where luminaries like the modern composer Günter Bialas have been teaching for fifty years, was a friendly looking place, with classroom buildings scattered about a grassy slope under the treetops of the English gardens and the stately palais that accommodates the pianists and organists. The musicologists were housed in an art deco villa on the edge of the garden and all other factions used tailor-made flat-roofed buildings that are dispersed across the spacious campus. Singing students had the historical summer theatre on the edge of campus at their disposal for podium training and scenic performances. There was even a large concert hall with professionally equipped recording studios.

At the end of our tour Hilde addressed the question of accommodation: "If you start here you don't even need to rent an apartment. Just do as I do. Stay in the hotel and let the pretty girls there bring you everything you need."

Shortly afterwards we were sitting in Schuster's bistro in the rustic Detmold courtyard where 1560, the year of construction, is engraved in gilded letters above the door.

Over a beer and excellent venison we discussed a potential arrangement. Herr Schuster offered me a room at a preferred rate, and it would be held for me even while I was traveling. For the next eight years I would feel happy as a clam in this situation, for due to the endless encouragement of Hilde, my parents, and Micha, I really did end up applying and was promptly accepted. My breakup with my girlfriend Eva had brought about a change of heart in me, and Detmold no longer seemed so awful. She and I had lived together for almost six years, and the dissolution of the relationship was painful and difficult. In fact, you could say I was suffering like a dog (which seemed to be my karma in all relationship matters). I tried to drown my sorrows in work but collapsed after three weeks and had to cancel all appearances for a month.

So once I was back to normal a professional challenge and

change of place seemed just what the doctor ordered. In the summer of 1996 I was greeted by the dean and professor Martin Redel and a circle of colleagues. Most of them eyed the new guy skeptically at first. A disabled lecturer? They'd never seen that before. Besides, none of the others were professional musicians, and so my teaching methods and evaluations were rather unorthodox— that is to say, realistic.

For example, I took my class to my colleagues' seminars at the beginning of the term, leading to widespread disapproval and confusion. My colleagues said I wanted to prove that I could do it better. That was nonsense. I just wanted my students to get a sense of the breadth of the pedagogical spectrum, so they could decide for themselves what would work best for them. After all, I have no monopoly on wisdom, and I would not be offended if anyone wanted to leave my class. Apart from that, most of the academic practices I was apparently violating were to me as mysterious as the rites of a secret society.

But even an oddball like me can get used to anything. In just a few weeks the irritations had subsided and the best time of my life was beginning. Half of the time I was on tour around the world, and the other half I spent with my students. Watching their progress was extremely gratifying. In general, graduates of the Detmold Academy take more than their fair share of the awards, outstanding competitions, and the important stages and podiums of the world. This is in part because of the academy's special emphasis on the practical and public exercise of music. The academy organizes more than two hundred fifty concerts per year in its numerous concert halls, studio stages, and in the Detmold Theatre.

In my private life, too, things were looking up. In one of my courses I met Nadja from Limburg, a singer with sassy, short hair and two little children who enriched my life. After getting along famously for a while we became an item. Since that trio liked to eat as much as I do, we did quite a lot for the Detmold gastronomical market.

But after two ravishing summers of love, the problems began. Nadja wanted a more committed relationship. She wanted me to move to Limburg because she owned a house there—a house in which her ex-husband still lived. I liked her children, Maja and Jaro, very much and could certainly imagine a family union in the future, but it just wasn't in the stars for me at that moment. Besides, with my touring and teaching responsibilities, I simply could not afford to uproot my life just like that. It would mean winding my career down before I had reached my full musical potential, and I was not willing to do this. I told her so openly. Nadja, who had converted to radical vegetarianism, countered by peevishly insisting that "you smell like meat" and urging me to embrace a plant-based diet. You can imagine how that went. After three years of cozy togetherness we had to go our separate ways, but I could not regret the joy these dear Detmold friends brought to my life.

In the winter semester of 2004 my days in the Teutoburg Forest came to an end. I had to follow a call to the Hanns Eisler Academy in Berlin. Some might say I left because a few awards and some positive rewards had given me a big head, but my true reasons for moving were practical. A year earlier I had acquired a beautiful house in the Hanover district of Kirchrode, having decided that this was where I wanted to get old. My parents, my brother Micha and Renate, and several good friends lived there by that time, but at least as many people I care about had moved to Berlin, like Uwe-Carsten Heye and his wife Sabine, the artist Andy Hahn, and the writer Felicitas Hoppe. I had seen far too little of all of them in the past few years because I was always traveling or in Detmold. Now that would all change, and I didn't even have to worry that an overdose of the capital would spoil my mood: the Intercity railway between Berlin and Hanover could get me home and sitting in my garden within two hours, half the time the trip to Detmold took me.

Of course, a not insignificant factor in my decision was the excellent reputation of the Hanns Eisler Academy, which is considered one of the best educational institutes in Europe. It isn't the kind of place whose offers you reject, and I had been offered a teaching position. Many musicians of the Berlin Philharmonic, with whom I will have a lot to do in the near future—as Simon Rattle assured me—were teaching at "the Eisler."

You may think I'm styling myself a star, but I hope I will be able to convince you otherwise. Let me tell you a little bit about the recognition I enjoy. I'll begin with an anecdote.

"I will never forget how this lady flipped out. She jumped onto the stage and laid me flat on my back. There I was on my back with her sitting on top of me. I couldn't get up, and she became really wild. Finally, John and Scott were able to tear her loose and drag her offstage." Honored reader, who might have told this tale? Arturo Toscanini? Herbert von Karajan? Luciano Pavarotti? Or Elvis Presley? The answer should be obvious: these are the King's memories. Rock 'n' rollers have fans; so do soccer players and movie stars, maybe even a politician like Guido Westerwelle, but a classical stage artist? Do conductors, soloists, opera and concert singers have real fans nowadays? I don't believe so. As is generally known, the word "fan" finds its root in the Latin *fanaticus* (raving, obsessed), which has attached itself to heretics, utopists, and troublemakers of all kinds since antiquity. Back then this type fell into the department of the Inquisition. Nowadays psychology takes an interest in fans and fanatics, ascribing "neurotic insecurity" and "psychotic traits" to them and prescribing treatment.

That does not seem entirely fair, since the psychoanalytic branch of this science is no stranger to fanaticism. But Freudians, even when they mass together at a conference, have a certain degree of self-control due to their professionalism. Self-control is rejected by the true fan outright. True fans send their inhibitions packing with all kinds of drugs, they faint in droves, they tear their hair out, scream like crazy, and carry semantically challenged signs. They toss their still-warm underwear onstage and every now and then have been known to demolish a hall full of chairs, only to beat up the police when they arrive. As you might imagine, this behavior would be completely unwelcome in a concert hall or theatre, and so thank goodness the true fan is seldom found there.

Maybe it's because fans find few performers worthy of idolization in the staid houses of high culture. Everyone knows a few figures with that divine pull. Depending on your tastes, there's Margaret Thatcher, Heidi Klum, the Heroes from Bern, Zinedine Zidane, the Dalai Lama, John Lennon, Madonna, Kim Jong Il, and Dean Martin, whom women were crazy about despite the fact that he sang things like "When the moon hits your eye like a big pizza pie, that's amore."

The classical music world has not seen an idol of these unearthly dimensions since Maria Callas left us, and that doesn't seem a bad thing to me, in light of the aforementioned fan excesses. Nowadays interpreters of the classics are, at most, well known. This means that there is a very specific special interest audience in whom they evoke a degree of interest and attention. It might get you onto television once or twice a year, and the local baker will greet you like an honored relative, but the rolls aren't any cheaper because of it. And why should they be? Prominence alone does not bestow merit, though I cannot deny that it does offer some satisfactions.

I once went to Passau to teach a master class and had my agency reserve a room for me. When I first entered the hostelry the woman at the reception desk took in my unorthodox appearance and stared at me like a walking trash bag. Clearly she had a problem with dwarfs, though she herself didn't exactly look like Miss Danube. More like a lump of unbaked dough near the end of its second rise, with a hairpiece.

"Everything is booked," she grunted before I could even open my mouth. When confronted with the fact of the reservation she found my name and grunted again. Apparently she really would have to accommodate this homunculus. She advised the porter to carry my luggage up seven flights into a chamber which, if one were to call it a guest room, would be an insult to every mountain hut. It was a small, dark, and musty place with a filthy bathroom. Without unpacking my bags I went right back down to the reception to wait under her suspicious gaze for my pianist, Charles Spencer. He was scheduled to arrive any minute and sure enough he soon came bouncing in and greeted me with his usual enthusiasm:

"Well, Professor, glad to see you."

"Yes, same here, but you can take your suitcase right back outside. We are not welcome here."

The matron sat as though struck by lightning, her complexion going from yeast grey to flour white. "Jesus Mary and Joseph," she stammered.

"No," I said, "it is just Professor Quasthoff from the Detmold Music Academy, and he wants his luggage brought down from your garret to the foyer." She squeezed out from behind the desk.

"Excuse me, Professor, excuse me. I am very sorry indeed." Then she mumbled something about "switching the room" and "embarrassing misunderstanding," but this time I brushed her off like a pesky fly.

"Dear lady, it is embarrassing but certainly no misunderstand-ing. Please call a taxi. I will not be staying here."

After I had gained a bit of prominence and shown my face on tel-evision once or twice, such things never happened to me again. I'm not conceited, but I can't say I mind the respect people accord me just because they know I am "somebody." For instance, now no train conductor dares to demand a penalty fee because I have forgotten my disabled ID. On the contrary, I am treated with kid gloves, and that is "a really good feeling" to quote from Helmut Dietl's *Rossini*.

· Sometimes I still have to pinch myself. When I did my first recording after winning the ARD Competition, the record com-pany made a few tentative attempts to promote the product on music and talk shows, but in the late eighties a gnome was not considered suitable on-air material, not in an official, legal sense and not in a private sense—and definitely not as a serious artist.

The only TV person who took an interest in me at first was Alfred Biolek. In 1992 his office called to ask whether my girl-friend Eva and I would like to appear on his talk show *Boulevard Bio*. Of course, it was not really music they wanted to hear about but thalidomide and a human being who refused to let even the most severe disability spoil his good mood. My excitement was limited. I was familiar with this story of the happily chirping pill victim, and while it is true that I am no weeping willow, I do not like being presented as a model handicapped person.

I am not a role model or life counselor, and I am not here to assuage the guilt of a society that equips certain office buildings with special entrances but otherwise punishes its physically incapacitated with constant disrespect. What good are my experi-ences for someone with a thalidomide disability if he cannot sing, or paint like Picasso but with his mouth? No good at all.

Less spectacularly disabled people still have a hard time finding employment. (Though German employers of a certain size are required to hire a number of disabled employees, those who do not are penalized with a meaningless fine.) Most of the disabled population is left to vegetate on welfare, or packed away in homes and exploited as cheap labor. Thank God, I was able to flee this ghetto after my ninth birthday—thanks to the loving care of my parents, my musical talent, the tolerance of a select few, and a lot of luck. I therefore find it hypocritical to join an organization for the disabled and make thalidomide the central fact of my life. Unlike most of those who share my fate, I have had the opportunity simply to accept my physical deficits as fact, much as others see their bunions, even if it was a long and painful process. The reader who has followed me patiently up to this point knows that I have not led a typical disabled life. I got the same smacks on the head as my brother, had the same normal friends, the same problems and formative experiences: the first beer, the first cigarette, the deciding goal that I shot once against the gang from the neighborhood, the first kiss, and—music. When press, radio, and television come at me with the old handicap stories, I now find it exhausting and growl my standard sentence: "I am one of eighty million disabled Germans—I just happen to be more visible."

We did make it to Biolek's show after all, because my agency asked me to and because I—accompanied by Peter Müller—was allowed to sing "Erlkönig." I do not regret the appearance. Bio is a charming host and the information about me and my girlfriend Eva his editors had written out for him on index cards was correct. Only when the star talker wrinkled his face and in his usual harmless, mumbling way began to steer the conversation towards the intimate part of our life—only then did I get queasy.

"Tell me, dear Eva," Bio began, grinding his lower jaw, "it is obvious that you two get along very well—our audience can see that, but how was it when you hm, well, how should I say, when you first spent the night together—?"

Embarrassed, I immediately threw myself in, protesting (falsely) that I consider sex less important than other things. But Eva wouldn't stand for it: "I don't agree. I like Thomas physically, too. He is good-looking and has a wonderful mouth for kissing."

That was very sweet. Still, my head turned ketchup red.

"Went great," Bio said when we were sitting in a pub in the old part of Cologne, a pub the busy media professor, TV moderator, and cookbook author happened to own. Well, I don't know about great, but it went better than I anticipated. Bio turned out to be a good guy in private as well, much more wickedly funny in private than in front of the camera. It soon became clear why it was he who brought the British comedy group Monty Python to Germany. We have since become good friends. He once cooked for me, and I quickly agreed when he invited me to his last talk show.

Sometimes it doesn't go quite so well. On the Radio Bremen talk show *III nach Neun (After Nine)*, I made a fool of myself, completely my own fault. I hadn't wanted to go in the first place, and I was right in the middle of Schönberg's *Gurrelieder*, which Simon Rattle was to perform with the Berlin Philharmonic, a work as difficult as it is monstrous, surpassing even Strauss's *Elektra* and Mahler's Eighth Symphony in the sweepingness of its late Romantic wide-screen format. I was singing the part of the speaker and that of the farmer and accordingly had a lot to do. But I let Deutsche Grammophon talk me into doing the radio show to promote our new CD of Schubert and Brahms lieder. The disaster began when one of the show's editors tied up my cell phone for days to negotiate the date for the interview. I asked that the subject of disability not be raised, nor the rejection by the University of Hanover, nor the work of my colleagues, having discussed all that already with Bio, the Kerner show, and the magazine *Stern*.

"You bet," the editor assured me. "The moderator, Giovanni di Lorenzo, will talk to you about the music business and the new record."

I thought I was in good hands. Di Lorenzo is from Hanover and wrote first-rate stories for the *Süddeutsche Zeitung* before rising to first *Tagesspiegel*, then *Zeit* editor in chief. But instead of di Lorenzo, his comoderator Amelie Fried led the discussion. As an author of women's novels, she is responsible for the show's take on "human warmth" and had only three questions on her agenda: my disability, the rejection by the University of Hanover, and what I think about the work of my colleagues. I was furious but naturally could not say so in front of the running cameras. I really didn't want to say anything and so switched to short, simple, curt sentences. Five minutes later Ms. Fried realized that this wouldn't do. I realized the same thing and hoped she would give up, but instead she redoubled her efforts to get me to say something negative about my colleagues. I said I had nothing to say on the matter, but she ignored my objections and kept digging until my at this point very bad mood released itself in a tirade against the hams Bocelli, Rieu, and company. I do not need to revoke any of it, but still, it was foolish to let myself be provoked like that. I confronted the producer afterwards about his broken agreement, and his response, "Well, that's television," taught me an important lesson.

I internalized that and never let myself be surprised, much less get excited, again on talk-show appearances, taking the chats for what they are instead—a business transaction with benefits for both sides. I advertise my work, the program gets fodder for its viewers, and if everything goes right the consumer gets an hour of relaxed entertainment.

I first truly realized the power of television when Jussi and I went on our first lied tour through the United States. CBS aired a *60 Minutes* segment about us, and we felt like real stars for the rest of the tour. We were greeted on the street and asked to sign autographs wherever we appeared. When ARD aired *Die Stimme (The Voice)*, a portrait filmed by my friend Michael Harder, things in Germany got similarly crazy before the attention level dropped back to normal. And, thank goodness, it did. The disruptions to your life begin even before a television program airs, since its producers must shoot hours and hours of footage just to get their three-minute clip.

Micha and his friend Dietrich zur Nedden have their own television experience as the hosts of the *Fitz Oblong Show*, a constant source of pleasure for me. The name comes from Robert Bolt's classic children's book *Der kleine dicke Ritter Oblong-Fitz-Oblong* in the black-and-white version of the *Augsburger Puppenkiste*, the Augsburg Puppet Theater, a formative force from our prepubescent days. Dietrich and Micha have been running it for more than ten years, first in the Künstlerhaus, and now in the Cumberland Gallery of the Schauspiel Hannover. The "literary chorus line" looks like the kind of lineup that the arts pages in Berlin recommend as "culty." The hosts sit behind a simple table and offer short stories, essays, songs, and poems. Dietrich, a Bob Dylan expert, is our razor-sharp analytical mind. His songs are ". . . und irgendwo bellt immer ein Hund" ("There Is Always a Dog Barking Somewhere"), "Denkwerkstatt Deutschland" ("Thinking

Workbench Germany"), or "Wenn das Umfeld umfällt" ("When the Environment Collapses"):

> Whether professional kicker or tennis queen,
> Show master, mason, or referee,
> Whether toilet woman, dentist, or therapist,
> Without an intact environment even the president's amiss.
> Success nowadays is simply a group thing,
> The motto being: together we're strong.
> When the environment is right everything's kicking,
> If not, there are only very slim pickings.

Refrain:

> When the environment collapses, you have no one at all
> When the environment collapses, you feel rather small
> When the environment collapses, no one takes your check
> When the environment collapses, you're nothing but *dreck*.

Micha, for his part, cultivates the melancholy hedonism of the American South, even when singing about the mid-European winter:

> Deathly silence where birds used to sing,
> Yesterday it was summer but now it is gone.
> You turn up the heat, rum with tea you drink,
> You sit at the window and wait for the snow to come.
> Others are waiting for reforms, the man from Bofrost or for Godot,
> For luck in the lottery, free trip to stop and go,
> They wait for love, for the bus, and I don't know
> Some wait forever and bite the dust.
> And you sit by the window drinking rum pure by now,
> You feel sorry for yourself and ask why and how?
> Then you remember with a sudden jolt:

Refrain:

> Welcome to the melancholia club
> Take off your coat, we've been waiting for you.
> On the left is the moping hall, the toilet is over there.
> Welcome to the club and see you at the bar.

> We drink Scotch to the ladies who give us a smile
> And two more tequilas to all those who deny us.
> Three beers on each penalty kick we shot into the sky,
> And please bring a mop, we are going to cry.
> We see the general double, the particular without contour
> We are so sorry for ourselves and why?
> Maybe we'll know after the next sip!

I take part as often as I can, reading stories and doing some singing. I read the texts cold. A half-hour rehearsal is enough for the songs. The Oblongs and I dive in blindly. Micha thinks that if you still need to rehearse at thirty you should probably just give it up. (He sounded pretty much like that already at twenty-five.) For the annual "best of" Oblong CDs we try a little bit harder of course, and, in order for the two hosts not to get too bored, they ask a guest author to the table each time—which has the added advantage of introducing them each month to some interesting new people who then must return the invitation. Over the last decade a veritable roster of contemporary German literary greats has passed through the studio, though heavier types like Durs · Grünbein must be left out of the fun on account of their lack of irony.

We have especially enjoyed as guests Bernd Rauschenbach and Jörg Gronius. The notorious drama duo is part of many *Fitz Oblong Shows*' inventory, so to speak, never missing one of the legendary Christmas revues, always sold out months in advance, that stage the year's highlights on the day before Christmas Eve. Rauschenbach is the head of the Arno Schmidt Foundation in Bargfeld, and a very in-demand reader for audio books. Gronius earns money and merits as opera librettist, dramatic advisor, and freelance writer. Since their school days Gronius and Rauschenbach have been writing absurd plays—the shortest on the planet. The shortest of all is *Sine Loco et Anno* and goes like this:

> *When the curtain rises*
> *one sees neither time nor space.*
> *Dark.*
> *Curtain.*

This is absurdity in the name of art, but a semiprominent person such as myself cannot avoid another contemporary absurdity: politics and politicians. Hey, you have to take the bad with the good. And the politicians aren't all so bad, anyway.

Gerhard Schröder, for example, is someone I got to know as a witty, artistically minded, and—contrary to his popular image—serious person when I sang some benefit concerts for the foundation Children of Chernobyl. I still do this today and have by now taken over the patronage from his former wife Hiltrud.

Schröder's successor as president of Lower Saxony, Sigmar Gabriel, was a lightweight in comparison, despite looking as heavy and round as a barrel. Six months before the election he asked me to join a circle of advisors for cultural issues. My coworkers were notables such as the writer Thea Dorn; *Zeit* publisher Michael Naumann; Ulrich Krempel, the director of the Sprengel Museum in Hanover; the head of Viva Dieter Gorny; and several other figures whose names I forgot because they did not show up at all. I only made it twice. At least the catering in the state agency is at

a top level, something that can't be said of the introductory presentation by Mr. Gorny. The former member of the Bochum Symphony subjected us to a neoliberal vocabulary featuring words
such as "bench-marketing," "employability," and "webucation."
He was always "triggering" one project or another and propagat-
ing shady ideas about "image-optionism" and crossover marketing. At first I thought, Okay, the media guru simply hasn't noticed
yet that this kind of new-economy talk is as out as a Flock of
Seagulls CD, but at least there is a president who lets people
think about culture. But during my second visit, I heard people
snore despite their open eyes and had to concede that Gorny
might be right. Maybe we really were just staging some kind of
puppet show to shine up a campaigning politician's image. This
seemed especially likely given the way Gabriel's press department insisted on trumpeting the circle of cultural advisors to the
media despite the fact that we all had only unofficial status.

He lost the election by a landslide and the Christian Democrat
Christian Wulff now reigns at the state chancellery. He is a man
whose cultural horizon can be staked out exactly on the "Day of
Lower Saxony" between pickles, oldies rock, and folk dance. It is
always the same in Germany, the country of thinkers and poets:
when cash runs short, cultural funding is cut first, even though
the amount per capita spent on culture is minute as compared to
other expenses. The government slashed the Hanover State Theatre's budget by two million euros, and Wulff's cultural killer
Lutz Stratmann didn't seem to understand that even in the
arts, you can't just cancel the show and pack everything in at a
moment's notice. There exist, after all, long-term contracts and
obligations that cannot be thrown to the wind as Stratmann
demanded. He seemed terribly surprised when throngs of angry
demonstrators occupied his offices for weeks. I participated in
the final protest meeting in front of the opera house. By then it

had become clear that Stratmann was being kept on a tight leash by the president and could not reverse the cuts.

"Even the least significant word sung in this house touches me more than some politician's speech," citizen Quasthoff called somewhat pathetically into the crowd. The dramatist Marius von Meyenburg described the Christian Democratic strategy more precisely:

"A cultural institution is put on the list of cuts, and at first people are upset, but already at the second mention of the institution the talk gets more quiet, and finally one hears a mere grumbling."

To top it off the aging Kraut-rocker Heinz Rudolf Kunze ("Warum bin ich nicht Grönemeyer," "Why Aren't I Grönemeyer"), of all people, has been hired to stage Shakespeare's *As You Like It* as a musical at the very moment the state has cut 220,000 euros from the Sprengel Museum's budget. The museum is one of the few institutions of Lower Saxony that is important outside the region as well, and my brother was in charge of its public affairs. He hates watching how the political spendthrifts gravitate towards the podium during the exhibition openings in order first to bore the audience with empty phrases and then to pose with the artists and director for the media.

The attitude towards culture in Lower Saxony is pretty well summed up in a farce that took place in 2001 revolving around an art investment of 800,000 deutsche marks. For this sum the traffic club (!) acquired eight bronze statues by the street decorator Seward Johnson—crude depictions of human mediocrity, completely without irony, they had already been lent to the EXPO 2000 and displayed outside the department store Karstadt. "Aesthetic bulk rubbish," as the Sprengel Museum director Ulrich Krempel remarked publicly, thereby triggering an angry debate among newspaper readers. Uneducated contemporaries consider the homunculi "art" that brings "joy to thousands of people," such as the CDU faction in the city council among others. The Christian Democrats even came up with the idea of incorporating the Johnson figures as "Fellow Humans" into the community.

The reason for their warmth was obvious. The townsmen felt recognized and—art or not—one thing was true: the sculptures were shockingly true to life. The mayor of Hanover at that time, Herbert Schmalstieg, was repeatedly observed trying to squeeze the Social Democrats' election pamphlet into the hand of one of our bronze "fellow humans."

"Die Welt ist arm, der Mensch ist schlecht / Da hab ich eben leider Recht" ("The world is poor, and man is bad. / In this unfortunately I am right"). Brecht said it first, and now Micha, dressed in Portugal's colors, moans it as he sits in front of the television and watches the soccer championship of Europe in disbelief as underdog Greece steals victory from the great Portugal forward Louis Figo.

But I cannot agree with this pessimistic assessment. Life could not be better. I respect Figo, but I love only the blond Claudia who sits next to me on the sofa nibbling on chips while I nibble at her earlobe and while daughter Lotte plays in the garden. I got my little family after all and am as happy as a clam with it. Claudia is editor at the MDR, living in Leipzig. She was ordered to assist the singer Quasthoff on the talk-show *Riverboat*. I was head over heels immediately and luckily it was mutual. We like the movies, are fanatical bookworms, and have a weakness for cooking, love to vacation by the sea, and in general fit like the proverbial Jack and his Jill. This was the woman of my life. Thankfully, my parents like her, too. It was clear that little Lotte would conquer their hearts by storm, but I wasn't so sure about Claudia since Father, in particular, thinks that my judgment about the female sex is rather dim. When they were introduced, though, his eye lingered with pleasure on my chosen one and suddenly he was an old school charmer offering Claudia and Lotte the place of honor at the golden wedding anniversary my parents celebrated in July, right behind the honored couple.

If I could take a snapshot of myself and my life right now, it would show a happy person riding an amazing professional wave. My voice works beautifully and the schedule is full until 2010.

I only pray that my parents will be around for a long time to enjoy the fact that I have mastered my life. I also want to stay healthy myself, in order to carry out all the musical projects that interest me, though I notice that due to my disability the first signs of age have already crept up in my body. Knock on wood, spit across the shoulder. I never again want to experience losing my voice in the middle of a concert with the Berlin Philharmonic. It happened, and I had to leave the stage. I spent two days in utter panic until a doctor told me that my vocal cords simply needed a little rest. When I apologized to Simon, who stood at the podium, he only shrugged: "There's no reason why, Tommy. Take it easy."

Simon says he has stopped getting worked up about things that cannot be changed, and that he has felt a lot better since then. How good to have a friend to offer support and wise counsel in such situations.

My friend Dietrich always maintains that "everybody is an island," a nice picture, but still I find that human existence is rather planetary in nature. Don't we all spin through a mute and dark nothingness from birth on? It doesn't matter whether with hot or cold surfaces, rings around the hips, or a few scarred moons in the crown. Every now and then another celestial body hits you and all hell breaks loose. When the frenzy is over one goes back to traveling alone across the circle of gravity around the sun, always searching for a little warmth, often wondering what it's all good

for. It is assuring then to know where one belongs, no small matter in our unsteady world. I have a beautiful house surrounded by
big walls. I have a pool and a sauna to trump each meteorological
mood of the universe, but to regulate the inner temperature one
needs to leave one's home every now and then to find those
places referred to as "pub" in English, "bar" in Italian, and *Gastwirtschaft*" in German.

Honored and patient reader, you've traveled far with me, and I
want to take you into my absolute favorite *Gastwirtschaft* as a
celebration of the hours we've spent together. You can find it in
the quadrant M8 on the map of Hanover, in an area that is notorious for its black holes hiding as hairdressing salons, nail and tan-
ning studios, lotto booths, and driving schools, the deepest one
being an Indian restaurant where cooks regularly disappear. Until
today there are eight Indians, three Vietnamese, and two Ghanese.
The latest man to cook the basmati rice was a Czech, and he, too,
has gone missing since last week.

In other words, one could not possibly bear the M8 quadrant if
at the corner of Lavesstrasse and Warmbüchenstrasse there was
not a gastronomical star called Father & Son, though father Guido
has by now fallen into a black hole himself, leaving son Aribert
with a liquor license, a cabbage field, and a potato plantation, as
well as several hundredweights of marinated meat, a shipload of
herring, and a snow-white apron. Aribert wears it with pride, just
like his manicured mustache. His motto is: "Please don't race us.
We are working here, not running a marathon." If one sticks to it,
beer flows like a steady river. If not—well, let's just say Aribert
gets less cozy, issuing bans on entering the locale. Anyone who
has ever witnessed one of his sudden meltdowns refuses to speak
of it except in a whisper. They say he explodes from the kitchen
like a supernova and turns the troublesome party into stardust.

"That will take a terrrrible end," predicts Hansen, who claims to have been present on one such occasion. The "r" grinds through his throat like a rusty pipe, which it probably is. Hansen, a cracked chap whose liver values are "Prractically not ascerrrtainable any longer," is the Uranus in this father-and-son system, so to speak, which is why the regular clientele has been expecting things to turn out terribly for years, but by the next morning he usually walks through the locale quoting Heine or the Stones. He is discreetly watched, that is, supported by Richie Krauskopf, his friendly counterpart. Richie is one of my best friends—round as a ball, he is married to the headwaitress Anne. Unfortunately, he is also an unlucky fellow whose way in the world could be characterized by the middle forward Jürgen "Cobra" Wegmann's quote: "First, we had no luck and then we had a bad break," which is why he often appears in bandages.

The regulars take the place's character in stride. Anne, the pub's heart and soul, makes sure of that. She is in charge of operations, managing weekly rounds, state politicians, sensitive actors, and other VIPs that sit down to Aribert's excellent menu—always with a steady, mild firmness. She also tops everyone off when midnight approaches, the blue hour, when the Father & Son reveals its real splendor and my social environment gravitates towards the bar. At the stroke of midnight figures like von Nedden appear, holding a sparkling beer in the light, and as if by magic the dramatic duo Gronius and Rauschenbach appear, with a baroque thirst and appetite, flaunting even more baroque stories from distant galaxies. After the *Fitz Oblong Show* the poet Gerhard Henschel peeks in, happily showing a picture of his family to anyone who is interested in a free beer while Mr. Foxx tries to pay off his drinking debts with copied artworks—in vain as usual. On very special nights one can hear Andy Hahn and Aribert sing recipes while the poet Felicitas Hoppe plays piano in a minor key. That is when critics from Berlin traveling through cry because they cannot find such beauty at home any longer. To console them Aribert offers up a round of vodka and all the women suddenly look like Sharon Stone. In such moments even I understand what Heisenberg was talking about when he spoke of the uncertainty principle, according to Lessing's motto: "Though one can drink too much, one drinks never enough."

Maybe we'll meet there sometime, or perhaps in your local concert hall. I look forward to it.

Until then!

CODA

Three years have passed since I wrote those last sentences for the German edition. What has happened since? I am pleased to share the latest update.

The most important change in my life is also a tax benefit: in June 2006, Claudia and I got married. Now I supply my sweet daughter Lotte with pocket money and her guinea pigs with fodder. We had a huge garden party at home—about one hundred relatives, friends, students, and colleagues gathered to celebrate my farewell to bachelorhood, a condition I haven't missed for a single second.

Not long after the big day, Claudia, little Lotte, the pigs, and I moved our lives to Berlin, where Professor Quasthoff teaches every day at the Hanns Eisler Academy, that is, when he is not on tour. I try to limit my appearances now, for I must make time for my family. Nevertheless, I am a concert singer by profession, and a professional cannot always say no. There are too many wonderful projects, too many fantastic colleagues with whom one has always wanted to work or would like to work again. My schedule simply refuses to lighten up and by now reaches into the year 2015, from New York to Los Angeles, Tokyo, Saint Petersburg, Stockholm, Amsterdam, Milan and London, and back. I have no choice but to take my two ladies with me as often as possible. We attended the festival in beautiful Lucerne, where I got to sing Schubert's orchestral lieder under the direction of Claudio Abbado in 2005 and Frank Martin's "Jedermann" monologues in 2006. We traveled to Verbier in French Switzerland, where Europe's most important classical festival takes place every year, attracting stars like Martha Argerich, Anna Netrebko, Lang Lang, Maxim Vengerov, James Levine, and Evgeny Kissin. My friend Martin Engström, the former director of Deutsche Grammophon, founded the Verbier Festival. In 1994 he had the brilliant idea of bringing this winter sport hot spot to life in the summer as well. The place offers everything a classical aficionado could dream of: a magnificent natural stage with a view of the ice walls of the Grand Combin Massif, exquisite Franco-Helvetian cuisine, and an atmosphere that is both cordial and sophisticated. Musicians are drawn to it like moths to a flame—myself included. I will forever remember a *Winterreise* I did with James Levine in 2004, as well as a jazz duo with the pianist Gabriel Kahane in 2006.

When I mentally conjure up the highlights of recent years I see concerts given with old, revered friends such as Simon Rattle, Seiji Ozawa, Helmuth Rilling, and Daniel Barenboim, rare occurrences in the fast-paced and overscheduled global climate of today's concert world. When Seiji asked me whether I would like to perform Britten's *War Requiem* with the Vienna Philharmonic Orchestra in May 2005, I obviously agreed right away, especially since Seiji was the conductor at the Wiener Staatsoper but also because I consider the *War Requiem* one of the most beautiful pieces of recent classical literature.

In 2006 the world celebrated not only my nuptials but the 250th anniversary of Mozart's birth. This brought me the pleasure of studying a few pieces for a Mozart tribute album, among them "Fuggi, crudele, fuggi!," Anna and Ottavio's duet from *Don Giovanni*. The soprano superstar Anna Netrebko was my partner; I had not met her before but can now say that she is even more beautiful in person than on TV and completely without affectation.

On top of that, in 2006 I received a third Grammy as well as the Amadeus Award and the BBC Music Award—all for my rendition of the Bach Cantatas with the Berlin Baroque Soloists. In the previous two years Deutsche Grammophon had issued *Die Schöne Müllerin*, an evening with my friend Justus Zeyen, and *The Voice*, a representative cross-section of my classic repertoire. But the most exciting CD project of my career was yet to come: *Watch What Happens.* Having always had a soft spot for blue notes, I had often dreamed of doing a jazz album, but it can be difficult for a classical singer to find a company willing to produce such a thing; it is hard for them to justify the risk of presenting a performer outside of his realm of established popularity. At least that was the conventional wisdom in the industry. The man who proved it wrong for me was Till Brönner, one of the world's best trumpeters and a wily fox of the business if ever there was one. In September 2004 I had met him in Munich at a gala benefit for the Alternative Nobel Prize (Right Livelihood Award), where Till played with his band and I appeared with the Berlin Philharmonic Jazz Group. After the event we sat down together with a glass of beer and knew right away that we liked each other.

"We'll go to [Deutsche] Grammophon," Till said, and so it happened.

It took a year, but finally Grammophon agreed, not least because the repertoire—taken largely from the Great American Songbook—had classic status, at least in the United States, as did the musicians assembled by Till. When I saw the lineup I got a little nervous. It read like the "Who's Who" of the Blue Note elite: Chuck Loeb (guitar), Alan Broadbent (piano), Dieter Ilg (bass), Peter Erskine (drums) with Till Brönner as producer and, of course, playing the trumpet. The whole gang had played with legends like Woody Herman, Stan Getz, and Joni Mitchell and were seasoned solo artists in their own right. It blew me away. Luckily for me, they turned out to be stellar human beings as well as stellar musicians.

The recording session began in September 2006 at the Bauer

Studios in Ludwigsburg, where Miles Davis had blown a few notes in his time. At the end we had twelve pieces in the can, among them Duke Ellington's "In My Solitude," Richard Rodgers's "My Funny Valentine," "There's a Boat Dat's Leavin' Soon for New York" and "They All Laughed" by George Gershwin, as well as Charlie Chaplin's "Smile" from *Modern Times*, "Can't We Be Friends?" by Jay Swift and Paul James, "I've Grown Accustomed to Her Face," from Alan Jay Lerner and Frederick Loewe's *My Fair Lady*, Sammy Fain's "Secret Love," and my favorite piece on this CD: "You and I" by Stevie Wonder.

The album was introduced in the States and Europe with a small tour. First stop, of all places: New York, the mecca of jazz, with its tradition-laden Carnegie Hall, where I still had a credit for a concert as "artist in residence." We rehearsed in the S.I.R. Studios at 520 West Twenty-fifth Street between Tenth and Eleventh avenues. I was as nervous as a horse before the races and was not calmed when the even more nervous Beyoncé crossed my path, or when Paul Simon heartily wished me "good luck." The next morning, before the concert, this review appeared in the *Wall Street Journal:* "The marvel is that Mr. Quasthoff's jazz singing is not just at the stylistic antipodes from his lieder singing but idiomatically so right. With impeccable timing and phrasing he insouciantly tosses off these songs, leaning into just the right notes of each phrase." I am eternally grateful to the author, Mr. Barrymore Laurence Scherer. It was a good omen, and indeed everything went wonderfully well. The concert reviews and the sales figures were both so good that Grammophon is already casting about for the next jazz album.

So, honorable reader, that's about it. Or, wait. I have one more story. It takes place in the fall of 2004 and illustrates the perils of having a big mouth: maybe it helps you sing wonderfully, but it can also accommodate a lot of foot. One morning around eleven, my phone rang. A sonorous voice on the other end said, "Good morning. This is Horst Köhler." It's a common enough name, so I let it roll across my tongue, wondering which Horst Köhler this could be. I remembered my last semester at law school—the voice on the phone must be the gawky, blond guy with whom I had, after each particularly soporific seminar about contract law, gone to the pub Distille to consume a second liquid breakfast. Pleasantly surprised—it had been a while since I had heard from him—I droned into the phone, "Man, Hotte, you old bum. Where have you been?"

The old bum answered, "This is Horst Köhler, the president of Germany."

The head of state wanted not to invite me for an antemeridian pint but to inform me that I was to receive the Federal Cross of Merit. Mr. Köhler did not hold my misunderstanding against me but laughed heartily. A year later he hung the large Cross of Merit around my neck.

—Thomas Quasthoff,
Berlin, June 2007

DISCOGRAPHY

A Portrait (Bach, Beethoven, Mozart, Schubert), Charles Spencer, BMG, October 2001

JOHANN SEBASTIAN BACH

Edition Bachakademie Vol. 66 (Weltliche Kantaten), Bach-Collegium Stuttgart, Helmuth Rilling, Hänssler, June 1999

Edition Bachakademie Vol. 67 (Weltliche Kantaten), Bach-Collegium Stuttgart, Helmuth Rilling, Hänssler, February 2000

Edition Bachakademie (Weltliche Kantaten), Bach-Collegium Stuttgart, Helmuth Rilling, Hänssler, November 1997

Edition Bachakademie (Weltliche Kantaten), Gächinger Kantorei Stuttgart, Helmuth Rilling, Hänssler, July 2001

Edition Bachakademie Vol. 73 (Magnificat, Lukas-Passion), Gächinger Kantorei Stuttgart, Helmuth Rilling, Hänssler, January 2000

Edition Bachakademie Vol. 74 (Matthäus-Passion), Gächinger Kantorei Stuttgart, Helmuth Rilling, Hänssler, June 1999

Jagd-/Kaffee-Kantate, Gächinger Kantorei Stuttgart, Bach-Collegium Stuttgart, Helmuth Rilling, Hänssler, May 1997

Johannes-Passion, Chorgemeinschaft Neubeuern, Bach-Collegium München, Enoch zu Guttenberg, BMG, January 1992

Kantaten, Windsbacher Knabenchor, Münchener Bach-Solisten, Karl-Friedrich Beringer, BR, January 1991

Lateinische Kirchenmusik 2, Messe in g-Moll, Messe in G-Dur, Sanctus C-Dur, Gächinger Kantorei Stuttgart, Helmuth Rilling, Hänssler, September 1999

Magnificat D-Dur, Gächinger Kantorei Stuttgart, Helmuth Rilling, Hänssler, January 1997

Matthäus-Passion, Bach-Collegium Stuttgart, Helmuth Rilling, Hänssler, January 1997

Matthäus-Passion, Tokyo Opera Singers, Saito Kinen Orchestra, Seiji Ozawa, Philips, February 1999

Messe, Gächinger Kantorei Stuttgart, Helmuth Rilling, Hänssler, October 1999

Messe in F-Dur und A-Dur, Gächinger Kantorei Stuttgart, Bach-Collegium Stuttgart, Helmuth Rilling, Hänssler, January 1997

Messe in F-Dur und A-Dur, Gächinger Kantorei Stuttgart, Helmuth Rilling, Hänssler, August 1999

Messe in g-Moll und G-Dur, Bach-Collegium Stuttgart, Stuttgarter Kammerorchester, Helmuth Rilling, Hänssler, January 1997

Messe in h-Moll, Windsbacher Knabenchor, Deutsche Kammerakademie Neuss, Karl-Friedrich Beringer, Hänssler, January 1997

Messe in h-Moll, Windsbacher Knabenchor, Deutsche Kammerakademie Neuss, Karl-Friedrich Beringer, Hänssler, October 1999

Messe in h-Moll, Windsbacher Knabenchor, Deutsche Kammerakademie Neuss, Karl-Friedrich Beringer, Rop, November 2003

Weihnachtsoratorium, Windsbacher Knabenchor, Karl-Friedrich Beringer, Teldec, October 1994

LUDWIG VON BEETHOVEN

Neunte Sinfonie, Eric Ericson Chamber Choir, Schwedischer Rundfunkchor, Berliner Philharmoniker, Claudio Abbado, Deutsche Grammophon, April 2002

JOHANNES BRAHMS, FRANZ LISZT

Lieder, Justus Zeyen, Deutsche Grammophon, February 2000

ANTONIO CASIMIR CARTELLIERI

Gioas, Bachchor Gütersloh, Detmolder Kammerorchester, Gernot Schmalfuss, Mdg, September 1997

ANTONIN DVORAK

Stabat Mater, Bach Festival Oregon Chor, Helmuth Rilling, Hänssler, January 1997

GEORG FRIEDRICH HÄNDEL

Der Messias, Oregon Bach Festival Chor und Orchester, Helmuth Rilling, Hänssler, December 1997

Der Messias, Oregon Bach Festival Chor und Orchester, Helmuth Rilling, Hänssler, April 2002

JOSEPH HAYDN
Orfeo und Euridice, Leopold Hager, Orfeo, May 1994

CARL LOEWE
Balladen, Norman Shetler, EMI, November 1989

GUSTAV MAHLER
Des Knaben Wunderhorn, Anne Sofie von Otter, Berliner Philharmoniker,
Claudio Abbado, Deutsche Grammophon, April 1999

WOLFGANG AMADEUS MOZART
Arien, Württembergisches Kammerorchester, Jorg Faerber, BMG, September
1997
Credo-Messe, Profil 2004
Krönungsmesse, Rundfunkchor Leipzig, Staatskapelle Dresden, Peter Schreier,
Philips, October 1993

KRZYSZTOF PENDERECKI
Credo, Oregon Bach Festival Chor und Orchester, Helmuth Rilling, Hänssler,
September 1998

THOMAS QUASTHOFF sings Händel & Bach, Helmuth Rilling, Hänssler, July
2002

ARIBERT REIMANN
Lieder, Christine Schäfer, Ursula Hesse, Claudia Barainsky, Axel Bauni, Orfeo,
March 1996

ROMANTISCHE LIEDER (Schubert, Wolf, Schumann, Strauß), Justus Zeyen,
Deutsche Grammophon, March 2004

ARNOLD SCHÖNBERG
Gurrelieder, Berliner Philharmoniker, Simon Rattle, EMI, April 2002

FRANZ SCHUBERT
Goethe-Lieder, Charles Spencer, BMG, March 1995
Schubert-Lieder, Anne Sofie von Otter, Chamber Orchestra of Europe, Claudio
Abbado, Deutsche Grammophon, April 2003
Schwanengesang; Johannes Brahms: Vier ernste Gesänge, mit Justus Zeyen,
Deutsche Grammophon, April 2001
Die Winterreise, Charles Spencer, BMG, October 1998

ROBERT SCHUMANN

Genoveva, Arnold-Schönberg-Chor, Cleveland Orchestra, Nikolaus Harnon-
court, Teldec, September 1997

Dichterliebe Liederkreis, Op. 39, mit Roberto Szidon, RCA, August 1993

DIE STIMME (Deutsche romantische Arien), Orchester der Deutschen Oper
Berlin, Christian Thielemann, Deutsche Grammophon, March 2002

JAZZ

"Watch What Happens": The Jazz Album, mit Till Brönner, Alan Broadbent,
Peter Erskine, Chuck Loeb, Dieter Ilg, Deutsche Grammophon, March
2007.

INDEX

Abbado, Claudio, 123–25, 127, 147, 152, 156, 219
Achternbusch, Herbert, 140
Ághová, Livia, 96
Aida (Verdi), 159
Albers, Hans, 48
Alexander, Peter, 46
Allen, Woody, 9
"Allerseelen" (Strauss), 107
Amadeus Award, 220–21
Angelripper, Tom, 77
Apocalypse Now, 111, 112
applause, 169–71
Arnim, Achim von, 25
Arnold Schönberg Choir, 132
Asakusa-Kannon temple, 174
Associated Press, 140
As You Like It (Shakespeare), 213
Attig, Jürgen, 110
Augsburger Puppenkiste, 208
"Au Privave," 84
autism, 55, 56
Ave Maria (Gounod), 74, 79
Avery Fisher Hall, 8, 14, 15–16, 32, 35

Bach, Johann Sebastian, 74, 120, 121, 122, 127, 170–71, 193, 220–21
Bach, Mechthild, 97
Bangemann, Martin, 38–39
Banse, Juliane, 130, 148, 169
barbiturates, 38–39

Barenboim, Daniel, 152, 159, 220
Bartók, Bela, 187
Bashmet, Yuri, 186–88, 191
Bauer Studios, 221–22
Baumgart, Renate, 6, 8, 10–12, 30, 31, 35, 168–69, 189, 200
Bayreuth Festival, 134
BBC Music Award, 220–21
Beethoven, Ludwig van, 46, 102, 125, 127, 128, 129–33, 155, 192–93
Bergen-Belsen concentration camp, 193
Berger, Senta, 153–54
Beringer, Karl-Friedrich, 193
Berlin Baroque Soloists, 221
Berliner Festwochen, 124
Berliner Philharmonisches Orchester, 124–27, 130, 147, 201, 206, 215
Berliner Tagesspiegel, 132–33, 207
Berlin Philharmonic Jazz Group, 221
Berlioz, Hector, 18, 21, 22
Bernstein, Leonard, 14, 164, 165
Bernstein, Steven, 35
Bernwards Hospital, 35
Bertelsmann, Fred, 40
Bert Kaempfert Orchestra, 46, 67
Between Hamburg and Tahiti, 40
Bialas, Günter, 198
Bible, 157, 161
Biolek, Alfred, 204–6, 207
Birdland, 35, 108, 109
Bläsig, 55, 59–60

blues music, 66, 67, 181
BMG, 103, 155, 156
Bocelli, Andrea, 154, 207
Bohème, La (Puccini), 73
Böhme, Kurt, 46
Bolt, Robert, 208
Born, Nicolas, 144–45
Borosc, André, 182, 184
Boser, Volker, 132
Bostridge, Ian, 126
Botha, Johan, 133, 135, 140
Boulevard Bio, 204–6
Brahms, Johannes, 30, 85, 116, 118,
    121, 125, 149, 155, 157, 158,
    196–97, 206
brain damage, 39
Brauhaus School, 59–62
breathing exercises, 81–84, 122
Brecht, Bertolt, 79, 94, 160, 214
Brentano, Clemens, 25
Britten, Benjamin, 182–83, 220
Broadbent, Alan, 221
Broadcast Hall, 95–96
Brönner, Till, 221
Bruckner, Anton, 126
Büning, Eleanore, 140
Bunte, 97–98
Buñuel, Luis, 33

Callas, Maria, 202
Canetti, Elias, 23
Carnegie Hall, 35, 124–25, 222
Carreras, José, 152, 154–55
CBS, 10
Chamber Orchestra of Europe, 124
Children of Chernobyl, 211
Christian Democrats, 112–13, 214
clarinets, 83–84
classical music, 20–21, 143, 154–55,
    189, 191–92, 221

Clinton, Bill, 149 50
Clinton, Hillary, 149
Cocker, Joe, 154
Cole, Nat King, 163–64
Coltrane, John, 83–84, 108
Concierto de Aranjuez (Rodrigo), 107
Conradi, Hubertus, 114
Contergan, 38–39, 42
Coppola, Francis Ford, 111, 112
Crater Lake, 167–68
Crayfish, 177
Credo (Penderecki), 122–23
Cumella, Charles, 13, 29

Dam-Jensen, Inger, 22, 23, 24, 28, 29
Dannen, Fanny van, 64
Davis, Colin, 18, 21–22, 23, 25, 28,
    29, 30, 32, 110, 129
Davis, Miles, 107–8, 222
Debussy, Claude, 169
Decsey, Ernst, 27
"deep panting" exercise, 82–84
Denoke, Angela, 130, 133, 140
Detmold Music Academy, 117–19,
    195–201, 203
Deutsche Grammophon, 155–56,
    159, 206, 221, 222
Deutsches Requiem, Ein (Brahms),
    121
Dichterliebe (Schumann), 115, 155,
    156
Dietl, Helmut, 204
Doldinger, Klaus, 191
Domin, Hilde, 189–90
Domingo, Plácido, 152, 154–55
Don Giovanni (Mozart), 8, 24–25,
    220
Donizetti, Gaetano, 80
Dorn, Thea, 211
Down syndrome, 55

Dregger, Alfred, 38–39
"Drei Chinesen mit dem Kontrabass," 71
Dylan, Bob, 208

Echo Classic Award, 33, 148, 153
Einstein, Albert, 112
Eisenhower, Dwight D., 14
Elektra (Strauss), 206
Elijah (Mendelssohn), 91, 121
Elmau Castle, 188–89
Else, Grandma, 40, 49, 50, 72–73, 75–76
Ely Cathedral, 127
EMI, 147, 155
Engström, Martin, 220
Entsorgt (Reimann), 144–45
epilepsy, 55, 56
Erhard, Ludwig, 59–60
"Erlkönig" (Goethe), 106
"Erlkönig" (Schubert), 85, 206
Erskine, Peter, 221
Eva (girlfriend), 179, 198, 204, 205–6
Evans, Gil, 107
Everding, August, 137
EXPO (1992), 177–81

Father & Son, 216–18
Federal Cross of Merit, 222–23
Festival Hall (Salzburg), 128, 129–33
fetal deformations, 37–39
Fidelio (Beethoven), 128, 129–33
Fink, Walter, 138
Fischer-Dieskau, Dietrich, 102, 108
Fitz Oblong Show, 208–11, 217
"Five Rückert Songs" (Mahler), 125
Fontana, D. J., 180
"Forelle, Die" (Schubert), 116, 157–58

Frankenfeld, Peter, 6, 49
Frankfurter Allgemeine Zeitung, 63, 116, 140, 192–93
Franz Schubert und seine Lieder (Fischer-Dieskau), 102
Frec-Frec, 177, 179
Freiburg Symphony Orchestra, 24
Fried, Amelie, 207
Friedrich, Caspar David, 104
Froboess, Conny, 46
"Frühlingstraum" (Schubert), 142
"Fuggi, crudele, fuggi!" (Mozart), 220
"Furtiva Lagrima, Una" (Donizetti), 80

G8 meeting (1999), 148–50
Gabriel, Sigmar, 211, 212
German language, 82, 118
Gershwin, George, 164, 222
Gertz, Achim, 93–94
Gitte, 79
Glocke, Die (Schiller), 6
Glotz, Peter, 189
Goerne, Matthias, 122, 156
Goethe, Johann Wolfgang von, 4, 20, 59, 81, 99, 106, 155
Golden Camera, 148, 150–53
Golden Gate Quartet, 72
Gorny, Dieter, 211, 212
gospel music, 73, 164
"Gott, sei mir gnädig" (Mendelssohn), 96
Gounod, Charles, 74, 79
Grabbe, Christian Dietrich, 197
Graf, Heinz Otto, 77–78
Grammy Awards, 4, 5, 6, 124, 133, 147, 148, 220–21
Grass, Günter, 22–23
Greindl, Josef, 46

Gronius, Jörg, 210–11
Gross, Oliver, 110
Grünbein, Durs, 210
Grünenthal, 38–39
Gurrelieder (Schönberg), 206
Gymnasium Andreanum, 62–64, 67,
    85–86, 109

Haack, Sabine, 177, 178, 179
Habermas, Jürgen, 59
Hager, Leopold, 145
Hahn, Andy, 111–13, 200, 217
Hamburg Music Hall, 33, 153
Händel, George Frideric, 120–21
Hannover Jazz Club, 84
Hanns Eisler Academy, 200–201, 219
Hanover Music Academy, 3, 87–88,
    143–44, 179
Hanover State Theatre, 212–13
Hänssler Publishing House, 155
Harder, Michael, 208
Hauberg, Professor, 39, 45
Haug, Thomas, 177
Haydn, Joseph, 75, 125–26, 145
Heckmair, Anderl, 12
Heidenröslein (Schubert), 52,
    157–58
Heine, Heinrich, 197, 217
Heintje, 76–77, 78
Heisenberg, Werner, 218
Held, Alan, 131
Helfgott, David, 154
Henschel, Gerhard, 217
Herbert, Uncle, 42–43, 73, 77
Hercules Hall, 96–97, 98, 101
Hermannsschlacht (Grabbe), 197
Hesse, Hermann, 65
Hessian Broadcasting Corporation,
    51
Heye, Sabine, 149, 200

Heye, Uwe Carsten, 149, 178, 200
Hippetuk, 87
Hoffmann, E. T. A., 102
Hofmann, Peter, 154
Holender, Ioan, 133, 137
Holocaust, 189, 192–93
Hoppe, Felicitas, 200, 217
Hörzu, 150–53
Hotel Rose, 97
Hotter, Hans, 46, 108, 156–57
"Hound Dog," 180–81
Howell, Peg Leg, 66, 67
Huber-Contwig, Ernst, 80, 90, 140,
    143–45
Hüsch, Hanns Dieter, 113

"Ich Liebe Nur Dich Allein"
    (Puccini), 73
"Ich will 'nen Cowboy als Mann,"
    79
Ilg, Dieter, 221
"Im Frühtau zu Berge," 71–72
International Bach Academy,
    119–21, 145
"In the Ghetto," 181
Italienisches Liederbuch (Wolf),
    166, 191

Jabs, Matthias, 181
Jacobi, Professor, 88, 143–44
Jacobsen, Antonia, 177
jam sessions, 93–94, 109–10
Janis, Byron, 182
jazz, 35, 84–85, 87, 90, 93–94, 105,
    108–11, 162–69, 189, 191–92,
    220, 221–22
"Jazz Time," 110
"Jedermann" (Martin), 219
Jephtha (Handel), 121

João, Maria, 182
Johann, Archbishop, 77
Johannes Passion (Bach), 127
Johnson, Robert, 67
Johnson, Seward, 213–14
Joshua (Handel), 120–21
Joyce, James, 100
Juilliard Chorus, 14
"Junge, Komm Bald Wieder," 40

Kabuki theater, 171
Kaempfert, Bert, 46, 67
Kafka, Franz, 30, 112
*Kafka or Tibor (Apoelyps Now—a
    M(H)ystery Play in Two Half
    Times)*, 111–13
Kahane, Gabriel, 220
Kahane, Jeffrey, 162–66
Kähne, Ecki, 177
Kaiser, Joachim, 98, 140, 141, 142
Kant, Immanuel, 31
Karajan, Herbert von, 126, 201
karaoke, 174
"Karma," 109
Kaschnitz, Marie Luise, 190
Kennedy, John F., 124
Kern, Jerome, 74, 164
King Lear overture (Berlioz), 21, 22
Kinski, Klaus, 161
Kissin, Evgeny, 185–86, 220
*Kleine dicke Ritter Oblong-Fitz-
    Oblong, Der* (Bolt), 208
Klemperer, Otto, 127
Klu Klux Klan, 161–62
Klüwer, Heinz, 40
Knaben Wunderhorn, Des (Mahler),
    7–8, 12, 21–29, 124, 147, 156
Knitting Factory, 35
Kohl, Helmut, 113, 177
Köhler, Horst, 222–23

Kölner Stadtanzeiger, 132
Krauskopf, Richie, 217
Kremer, Gidon, 160
Krempel, Ulrich, 211, 213
Kronstein-Uhrmacher, Hilde,
    195–98
Krönungsmesse (Mozart), 145
Kuhlenbeck, Thomas, 177
Kunz, Ursula, 96
Kunze, Heinz Rudolf, 213

"Lachende Vagabund, Der," 40
Lake of Gennesaret, 193
Landgren, Nils, 191
La Scala, 123
Lehmann, Charlotte, 80–85, 86, 87,
    88, 90 92, 93, 95, 96, 101,
    110–11, 119, 144, 160
Lehnhoff, Nikolaus, 129, 130, 132
Leine Domizil, 93
Lessing, Gotthold Ephraim, 218
Levine, James, 220
"Lied des Verfolgten im Turm"
    (Mahler), 24–25
Liederabend, 32
Liederkreis (Schumann), 155
Lieschen, Grandma, 40, 48, 50,
    72–73, 81
Lincoln Center, 14, 101
"Lindenbaum, Der" (Schubert), 99,
    100, 101
"Literanover," 111–13
Live at the Village Vanguard, 83–84
Lockenhaus Festival, 160
Loeb, Chuck, 221
Loewe, Carl, 46, 91, 106–7, 155, 157
Lolita, 36
Lorenzo, Giovanni di, 207
Loriot, 189
Lortzing, Albert, 51

Los Angeles Times, 167
Louis Armstrong Memorial, 108
Low, Bruce, 46
"Low Down Rounder Blues," 67
Lower Saxony, 160, 175–81,
    211–14
Ludwig II, King of Bavaria, 133, 189
Luxemburger Wort, 116

"Mache dich, mein Herze, rein"
    (Bach), 96
"Machen Wur Die Beine von
    Dolores, Das," 46
"Mackie Messer-Song" (Brecht), 79
Maffay, Peter, 115
Magic Flute, The (Mozart), 156
Mahler, Gustav, 7–8, 12, 15, 21–29,
    124, 125, 126, 147, 156, 206
Mahlke, Sybille, 132–33
Malmquist, Siv, 37
"Mama," 77
Mancini, Henry, 164
"Man müsste nochmal zwanzig sein
    und so verliebt wie damals"
    (Schneider), 76
Mann, Thomas, 101, 134
Marder, Linda, 13–14, 29, 32, 147
"Marmor, Stein und Eisen bricht,"
    77
Martin, Dean, 202
Martin, Frank, 21, 22, 219
Matthäus-Passion (Bach), 96, 121,
    122, 170–71, 193
Mauthausen concentration camp,
    192–93
Meine, Klaus, 180
Meistersinger, Die (Wagner), 134,
    159
Mendelssohn, Felix, 96, 121
Mermoz cruise tour, 18–19, 181–86

Metropolitan Opera, 14, 161–62
Metternich, Josef, 46
Meyenburg, Marius von, 213
Meysel, Inge, 153
Michaelis Choir, 64
Mielitz, Christine, 133, 135,
    136–37, 138
Miles Ahead, 107
Mintz, Shlomo, 186
Monteverdi, Claudio, 19
Moore, Scotty, 180–81
Morini, Erika, 159
Mozart, Wolfgang Amadeus, 8, 18,
    24–25, 75, 80, 93, 145, 156,
    169, 220
"Müde bin ich, geh zur Ruh," 76
Müller (nurse), 56–58, 59
Müller, Heiner, 31
Müller, Johannes, 188–89
Müller, Peter, 95–96, 97, 98, 114–15,
    120–21, 160, 175–77, 206
Müller, Wilhelm, 99–101
Münchner Abendzeitung, 96, 98
Music der Romantik (Rosen), 102
musicology, 101–2
Mussorgsky, Modest, 96

Nadja (girlfriend), 199–200
"Naima," 83–84
Narcissus and Goldmund (Hesse),
    65
Naumann, Michael, 211
Nazism, 59, 134, 192–93
NDR, 40, 49, 77, 78, 93–95, 110
NDR Hörfest, 110
Nedden, Dietrich zur, 4–6, 208–9,
    215, 217
Neddermayer, Ms., 55–56
Netrebko, Anna, 220
Neville, Aaron, 164

New Testament, 161
New York Philharmonic, 7, 11, 13,
    20, 21, 24, 28
New York Times, The, 10
Nida-Rümelin, Julian, 152–53
"Nock" (Loewe), 85, 157
Nonsens, Reno, 51–52
Noriko, Miss (press agent), 171–72
Norman, Jessye, 97, 160
"Nussbaum" (Schumann), 118

"Ode an die Freude" chorus
    (Beethoven), 192
Oelze, Christiane, 126
"Oh, sancta justitia. Ich möchte
    rasen" (Lortzing), 51
Old Testament, 157
"Ol' Man River," 74, 164
"One for My Baby (and One More
    for the Road)," 162, 166
Onkel Pö, 109–10
opera, 21, 156–57, 161–62, 212–13
Oregon Bach Festival, 122–23,
    162–69, 182, 188
Orpheus and Eurydice (Haydn), 145
Orth, Uli, 180
Osterfestspiele (Salzburg), 129–33
Otello (Verdi), 161–62
Otter, Anne Sofie von, 124, 147
Ozawa, Seiji, 34, 220

Pachinko halls, 174
Paris Bar, 153
Park, Kyung-Shin, 96
Parker, Charlie, 84, 108
Parsifal (Wagner), 133–40
Pastorius, Jaco, 110
Pavarotti, Luciano, 154–55, 201
Pavlov, Ivan, 43–45

Peine District Hospital, 87
Penderecki, Krysztof, 122–23
Pergamenschikov, Boris, 182
Perzi, Niklas, 192
Peschko, Sebastian, 78–80
Petersburg Ensemble, 187–88, 191
Petite Symphonie Concertante
    (Martin), 21, 22
Petz, Katharina, 196
pharmaceuticals industry, 38–39
phocomelia, 39
Piano Concerto No. 1 (Brahms), 125,
    197
Piano Concerto No. 3
    (Rachmaninoff), 154
Poems from the Posthumously Left
    Papers of a Travelling French
    Horn Player (Müller), 99–101
Polgar, Laszlo, 131
pop music, 105, 162–69
Prefontaine Classic, 168
Presley, Elvis, 180–81, 201
Prey, Hermann, 78, 102–3, 108
"Prinz Eugen" (Loewe), 91, 157
Puccini, Giacomo, 73

Quadflieg, Will, 140–41
Quasthoff, Brigitte Fellberg, 5, 33,
    35, 36–37, 41–54, 58, 59, 60,
    66–67, 68, 71–72, 76–77, 79,
    83, 85, 87, 88, 89–91, 97, 109,
    135–36, 144–45, 150, 153,
    189, 191, 198, 200, 205, 215
Quasthoff, Claudia, 214–15, 219
Quasthoff, Häns, 5, 33–34, 37,
    41–54, 58, 62, 66–67, 68, 69,
    70–72, 77–79, 80, 83, 85, 86,
    87–91, 108, 109, 135, 144–45,
    150, 153, 189, 191, 198, 200,
    205, 214–15

Quasthoff, Lotte, 214, 215, 219
Quasthoff, Michael "Micha," 3–6, 8,
  12–13, 15, 28, 29, 33–34, 37,
  43, 46, 52, 53, 58, 60, 61,
  64–65, 66, 71–72, 77, 82–86,
  88, 89, 108–9, 111–14,
  135–36, 152, 163–64, 165,
  172–73, 177–81, 189, 198,
  200, 205, 208–11
Quasthoff, Thomas:
  accompanists of, 95–96, 97, 98,
    114–17, 120–21, 157, 158–60,
    175–77, 183, 195, 221
  Amadeus Award received by,
    220–21
  amateur recitals of, 74–78
  American Songbook concert of,
    162–69
  in ARD Competition (1988), 6,
    94–98, 121, 141, 143, 189,
    196, 204
  in Arnum, 80–82
  audiences as viewed by, 20–21,
    24–25, 75–76, 115–17,
    161–62, 169–71
  auditions by, 77–80, 88–89,
    120–21
  awards received by, 4, 5, 6, 33,
    92–98, 121, 124, 141, 143, 147,
    148, 150–53, 189, 196, 220–23
  bank apprenticeship of, 93, 94
  in Barcelona, 177–81
  as bass-baritone, 7–8, 92, 102–3,
    125–26, 184
  in Bavaria, 77, 188–91
  BBC Music Award received by,
    220–21
  in Berlin, 200–201, 219
  birth of, 35
  as BMG recording artist, 103,
    155, 156

Bodenau premiere of, 90–91
body cast worn by, 3–4, 6, 39,
  41–42, 45–46
in Braunschweig, 91–92
breathing exercises of, 81–84
in Buenos Aires, 122, 170
cabaret act of, 113–15
on Cape Cod, 5, 34
career of, 3–6, 10–11, 32–33, 121,
  200, 215, 218, 219–20
childhood of, 36–69
competitions entered by, 6,
  92–98, 121, 141, 143, 189,
  196, 204
concert tours of, 11, 32–35,
  103–4, 155, 169–83, 199, 200,
  215, 219–20
conductors known by, 119–28,
  see also specific conductors
contracts of, 110, 182
critical reviews of, 9, 32–33,
  96–98, 101, 116, 132–33, 137,
  138–44, 169, 177, 222
on cruise tours, 18–19, 181–86
at Detmold Music Academy,
  117–19, 195–201, 203
as Deutsche Grammophon
  recording artist, 155–56, 159,
  206, 221, 222
discography of, 225–28
discrimination experienced by,
  54–69, 79, 84–85, 92–93, 199,
  203–4, 207
early performances of, 16–17, 84,
  90–92, 101, 110–11, 160
Echo Classic Award received by
  (1998), 33, 148, 153
education of, 3, 53–64, 67, 85–90,
  207
elevators as difficulty for, 11, 22,
  176–77

at Elmau Castle, 188–91
in England, 127–28
in Eugene, Ore., 122–23, 162–69,
   182, 188
fame of, 3, 10, 29–30, 147–55,
   201–8, 222–23
Federal Cross of Merit awarded
   to, 222–23
financial situation of, 93, 110
girlfriends of, 179, 198, 199–200,
   204, 205–6, 214–15, 219
Golden Camera awarded to, 148,
   150–53
Grammy Awards received by, 4,
   5, 6, 124, 133, 147, 148,
   220–21
in Hamburg, 109–10
at Hanns Eisler Academy,
   200–201, 219
in Hanover, 3–6, 37–38, 54–60,
   78–80, 88–90, 111–13,
   146–47, 163, 200–201, 216–18
health of, 92, 103, 115–16,
   120–21, 172–76, 215
height of, 16–17
as Hildesheim native, 35, 41,
   46–47, 53–54 58, 62–63, 64,
   67–68, 84, 87, 93, 110, 161
illnesses of, 37–38
interviews of, 133, 148, 204–8
in Israel, 193–94
in Japan, 170–75
as jazz singer, 110–11, 220,
   221–22
legal studies of, 88–90, 111, 223
as lieder singer, 21–29, 32–33,
   84–85, 98, 99–108, 115–17,
   118, 142, 145, 155, 156–60,
   169, 195, 196, 206, 222
in Lugano, 144–45
in Luxembourg, 115–16

in Madrid, 175–77
management of, 13–14, 110, 143,
   145–47, 171–72, 182, 203
in Marrakech, 185
at Mauthausen concert (2000),
   192–93
media coverage of, 9, 32–33,
   50–53, 96–98, 101, 116,
   132–33, 137, 138–44, 148,
   169, 177, 192–93, 204–8, 222
in Munich, 94–98
musical talent of, 64, 74–85, 86,
   87–88, 90, 92, 93, 95, 96, 101,
   105–6, 110–11, 119, 144, 160,
   215
music industry as viewed by, 6,
   13, 140–41, 143, 145–47,
   150–56, 201–2, 207
as music teacher, 117–19, 122,
   195–201, 203
in New York City, 5, 7–35, 101,
   124–25, 222
as opera singer, 6, 24–25, 127–40,
   159, 165
orthopedic rehabilitation for,
   37–38
in Passau, 203–4
personality of, 15, 67–69, 85–86,
   89–90, 175–77, 215–16
physical disabilities of, 3–4, 6, 9,
   11, 12, 13, 15–16, 22, 37–46,
   53–69, 75, 77–78, 79, 84–88,
   92–93, 97–98, 133, 136–37,
   143, 147–48, 176–77, 199,
   203–8, 215
podium used by, 16–17
popular standards recorded by,
   162–69
prosthesis used by, 42–46, 79
pub performances of, 84, 87, 90,
   93–94, 109–15

Quasthoff, Thomas (*continued*)
  recordings of, 107, 124, 155,
    158–59, 220–21, 225–28
  rehearsals by, 22, 95, 127–40,
    144–45, 175–76
  at Saint Anne's Home, 6, 37–38,
    54–60, 70, 75
  in St. Petersburg, 169–70,
    187
  in Salzburg, 128, 129–33
  in Santiago de Compostela,
    121–22
  in school choir, 64, 85–86
  singing teachers of, 69, 77–85,
    86, 87–88, 90, 110–11, 119,
    122, 143–45
  social life of, 13–14, 29–31,
    64–67, 69, 170–76, 200–201,
    216–18
  stage performance by, 9, 10–14,
    16–17, 79, 90–92, 95–96, 97,
    115–17, 125–26, 129–35,
    147–48, 175–76
  tape recordings of, 70–74
  television appearances of,
    150–53, 204–8
  as thalidomide victim, 3, 35,
    36–69, 54–55, 56, 68, 87–88,
    97–98, 204–8
  at Verbier Festival (2006),
    219–20
  in Vienna, 128, 129–40,
    170
  vocal technique, 7–8, 9, 12, 22,
    81–84, 92, 102–7, 115,
    125–26, 175–76, 184
  Walter Kaminski Memorial Prize
    awarded to, 92–93
Quinichette, Paul "Lady Q,"
  108
Quinn, Freddy, 40

Raab, Karl, 127
Rachmaninoff, Sergey, 154
Radio Bremen, 206–8
Ramsey, Bill, 79
Rarebell, Herman, 181
Rattle, Simon, 123, 125–28, 129,
    130, 132, 133, 134, 192, 201,
    206, 215, 220
Raucheisen, Michael, 159
Rauschenbach, Bernd, 210–11
Real Filharmonia, 121
rectal stenosis, 39
Redel, Martin, 199
Reimann, Aribert, 144–45
"Revelge" (Mahler), 27
Richard Wagner Foundation,
  160
Rieu, André, 154, 207
Rilling, Helmuth, 11, 119–23, 155,
    163, 167, 170, 220
rock music, 77, 90, 177–81,
    201
Rodrigo, Joaquín, 107
Rohde, Achim, 189
Romantic period, 30, 85, 99–108,
    120, 206
Romantische Lieder, 107
Rosen, Charles, 102
Rosenkavalier, Der (Strauss),
  157
Rossini (Dietl), 204
Rost, Andrea, 182
Rostropovich, Mstislav, 18,
    182–84
Rothko, Mark, 35
Rotten, Johnny, 87
Rubens, Sybilla, 166, 191
Rückert, Friedrich, 8, 99
Rudzinski, Martin, 96
Runnicles, Donald, 136, 137,
    138

Saint Ann's Home, 6, 37–38, 54–60, 70, 75
Saltzman, Royce, 163, 164, 166, 167
Salzburger Festspiele, 129, 163
Sanders, Pharoah, 83–84, 109
"Sapphische Ode" (Brahms), 157–58
Sartre, Jean-Paul, 86, 119
saxophones, 84, 107, 109, 191
Schenk, Heinz, 51–52
Schenker, Rudolf, 181
Scherer, Barrymore Laurence, 222
Schiller, Friedrich von, 6, 20, 192
Schmalstieg, Herbert, 214
Schmid, Cornelia, 146–47
Schmidt, Andreas, 156
Schmiedeskamp, Katja, 177
Schneiderath, Grandpa, 83–84
Schock, Rudolf, 51–53
Scholl, Hans-Otto, 38–39
Scholz, Mr., 59–60
Schönberg, Arnold, 19, 30, 134, 206
Schöne Müllerin, Die (Schubert), 99–100, 221
Schopenhauer, Arthur, 135, 138
Schöpfung, Die (Haydn), 125–26
Schreier, Peter, 108, 145
Schröder, Gerhard, 35, 149, 150, 177, 178, 181, 211
Schubert, Franz, 30, 52, 85, 96, 98, 99–104 106–107, 116, 140, 142, 155, 157–59, 206, 219, 221
Schumann, Clara, 118, 196
Schumann, Robert, 85, 115, 118, 155, 156
Schütterle, Erwin, 97
Schwanengesang (Schubert), 158–59
Scorpions, 177–81
"seal extremities," 39
Seasons, The (Haydn), 126
"Sentry's Nightsong, The," 20

September 11 attacks (2001), 124–25
Sex Mob Featuring John Medeski, 35
Shakespeare, William, 213
Shalit, Tony, 6, 17–20, 28–29, 30, 129–30, 134, 136
Shetler, Norman, 155, 160
Shine, 154
Sibelius, Jean, 18
Siebold, Agathe von, 196–97
Sievers, Markus, 29
Sinatra, Frank, 162, 163, 164
Sine Loco et Anno (Gronius and Rauschenbach), 211
Sinnen, Hella von, 153
S.I.R. Studios, 222
60 Minutes, 208
Sketches of Spain, 107
Slezak, Leo, 161–62
Smeja, Marc, 182
Social Democrats, 38, 150, 189
"Sommer der Liebe," 113–14
"Spanish Eyes," 46
Spaun, Joseph von, 99
Spencer, Charles, 101, 103, 159, 160, 183, 203
Spivakov, Vladimir, 18, 169–70, 182
Spontanmukkens, 93–94
Sprengel Museum, 111–13, 211, 213
Steinmetz, John and Kazi, 166, 169
Stern, Isaac, 125
Stimme, Die, 208, 221
Stipe, Michael, 161
Strange Tune Pictures, 109
Stratmann, Lutz, 212–13
Strauss, Johann, 46–47
Strauss, Richard, 107, 157, 206
String Sextet in G-Major (Brahms), 197

Süddeutsche Zeitung, 15, 96–97, 98,
    132, 141, 207
Svensson, Esbjörn, 191
Swenson, Robert, 96
"Swing Low, Sweet Chariot," 72,
    73, 142, 164
Symphony No. 3 ("Eroica")
    (Beethoven), 125, 155
Symphony No. 8 (Mahler), 206
Symphony No. 9 ("Choral")
    (Beethoven), 127, 192–93
Symphony Orchestra of the
    Bavarian Broadcasting Corp.,
    129
Szidon, Roberto, 155

Tannhäuser (Wagner), 19
Tavern on the Green, 30–31
Taylor, James, 164–65
Taylor, Jimmy, 172–73
Teatro Colón, 122, 170
"ten-minute smile," 13, 29
tenors, 102, 154–55
Terfel, Bryn, 159
thalidomide, 3, 35, 36–69, 54–55,
    56, 68, 87–88, 97–98, 204–8
Theater am Aegi, 195
Thielemann, Christian, 134, 159
Thomas, Ross, 11
"Three Tenors," 154–55
"Tiroler sind lustig, die Tiroler sind
    froh, Die," 76
Todd, Rick, 165–66, 167, 169
Toi, Toi, Toi, 49–51
Tommasini, Anthony, 10, 32
Toscanini, Arturo, 201
Traber, Habakuk, 27
Trost, Rainer, 130
trumpets, 107
tz, 98

Über Religion und Kunst (Wagner),
    134
Union of German Musical
    Educators and Concert
    Artists, 92–93
"Unter Blüten des Mais spielt' ich
    mit ihrer Hand" (Brahms),
    197
Ustinov, Peter, 150, 152

Valentin, Karl, 75, 104, 113
Vanessa-Mae, 154
Verbier Festival, 219–20
Verdi, Giuseppe, 46, 135, 142, 159,
    161–62, 181–82
Vienna Philharmonic, 192–93,
    220
Vienna State Opera, 133–40, 220
Vier ernste Gesänge (Brahms), 116,
    118, 149, 157
Villars, Jon, 130
violas, 186–88, 194
Violin Concerto in C (Bartók),
    187
violins, 159, 169, 187
Vishnevskaya, Galina, 18, 182–83,
    184

Wagner, Richard, 30, 92, 133–40,
    154, 158, 159, 160
Wagner, Wolfgang, 134
Waldersee, Countess, 188
Walküre, Die (Wagner), 92
Wall Street Journal, 222
Walter Kaminski Memorial Prize,
    92–93
"Wandering Star," 46
War Requiem (Britten), 182–83,
    220

Watch What Happens, 221–22
Weather Report, 110
Wegmann, Jürgen "Cobra," 217
Welt, 132
Werner, Ilse, 48
Westerwelle, Guido, 201
West Side Story (Bernstein), 164,
    165
Wiener Kurier, 133, 139–40
Wilde, Oscar, 70
Willemsen, Roger, 153–54
Williams, Tony, 110
"Wind of Change," 178
Windsbach Boys Choir, 193
Winterreise (Schubert), 98, 99–104,
    155, 182, 220
"Wo die schoenen Trompeten
    blasen" (Mahler), 26–27
Wöhr, Lia, 51–52
Wolf, Hugo, 85, 102, 118, 122, 166,
    191

Woolf, Virginia, 191
Wulff, Christian, 212

Young, Lester, 108

Zar und Zimmermann (Lortzing),
    51
Zawinul, Joe, 192
Zeyen, Justus "Jussi," 115–17, 157,
    158–60, 168, 169, 175, 185,
    191, 195, 208, 221
Zigeunerbaron (Strauss), 46–47
Zombie Club, 17
"Zukerpuppe aus der
    Bauchtanztruppe, Die," 79
Zum Blauen Bock, 51
Zurich Opera, 196
Zur Nedden, Dietrich, 4–6
"Zur Ruh, zur Ruh" (Wolf), 122

ABOUT THE AUTHOR

THOMAS QUASTHOFF was born in 1959 in Hildesheim, Germany. In 1988 he won first prize at the prestigious ARD International Music Competition in Munich, which launched his career. He has performed with the world's most distinguished orchestras and conductors (including Claudio Abbado and Simon Rattle). He has won three Grammy Awards: for Best Classical Vocal Performance in 2000, for his Bach cantatas and Schubert lieder in 2004, and for Best Choral Performance in 2008 for Brahms's *Ein Deutsches Requiem*. Quasthoff is a professor at the Hans Eisler School of Music in Berlin. He performs and records throughout the world.

A NOTE ON THE TYPE

The text of this book was composed in Trump Mediæval. Designed by Professor Georg Trump (1896–1985) in the mid-1950s, Trump Mediæval was cut and cast by the C. E. Weber Type Foundry of Stuttgart, Germany. The roman letter forms are based on classical prototypes, but Professor Trump has imbued them with his own unmistakable style. The italic letter forms, unlike those of so many other typefaces, are closely related to their roman counterparts. The result is a truly contemporary type, notable for both its legibility and its versatility.

Composed by Creative Graphics,
Allentown, Pennsylvania

Printed and bound by R. R. Donnelley,
Harrisonburg, Virginia

Designed by M. Kristen Bearse